Town Meeting Time

A Handbook of Parliamentary Law

TOWN MEETING TIME

A Handbook of Parliamentary Law

Prepared (1962) by a Committee of the Massachusetts Moderators Association

RICHARD B. JOHNSON, *Moderator of Swampscott*
BENJAMIN A. TRUSTMAN, *Moderator of Brookline*
CHARLES Y. WADSWORTH, *Moderator of Lincoln*

SECOND EDITION

Revised and Amended (1983) by a Committee of the Massachusetts Moderators Association

RALPH C. COPELAND, *Moderator of Medfield*
JOSEPH HARRINGTON, JR., *Moderator of Wenham*
JOHN B. HOWARD, *Moderator of Chesterfield*
CHARLES L. KIRKPATRICK, *Moderator of South Hadley*
DOUGLAS D. NICHOLS, *Moderator of Ludlow*

THIRD EDITION

Revised and Amended (2001) by a Committee of the Massachusetts Moderators Association

ROSLYN GARFIELD, *Moderator of Provincetown*
HENRY L. HALL, JR., *Moderator of Belmont*
JOSEPH HARRINGTON III, *Moderator of Westborough*
JOHN M. RUSSELL, JR., *Moderator of Hull*

Massachusetts Moderators Association
2001

Original Edition 1962 published by Little, Brown and Co.
Second Edition 1984 with additions published by Robert E. Krieger Publishing Co., Inc.
Third Edition with amendments published 2001 by Massachusetts Moderators Association.
First Printing by Quinn-Woodbine, Inc.
Third Printing

**Published by
Massachusetts Moderators Association**

Copyright © 1962 by Little, Brown and Company
Transferred Sept., 1981 to Massachusetts Moderators Association
Reviewed and amended Sept., 1983 by a Committee of the Association under the Chairmanship of Joseph Harrington, Jr.
Copyright © 1984 by the Massachusetts Moderators Association
Reviewed and amended June, 2001 by a Committee of the Association under the Chairmanship of Joseph Harrington III
Copyright © 2001 by the Massachusetts Moderators Association

All rights reserved. No part of this book may be reproduced in any form or by any electronic or mechanical means including information storage and retrieval systems without permission in writing from the Massachusetts Moderators Association.

Printed in the United States of America by Thomson-Shore, Inc., Dexter, MI

ISBN 13: 978-0-9711679-0-2
ISBN 10:   0-9711679-0-7

Introductory Report

THE HONORABLE RAYMOND FESSENDEN
PRESIDENT, THE MASSACHUSETTS MODERATORS' ASSOCIATION

DEAR DR. FESSENDEN,

    The committee appointed by your predecessor, the late Rudolph F. King, of Millis, pursuant to a vote of the Association at its Annual Meeting on December 16, 1960, to prepare a new handbook for town meetings, has the honor to submit the following report. We hope that it will prove useful not only to our fellow moderators in Massachusetts but also to fellow moderators in the other New England states, to town clerks, town counsel, finance committee members and others who play a leading part in town meetings, to the rank and file of voters and town meeting members and, in fact, to persons concerned with parliamentary law in many other settings.

    We recognize that many meetings have run smoothly and well for years under experienced moderators, and we do not suggest that they should change their ways to suit ours. Yet the fact of our appointment reflects a realization that none of us holds office in perpetuity and that from time to time a town will acquire a new moderator who will find a handbook useful. Furthermore, the migration from the cities to the suburbs is introducing to town meetings a large number of potentially useful voters and town meeting members who may welcome a guide until they learn the ropes.[1]

    In preparing this report we have consulted fellow moderators of experience, read cases and statutes from the six New England states and procedural by-laws from some two-score Massachusetts towns, and examined a number of manuals on procedure.

    Our research into town by-laws makes no claim to be exhaustive or up to date. It has consisted of sampling a collection of Massachusetts town by-laws accumulated over a period of forty or fifty years for various office purposes. The sample thus produced seems to be reasonably representative, and by-laws in this field are changed so infrequently that it has not seemed worth while for our purpose to try to verify them all as of this moment. Towns in the other five New England states (other than Connecticut towns with representative meetings) do not seem to make a practice of regulating their proceedings by by-law.[2] Although we have

---

[1] See Tilden, Town Government, 38 B.U.L. Rev. 347 (1958).
[2] Unless otherwise indicated, the references to towns in the text and footnotes are references to Massachusetts towns. See §3, final paragraph.

examined and discussed pertinent statutes and decisions in other New England states, it should be remembered that as Massachusetts lawyers we do not claim to be experts in the laws and customs of these other states. The manuals we have examined consist of Geoffrey Bolton's *Handbook for Town Moderators* (2d ed. 1954) (cited as Bolton); Cushing's *Manual of Parliamentary Practice* (revised and amplified by Paul E. Lowe, 1925) (Cushing); Demeter's *Manual of Parliamentary Law and Procedure* (Universal ed. 1953) (Demeter); Frank W. Hackett's *The Gavel and the Mace, or Parliamentary Law in Easy Chapters* (1900) (Hackett); and Robert's *Rules of Order* (rev. ed. 1943) (Robert). Bolton prepared his handbook for the Massachusetts Federation of Taxpayers' Associations, Inc. It is an excellent account of Massachusetts practice.[3] We all know that Luther S. Cushing was clerk of the Massachusetts House of Representatives from 1832 to 1843. His manual has been officially adopted by at least thirteen Massachusetts towns.[4]

Demeter does not seem to have a friendly feeling for moderators.[5] *The Gavel and the Mace* is a delightful book,

---

[3] Bolton includes material respecting the conduct of elections. We have omitted such material partially because of the impracticability of including it for all the New England states, and partially because of the recent changes in the Massachusetts law which appear to eliminate the moderator's duties in the conduct of elections. See Mass. Acts of 1960, c. 431, and Acts of 1961, c. 288, amending Gen. Laws, c. 54, §§12 and 71A respectively.

[4] Acushnet, Bedford, Bernardston, Essex, Framingham, Hopedale, Ipswich, Shrewsbury, Swampscott, Uxbridge, Wakefield, Westminster, Winchester. The Massachusetts Federation of Taxpayers' Associations once expressed an opinion to the effect that such incorporation by reference is illegal. See Model By-Laws for Massachusetts Towns 20 (1940). See also Cawley v. Northern Waste Co., 239 Mass. 540, 132 N.E. 365 (1921). The towns listed above and in footnotes 7 and 8 represent a considerable weight of opinion to the contrary, and in 1954 the Federation expressed a different view. See its Tax Talk, Vol. 21, No. 1. Blomquist v. Arlington, 338 Mass. 594, 156 N.E.2d 416 (1959), appears to assume that generally a manual may be incorporated.

[5] "Tyranny in Town Meetings. Town meeting business is conducted tyrannically to-day. The moderator is a virtual dictator. He does not entertain appeals from his decisions, nor reconsideration, rescission and other basic parliamentary motions. He defends his misrulings and misconduct of business with the arbitrary edict 'this has been our usual practice.' Town meeting members passively assent to such edicts out of a sense of delicate restraint. Consequently, members *haven't* a chance with the moderator; he has *two strikes* on them before they start. In the main, he fabricates and applies his *own* rules instead of applying the rules of a reliable and up-to-date manual of parliamentary law *with which town members* are familiar. It is high time selectmen

INTRODUCTORY REPORT   v

unfortunately not easy to obtain. General Robert's *Rules of Order* has sold some 2,000,000 copies, has been printed in Braille, has outsold such favorites as *Tarzan of the Apes,* Emily Post's *Etiquette,* and *Little Lord Fauntleroy,*[6] and has been officially adopted by at least four towns.[7]

We have also found a mine of useful information in House Document No. 459, 86th Congress, 2d Session (1960), published by the United States Government Printing Office. This contains the Federal Constitution (which includes a surprising number of parliamentary rules), Thomas Jefferson's Manual (which he compiled, mostly from British sources, for his own guidance when as Vice President he presided over the Senate, and which is as enjoyable to read as *The Gavel and the Mace)* and *Rules of the House of Representatives,* all annotated by Lewis Deschler, Parliamentarian. References to "Jefferson," "Deschler" or "House Rules" all relate to House Document No. 459, and "Congress" (meaning no disrespect to the Senate) is shorthand for the House of Representatives of the United States. We will refer often to House Rule XVI, 4. The Manual which Massachusetts publishes each year for the use of its General Court contains its Senate Rules and House Rules and a collection of rulings thereon (and on the Massachusetts Constitution, which also contains parliamentary rules) by presiding officers.[8]

The question may be asked why we venture to compete with such formidable rivals. Fortunately for us, we have impressive authority for the proposition that technical rules of parliamentary law are not well adapted to the deliberations of a town meeting,[9] and are sometimes even contrary to law.[10] Illustrations of this will appear. Sometimes the manuals disagree with each other, and we

---

incorporated a modern manual in their by-laws, and thus give the members a *50-50* chance with the moderator. Such a reform is sadly and urgently needed in the interest of enlightened, progressive and orderly processes of democratic self-government. Outmoded and archaic or arbitrary parliamentary practice and procedure in our town meetings is bad influence on our democratic principles." P. 232. The emphasis and syntax are his. It is clear that the modern manual he has in mind is Demeter's.

[6] Saturday Evening Post 25 (Aug. 19, 1961).
[7] Arlington, Groveland, Lexington and Northboro.
[8] Westminster and Weymouth have officially adopted the rules of the Massachusetts House.
[9] Wood v. Milton, 197 Mass. 531, 84 N.E. 332 (1908); Hill v. Goodwin, 56 N.H. 441 (1876); Bullard v. Allen, 124 Me. 251, 127 Atl. 722 (1925).
[10] Blomquist v. Arlington, 338 Mass. 594, 156 N.E.2d 416 (1959).

have recommended what seems to us the better view. We have even had the temerity to proclaim, like the little boy in "The Emperor's New Clothes," that some of the rules prescribed for us by the manuals make no sense.

There are no pictures in this book. The reader who wishes to see what a town meeting looks like is referred to John Gould's *New England Town Meeting: Safeguard of Democracy* (1940) (Gould).

Some duplication has seemed to be a necessary evil. For example, half of our readers who wish to know in a hurry whether a motion to commit may be amended will look under "Commit" and the other half will look under "Amend." Neither half will be pleased with being told to look somewhere else, so where the answer is short, we have put it in both places. Where the discussion is lengthy, we have tried to insert cross references.

The form of motion set forth in each section on subsidiary, incidental and privileged motions is merely suggested as an aid to the inexperienced. There are many recognized variations.

We hope that you will find that we have presented a simple handbook useful at town meetings and at other meetings as well.

                              Very truly yours,

                              RICHARD B. JOHNSON
                                Moderator of Swampscott
                              BENJAMIN A. TRUSTMAN
                                  Moderator of Brookline
                              CHARLES Y. WADSWORTH
                                  Moderator of Lincoln

Boston
October 1962

INTRODUCTION TO THE SECOND EDITION

It was twenty-one years ago, in October 1962, that Moderators Johnson, Trustman, and Wadsworth penned the modest conclusion to the Introductory Report that prefaced the first printing of "Town Meeting Time":
> "We hope that you will find that we have presented a simple handbook useful at town meetings and at other meetings as well."

How well they achieved their objective is seen in a single example. In *MacKeen v. Town of Canton,* 379 Mass. 514, 399 N.E. 2d 22 (1980), Town Meeting Time is cited as an authority no fewer than seven times.

Messrs. Howard, Kirkpatrick, and Nichols—three brave but somewhat less than lionhearted moderators[1]— undertook a review of both reported case law and of statutory developments of particular interest to the parliamentary concerns of moderators, arising between the first and this edition of Town Meeting Time. They found no surprises. They will go to their next meetings with either their 1962 or this second edition as secure armor to support their actions. The newest, eager moderator can do likewise. The words written and the principles expounded twenty-one years ago are all as valid now as they were then.

A word of caution, however, is in order. The secure moderator is one who regulates the proceedings of the town meeting in conformity with accepted parliamentary procedures, and leaves questions of law to town counsel. This is treated in §6 and §9. However, Town Meeting Time was originally written in the early 1960's; we live now in a more litigious society. More than ever it now behooves the moderator to confine his rulings to the conduct of the meeting. In that area the moderator is entirely safe; outside it trouble may lie. If you need more, read *Ellis v. Board of Selectmen of Barnstable,* 361 Mass. 794, 282 N.E. 2d 637 (1972). However, an informed moderator may act to ensure that the meeting is made aware of the potential legal problems following upon some proposed action.

As originally stated in §11, Massachusetts moderators had in the past been faced with potential problems when presented with a motion to reduce the budget requested by the school committee. The adoption in 1980 of a new Section 34 to Chapter 71 of the Massachusetts General Laws solved the problem. A town can now reduce a school committee budget without fear of a suit and the sure loss of that suit by the town. Effect of Proposition 2½ (Section 21C

---

[1] For what constitutes a lionhearted moderator, see §32.

of Chapter 59) is within the province of the finance committee and the town counsel, and not that of the moderator.

While Messers. Johnson, Trustman, and Wadsworth did not tinker with the doctrines of the older manuals in regard to the rank or precedence of various motions, they seemed to question the rank of "Postpone Indefinitely" at the lowest level of subsidiary motions. Review their comments in the first footnote in §39; it suggests such motions rank ninth.

Ten additions to the list of Massachusetts general statutes requiring a town meeting affirmative vote in excess of a majority for adoption have been entered in the Appendix.

At the 1975 Annual Meeting of the Association, the President presented a paper on "The Town Meeting: Its Development as a Form of Government." By vote of the Association, this monograph has been included as an addendum to this edition of Town Meeting Time.

>Respectfully submitted,
>>Ralph C. Copeland, *Moderator of Medfield*
>>Joseph Harrington, Jr., *Moderator of Wenham*
>>John B. Howard, *Moderator of Chesterfield*
>>Charles L. Kirkpatrick, *Moderator of South Hadley*
>>Douglas D. Nichols, *Moderator of Ludlow*

INTRODUCTION TO THE THIRD EDITION

Once again a committee of contemporary moderators has thoroughly reviewed "Town Meeting Time" and found the earlier editions to be essentially as valid today as when written. Indeed, the motivator for undertaking a third edition was not perceived failings in the content, but in the quantity on hand. All the unused copies have been sold.

Why not simply reprint the second edition? With the passage of time have come some subtle and not so subtle changes in practice. We submit, for example, that a moderator who encouraged that there be separate voting lists (and separate entrances to the hall) for men and for women would add a new dimension to the term "lion-hearted moderator."

There have been a few changes in Massachusetts law, two of them at the suggestion of the Massachusetts Moderators Association (referred to in §4, footnote 30, and §67, footnote 16). Considerably more experience has been gained with the application of Proposition 2 ½ legislation, some of it very much in the province of the moderator. (§11, §20) There is some case law, which clearly contradicts one piece of advice appearing in the earlier editions. (§59, footnote 10)

Notwithstanding the disclaimers in the Introduction to the First Edition, we have admired the grasp of law and practice in the other five New England states displayed by the original three authors. Much of the resulting material, we are sure, is still valid today. We believe, however, that the readership of "Town Meeting Time" consists overwhelmingly of Massachusetts readers, for whom the observations on practice in neighboring states are of interest but no great practical value. We have decided to leave these passages alone; the reader is hereby warned that they were penned in the early 1960s, and for the most part have not been updated since then.

Chapter 10, dealing with conflict of interest, was in serious need of updating due to the increase in formality brought to this area by the passage of the Massachusetts Conflict of Interest statute starting around the time of the publication of the first edition. We drew heavily on a monograph prepared by Harry Terkanian, former moderator of Wellfleet, who reviewed the text and improved upon it; we thank him.

Many other moderators have contributed suggestions; we thank them all. We also wish to thank Donald Hyde, former moderator of Stow, for his assistance with the publication of the volume. Jacqueline Lapidus supplied professional editing services that improved and updated the text to modern standards. The law firm of Ropes & Gray assisted with a thorough review of the legal citations, with substantial stenographic assistance, and also by graciously hosting all the committee's meetings.

INTRODUCTION TO THE THIRD EDITION

We hope that you will find that we have preserved all that is of value in this marvelous reference work, and extended its life to make it fully suitable for application at Massachusetts town meetings as we, and the institution of the town meeting, enter the 21st century.

Respectfully submitted,
 Roslyn Garfield, *Moderator of Provincetown*
 Henry L. Hall, Jr., *Moderator of Belmont*
 Joseph Harrington III, *Moderator of Westborough*
 John M. Russell, Jr., *Moderator of Hull*

CONTENTS

Introductory Report iii
Introduction to the Second Edition vii
Introduction to the Third Edition ix

CHAPTER 1

THE TOWN MEETING

§1.	History	1
§2.	Representative Town Meetings	5
§3.	Necessity for Rules of Procedure	8
§4.	The Warrant	12

CHAPTER 2

THE CAST OF CHARACTERS

§5.	Quorum	....	17
§6.	The Moderator	....	20
	1.	Election of the Moderator.	22
	2.	Powers and Duties of the Moderator.	24
§7.	The Town Clerk	....	26
§8.	The Selectmen	....	28
§9.	The Town Counsel	....	30
§10.	The Finance Committee	....	31
§11.	The School Committee	....	34
§12.	Select Committees	....	35
§13.	Constables, Checkers, Tellers and Pages	....	40
§14.	Strangers	....	41

CHAPTER 3

PRELIMINARY CONSIDERATIONS

§15.	Preparation for the Meeting	....	44
	1.	The Warrant.	44
	2.	Motions.	45
	3.	Procedural Questions.	46
	4.	Officials.	46
	5.	Physical Equipment.	46
§16.	Opening the Meeting	....	48
	1.	The Return of the Warrant.	48
	2.	Swearing in Newly Elected Officers.	49
	3.	The Anthem and the Prayer.	49

CONTENTS

4.	Distinguished Visitors.	50
5.	Complimentary Resolutions.	50
6.	Introductory Comments.	50
§17.	Reports of Committees	51
§18.	The Order of Consideration of the Articles	52
§19.	The Reading of the Articles	54
§20.	Handling the Budget	54
§21.	Two Meetings in One Night	57
§22.	Broadcasting and Recording	58

CHAPTER 4

MOTIONS

§23.	In General	61
§24.	Seconding and Stating the Motion	63
§25.	Motions of Doubtful Legality	64
§26.	Withdrawal	65

CHAPTER 5

MAIN MOTIONS

§27.	In General	66
§28.	Detailed Affirmative Main Motions — Scope	66
§29.	Brief Affirmative Main Motions	71
§30.	Negative Main Motions	72
§31.	Reconsideration and Rescission in General	77
§32.	Who May Move Reconsideration	78
§33.	Limits to Reconsideration	79
§34.	Exceptions to the Power to Reconsider	81
§35.	Rank and Application to Certain Motions	83
§36.	Reconsideration by Ruse and by Thin Slices	85
§37.	The Tradition Against Reconsideration	86

CHAPTER 6

SUBSIDIARY MOTIONS

§38.	In General	88
	1. Subsidiary Motions Competing with Each Other.	88
	2. A Subsidiary Motion as Applied to Another Subsidiary Motion.	89
§39.	To Postpone Indefinitely (as a Subsidiary Motion)	91

§40.	To Amend (or Substitute)	93
§41.	To Commit (or Refer)	96
§42.	To Postpone to a Time Certain	99
§43.	To Limit or Extend the Limits of Debate	101
§44.	The Previous Question	102
§45.	To Lay on the Table	104

CHAPTER 7

INCIDENTAL MOTIONS

§46.	In General	107
§47.	Point of Order	109
§48.	Appeal	110
§49.	Division of a Question	113
§50.	Separate Consideration	114
§51.	To Fix the Method of Voting	115
§52.	Nominations to Committees	116
§53.	Motions for Leave to Withdraw or Modify a Motion	118
§54.	Suspension of the Rules	120
§55.	Inappropriate or Unnecessary Incidental Motions	121

CHAPTER 8

PRIVILEGED MOTIONS

§56.	In General	123
§57.	A Question of Privilege	123
§58.	To Fix the Time to (or at) Which to Adjourn	125
§59.	A Point of No Quorum	127
§60.	To Adjourn to a Fixed Time or to Recess	128
§61.	To Dissolve or Adjourn Sine Die	131

CHAPTER 9

DEBATE

§62.	Decorum in Debate	134
§63.	Slander	137

CHAPTER 10

CONFLICT OF INTEREST

§64.	In General	139
§65.	For the Moderator	142
§66.	For Attorneys	145

CHAPTER 11

VOTING

§67.	In General	146

Appendix 155
Addendum 161
Index 171

Chapter 1

The Town Meeting

§1. History

The basic unit of local government in New England is the town. Sometimes a town grows into a city, or acquires a city within its boundaries; sometimes it develops villages, boroughs and school, water, fire and other special purpose districts within its boundaries. Sometimes two or more towns will join for special purposes in districts that extend beyond the boundaries of one town. The cities have a different scheme of government altogether; the villages, boroughs and districts may have a different scheme, or they may be modeled on the towns.

"The village or township is the only association which is so perfectly natural that, whenever a number of men are collected, it seems to constitute itself.

"The town or tithing, then, exists in all nations, whatever their laws and customs may be: It is man who makes monarchies and establishes republics, but the township seems to come directly from the hand of God. . . ."[1]

The distinctive characteristic of town government, and of the villages, boroughs and districts modeled on it, is the town meeting (or village, borough or district meeting), in which are vested the traditional powers of the legislative branch of any level of government the power to make laws (called by-laws in these cases) and the power of the purse. (In Rhode Island these powers are divided; by-laws are made by a smaller body, called the town council, while taxes and expenditures are voted at a "financial town meeting.")[2]

"Town meetings are to liberty what primary schools are to science; they bring it within the people's reach, they teach men how to use and how to enjoy it."[3]

"By experience there was wrought out the matchless

---

§1 [1] De Tocqueville, *Democracy in America* 60 (Bradley ed. 1945).
[2] R.I. Const., Amend. Art. XXIX, §2.
[3] De Tocqueville, op. cit. *supra* at 61.

mechanism of the town meeting."[4]
"The attendance is usually good; the debates sensible and practical."[5]

These are splendid words, but they should not make us too complacent. Others have written in different terms about towns[6] and have criticized town meetings as "government by wisecrack . . . mechanisms too cumbersome to make real decisions."[7]

Nevertheless, "There are aspirations behind the town-meeting conception of democracy, however, which must be recognized as indelible parts of the democratic creed. The town-meeting conception of democracy is an idealized way of expressing the democratic hope that those who are governed will be able to reach those who govern them, that they will be able to make their voices heard where it counts and will be recognized as persons and not as faceless cogs in an efficient machine. It speaks for the belief that a society is safer and freer when the bulk of its citizens understand the programs and goals that their government has chosen and when they have achieved this understanding because these programs and goals have been honestly debated in public.

"Not least, the town-meeting ideal catches an important meaning of freedom and expresses a classic conviction of believers in democracy. The ordinary man may or may not be the best judge of his own interests, but if he does not exercise effective authority over matters that are in his immediate range of interest and competence, he may be a well-tended animal, but he will not be a free man. Freedom in the concrete, freedom as it is experienced in daily life, is the experience of having a hand in the determining of issues that

---

[4] Tercentenary Oration of Chief Justice Rugg, Oct. 20, 1930, printed in 273 Mass. 589, 599. "In a town-meeting, the great secret of political science was uncovered, and the problem solved, how to give every individual his fair weight in the government, without any disorder from numbers." 11 Emerson, Complete Works 46-47 (1904).
[5] Bryce, *The American Commonwealth* 601 (1911). This is quite true, of course, and only a cad would wonder how many town meetings Lord Bryce had time to attend.
[6] Lerner, *America as a Civilization* (1957) entitles Chapter 3, §8, "The Decline of the Small Town."
[7] Wood, *Surburbia* 162 (1959).

§1 1: THE TOWN MEETING 3

touch the individual closely and intimately."[8]

Each town is required to hold at least one meeting each year, called the annual meeting,[9] and is authorized to hold as many other meetings, called special meetings, as it wishes.[10] In the beginning, attendance at town meeting was compulsory, and fines were levied for tardiness.[11] Since everyone was required to attend, the only notice needed was of the time and place. There was no need to warn the voters of the business that might be taken up. This viewpoint gradually gave way to a recognition that it was unduly onerous to require people to attend special meetings on matters they did not care about,[12] and so the definition, by articles in the warrant, of matters that might be acted upon at special meetings became important. Now annual meetings are similarly defined.[13]

The difference between annual and special meetings, as to the notice of business to be taken up, still prevails in Rhode

---

[8] Rockefeller Panel Report on American Democracy: The Power of the Democratic Idea 39-41 (1960). See also Hernane Tavares de Sá, "Town Meeting Tonight," in *Americas* (a magazine published in English, Spanish and Portuguese by the Pan-American Union), June, 1949, p. 8: "The town meeting, oldest expression of democracy in the Western Hemisphere, survives with unabated vigor in the rural sections of the New England States. It has much to say to Latin America, where many of the set backs suffered by democratic government are due to a flaw in origin."

[9] Conn. Gen. Stat., tit. 6, c. 90, §7-1 (on the first Monday in October); Me. Rev. Stat., c. 90-A, §35 (in March); Mass. Gen. Laws, c. 39, §9 (in February, March or April); N.H. Rev. Stat. Ann., c. 39, §1 (on the second Tuesday of March); R.I. Gen. Laws, tit. 45, c. 3, §§1, 2 (at such time as is or may be by by-law or vote provided); Vt. Stat. Ann., tit. 24, c. 31, §702 (on the first Tuesday of March).

[10] Conn. Gen. Stat., tit. 6, c. 90, §7-1; Me. Rev. Stat., c. 90-A, §32; Mass. Gen. Laws, c. 39, §9; N.H. Rev. Stat. Ann., c. 39, §1; R.I. Gen. Laws, tit. 45, c. 3, §4; Vt. Stat. Ann., tit. 24, c. 31, §705.

[11] Garland, New England Town Law 48 (1906).

[12] See Boston Town Records, July 26, 1779: "A Motion was made by General Hancock relative to Beacon Hill, but not Acted upon as the same was not inserted in the Warrant for calling a Meeting." General Hancock should have known better, as he had been not only President of the Continental Congress but also, from time to time, moderator of the Boston Town Meeting.

[13] Bloomfield v. Charter Oak Bank, 121 U.S. 121 (1887).

Island except for disposing of land or making a tax[14] and lasted longer in Vermont than in the other four states.[15]

Also, in the beginning, town meetings exercised judicial and administrative as well as legislative functions,[16] but the judicial and administrative functions were soon transferred to regular courts and to the selectmen and others. The meeting still retains the traditional legislative power of appropriating funds and making substantive by-laws.

There was a time when the town meeting exercised more influence outside the boundaries of the town than it does today. The town was the "tap spring" of the Revolution;[17] and town meeting resolutions initiated the convention that drafted the Massachusetts Constitution.[18]

Meetings were held much more frequently in those days than they are now. For example, in 1780, Boston had eleven meetings occupying, with adjournments, 40 days in all. Part of this was for fun,[19] but most of it was for the regular serious business of raising troops, supplies, fortifications and money for the war,[20] and considering, paragraph by paragraph, the constitution being drafted for the Commonwealth, and

---

[14] R.I. Gen. Laws, tit. 45, c. 3, §§6, 12; Lonsdale Co. v. Taft, 34 R.I. 496, 84 Atl. 795 (1912).

[15] Compare Schoff v. Bloomfield, 8 Vt. 472 (1836), with Moore v. Beattie, 33 Vt. 219 (1860).

[16] Eaton, "The Right to Local Self-Government," 13 *Harv. L. Rev.* 441, 450-451 (1900).

[17] Wheelock v. Lowell, 196 Mass. 220, 81 N.E. 977 (1907); Lerner, op. cit. *supra* at 149.

[18] Morison, The Formation of the Massachusetts Constitution 3 and 13 (1955).

[19] See the Boston Town Records for March 5 in 1778, 1779, 1780, 1781, 1782 and 1783 for accounts of entire meetings devoted to orations "to perpetuate the Memory of the horrid Massacre perpetrated on the Evening of the 5th of March 1770, by a Party of Soldiers under the Command of Capt. Thomas Preston of the 29th Regiment." The routine began with a report by the committee which selected the orator, accepted; consideration and a vote on when and where to hear the oration (the Old Brick Meeting House at half-past twelve); appointment of a committee to inform the orator; adjournment to the Old Brick Meeting House; report of the committee to inform the orator; the oration; applause; appointment of a committee to thank the orator and another committee "to apply to a proper Gentleman to deliver an Oration on the 5th of March next"; and a collection for one of the victims. The routine never varied until 1783, when the town voted to transfer the oration to the 4th of July.

[20] See Boston Town Records for May 6 and 13, 1778: Aug. 9 and 12, 1779.

ultimately accepting it.[21]

Ironically, the constitution that the towns initiated and ratified established a court, which proceeded to rule that towns are subordinate creatures of the Commonwealth and may exercise only such powers as the legislature may grant. In 1814, when Fairhaven undertook to fortify itself against the British Navy, it was firmly told it lacked the power to do so, even by a unanimous vote of those present.[22] Whatever the case in 1814, it must be confessed that today it is not very practical for a town to undertake military operations. In this instance, a page of logic outweighs a volume of history.

A 20th century development in town meetings is the representative meeting. During the 19th century, when a town outgrew the capacity of any hall available for its meetings, it was the fashion to apply to the legislature for a city charter, in which the meeting's functions were vested in a board of aldermen sometimes called a city council. Now a town that has grown too large for its hall may, by a special act of the legislature, adopt a representative town meeting form of government, in which all of the old forms are preserved, but the business of the meeting, other than elections, is carried on by town meeting members elected by the voters.[23]

§2. Representative Town Meetings

The representative town meeting developed in

---

[21] Id., May 3, 4, 8, 9, 10 and 12, 1780.
[22] Stetson v. Kempton, 13 Mass. 272 (1816). But it may celebrate the return of the veterans. Mass. Gen. Laws, c. 40, §5(27); N.H. Rev. Stat. Ann., c. 31, §4 X. Compare, however, N.H. Rev. Stat. Ann., c. 31, §5, in which appropriations for any military purpose in time of war are expressly exempt from limits imposed on appropriations at special town meetings.
[23] Mass. Const., Amend. Art. II, as amended (under which the Legislature has enacted Gen. Laws, c. 43A, and numerous Special Acts); Town of Trumbull v. Ehrsam, 148 Conn. 47, 166 A.2d 844 (1961). See a series of articles on this subject in the *Worcester Telegram*, March 3, 4, 5 and 6, 1959. A New Hampshire town of more than 5000 inhabitants does not need a special act. It may accept a standard form of representative town meeting. N.H. Rev. Stat. Ann., c. 40A, added by N.H. Laws 1961, c. 241.

Massachusetts and in Connecticut when towns found the open meeting unwieldy and often unrepresentative of a cross-section of the town population.[1]

In the representative (or "limited") town meeting, the citizens elect representatives to vote at the town meeting. Naturally the plan has its greatest appeal to the larger towns, where it is impossible to find physical quarters large enough to accommodate all those likely to attend the meeting. In 1915, Brookline, Massachusetts, then the largest town in New England and the country, was the first town to adopt the plan of the limited town meeting.[2] In each case the representative town meeting has been adopted by vote of the town accepting a special legislative act.[3] In Massachusetts the General Court was held[4] not to have this power until the adoption of an amendment to the Constitution of the Commonwealth,[5] but elsewhere the power of the legislature in this respect appears not to have been questioned. Its application was originally restricted, in Massachusetts, to towns with a population of 12,000 or more. Another amendment to the Massachusetts Constitution in 1926[6] extended the privilege to towns with a population of 6,000. By December 1999, 41 Massachusetts towns had adopted the plan, of which 36 had a population in excess of 12,000, four had a population between 6,000 and 12,000 and one (Lee) had a population less than 6,000, although its population at the time of adoption of the plan exceeded 6,000. In addition, nine towns,[7] each with a population in excess of 12,000, have adopted a city form of government since 1972, replacing the open or representative

---

§2[1] See "Participation in Representative Town Meeting" (Bureau of Government Research, University of Massachusetts; undated).

[2] Mass. Acts of 1915, c. 250, accepted by the town on Nov. 2, 1915.

[3] Although in 1931 the Massachusetts legislature enacted a "standard form" of representative town meeting (Mass. Gen. Laws, c. 43A) (which may be adopted only by towns that have already established a representative town meeting), only Brookline and Arlington have adopted the standard form in place of their special acts.

[4] Opinion of the Justices, 229 Mass. 601, 119 N.E. 778 (1918).

[5] Massachusetts Constitution - Amendments, Article II.

[6] Article LXX.

[7] Agawam, Amesbury, Barnstable, Easthampton, Franklin, Methuen, Southbridge, Watertown and Weymouth.

town meeting with a manager/council or mayor/council plan. Towns in Connecticut, Maine, and Vermont also have representative town meetings. A 1961 statute has authorized any New Hampshire town with more than 5,000 inhabitants to adopt this form of town meeting.

In Massachusetts the number of elected town meeting members varies from 50 in Saugus to 372 in Fairhaven, with half of the towns having approximately 240. A majority of the Massachusetts towns also have members at large or ex officio who are entitled to vote at the meeting, the number in such towns varying from two in Wellesley to 39 in Adams. The elected town meeting members are elected from precincts or districts, one third each year for terms of three years, as a rule. In Connecticut, and in Saugus, Massachusetts, they all stand for re-election every two years. The precincts, the number of members from each precinct, and the relationship between the number of town meeting members and the voters are determined in a great variety of ways. The meeting generally has authority to determine the election and qualifications of its members.

Elections to town meeting membership are nonpartisan in theory (the ballot may not carry political labels) and usually also in practice.

The representative town meeting itself is much the same as all other town meetings. The warrant is prepared, the moderator presides, the articles are considered and voted upon, and registered voters may attend and speak. One difference in procedure is that only the elected members of the town meeting may vote, except that some Massachusetts towns also give the voting privilege to certain town officials who are designated as members at large. A second difference is that a secret ballot may not be used when voting on any motion at a representative town meeting unless two-thirds of the town meeting members present and voting thereon vote that a secret ballot be used.[8]

"Fundamentally, the structure and powers of all representative town meetings are the same, although in detail

---

[8] Mass. Gen. Laws, c. 39, §15.

there is considerable variation in practices among the various towns. Most of the legislative acts are copied from similar acts for other towns, but each town appears to have made numerous changes to suit its own local situation."[9]

An important feature of the representative town meeting, which usually does not apply to the open town meeting, is a statutory provision that all votes in some towns, and certain types of votes in other towns, shall not be operative until after the expiration of a specified number of days after the dissolution of the meeting. This is done in order to provide an opportunity for obtaining, by petition, a referendum of the registered voters at large on the vote in question.[10] Sometimes it is provided that the vote of the representative town meeting will not be reversed by the referendum unless a specified minimum percentage of the registered voters votes so to reverse.[11]

The statutory period for filing a petition for a referendum is expressed in terms of a given number of days after "dissolution" of the meeting, rather than after the passage of the vote in question. One result of this statute is that in some towns no votes, and in other towns no votes of the categories mentioned in the applicable statute, take effect until after final dissolution of the meeting, no matter how many adjourned sessions may have followed the vote.[12]

§3. Necessity for Rules of Procedure

Town meetings, like all other assemblies, need rules of procedure for two reasons. The first is simple efficiency; the business of the meeting can be accomplished more accurately, with fewer errors and with less waste of time, if it is taken up and considered in an orderly, systematic way. The second is more important: It is the protection of the rights of individuals

---

[9] Guide for Establishing a Representative Town Meeting (Bureau of Government Research, University of Massachusetts, 1957).
[10] See, for example, Mass. Gen. Laws, c. 43A, §10.
[11] Mass. Gen. Laws, c. 43A, §10 (20 percent).
[12] See also §61 *infra*.

§3   1: THE TOWN MEETING   9

and minorities against illegal encroachment, unintentional or otherwise, by the majority.

"...as it is always in the power of the majority, by their numbers, to stop any improper measures proposed on the part of their opponents, the only weapons by which the minority can defend themselves against similar attempts from those in power are the forms and rules of proceeding which have been adopted as they were found necessary, from time to time, and are become the law of the House, by a strict adherence to which the weaker party can only be protected from those irregularities and abuses which these forms were intended to check, and which the wantonness of power is but too often apt to suggest to large and successful majorities...

"And whether these forms be in all cases the most rational or not is really not of so great importance. It is much more material that there should be a rule to go by than what that rule is; that there may be a uniformity of proceeding in business not subject to the caprice of the Speaker or captiousness of the members. It is very material that order, decency, and regularity be preserved in a dignified public body."[1]

These rules can become very detailed and elaborate. Bodies like the English Houses of Parliament and our state and national legislatures have long histories, full of precedents, and their members can be expected to acquire some substantial knowledge of them.[2] It has often been held, however, that it is unreasonable to expect town meetings to adhere to all the complexities of procedure appropriate to more sophisticated assemblies.[3] Some people think that this

---

§3 [1] Jefferson 116-118.
[2] "The Congress of the United States of America, as well as our State legislatures, when they have no special provision to cover the case, govern themselves by a sort of parliamentary common law, an heirloom which, like that mass of mingled wisdom and absurdity, the common law itself, has been handed down to us from Great Britain." Hackett 35.
[3] Bullard v. Allen, 124 Me. 251, 127 Atl. 722 (1925); Wood v. Milton, 197 Mass. 531, 84 N.E. 332 (1908); Hill v. Goodwin, 56 N.H. 441 (1876).

means that town meetings operate under no rules at all.⁴ We respectfully submit that they are mistaken. To anyone who has attended a meeting of the Massachusetts Moderators Association it is clear that, while there is a rich diversity of practice from town to town, the common denominator is the fact that each town has rules, written or unwritten, which it considers appropriate to its circumstances and which are consistently applied. All moderators consider themselves a custodian of the town's traditions, not least of which is the preference for a government of laws and not of people. For this, it is not necessary to follow a manual. A highly individualistic local practice will do, provided it is reasonable and consistent. "Decisions of presiding officers, I may here as well as anywhere remark, become precedents, just as do those of judges in courts of law."⁵

As noted in the Addendum, and as its very name makes clear, modern parliamentary procedure had its origin in the rules of procedure adopted by the British Parliament. In the Introduction to the First Edition the reader will find a thorough enumeration of the handbooks on rules of order which evolved therefrom on this side of the Atlantic. Most of

---

⁴ See the passage in Demeter quoted *supra* page iv, note 5. Wood, *Suburbia* 278-279 (1959) says: "The notion of systematic, regularized restraints filters down from higher levels of government; statutes, regulations, Robert's *Rules of Order* become the departure point for public action. But the most significant feature of small town politics is the frequency with which legal and procedural requirements are overlooked and ignored. They are always to be adjusted according to the 'common sense, down-to-earth' judgment of the participants, to take account of unique conditions and provincial peculiarities. Tickets can be fixed, favors granted, contracts awarded, not because these irregularities will remain hidden, but because they are acceptable on the basis of personal esteem. The successful town moderator is the one who moderates between the rules of the game and the disposition of the meeting." Professor Wood has also been quoted as telling students at Harvard Law School that the justice of the peace and the moderator of the town meeting, "individuals usually lacking a legal background," become the directive forces in the community. Harvard Law School Record, March 12, 1959. It is probably true that less than half of the moderators in Massachusetts have law degrees, so that "usually" may be statistically correct. However, those who do not have law degrees generally make a better impression on their fellow barristers than they seem to make on Professor Wood.

⁵ Hackett 36. See §37 infra. See Hunneman v. Grafton, 10 Met. 454, 457 (Mass. 1845).

these are of historical interest only, because in the overwhelming majority of cases today, organizations seeking guidance on democratic rules of procedure turn to Henry M. Robert's *Rules of Order*. Indeed, this well-known compendium was written precisely for small organizations with neither the resources nor the desire to evolve their own rules of order. It serves admirably in such situations, which typically involve regular meetings held to deal with the ongoing affairs of a club, lodge, religious body, or other affinity group.

A Massachusetts town meeting differs significantly from the meetings of such organizations. For instance, each town meeting is called pursuant to a separate warrant. It deals with the business laid down therein, in one or more sessions, and then it is literally dissolved or disbanded. There are other differences as well.[6] This volume attempts to incorporate the applicable parts of Robert's (and other manuals) and establish a model rules of order which takes full cognizance of the peculiarities of a Massachusetts town meeting. We recommend it as being particularly suitable for those who wish a single source to which to turn. Nevertheless, numerous Massachusetts towns use Robert's *Rules of Order* to good effect, simply recognizing through by-laws or local practices those places where the generic rules need to be modified or augmented to work within the framework for a town meeting set forth in the General Laws of the Commonwealth. Of most importance is not which manual is selected as a basis, but that there be a basis, known to and available to the public, and that the rules of order be applied fully, impartially, and consistently.

In 1962, the New Hampshire Supreme Court ruled that, in the absence of a statute, an open town meeting is not a continuing body, and one meeting may not adopt standing rules or by-laws to govern the proceedings of subsequent meetings. Each meeting is treated as independent and entitled to the privilege of adopting its own rules.[7] On the other hand, the Connecticut legislature has expressly authorized towns to

---

[6] For a discussion of some of these, see §55.
[7] Town of Exeter v. Kenick, 104 N.H. 168, 181 A.2d 638 (1962).

adopt rules of order for the conduct of their meetings.[8]

§4. The Warrant

The foundation stone of every town meeting is the warrant. Every town meeting, whether annual or special, is called pursuant to a warrant,[1] sometimes called a warning.[2] The warrant must state the time and place of holding the meetings[3] and the subjects to be acted upon,[4] and no action at a town meeting is valid unless the subject matter is contained in the warrant. This requirement does not mean that the warrant must contain verbatim the language of the votes to be taken,[5] but the warrant must contain a sufficient description of what is proposed so as to constitute an adequate warning to all the inhabitants of the town.[6] Every action taken at the meeting must be pursuant to some article in the warrant, and must be within the scope of such article.[7]

---

[8] Public Acts of 1961, c. 593.

§4 [1] Me. Rev. Stat., c. 90-A, §30; Mass. Gen. Laws, c. 39, §10; N.H. Rev. Stat. Ann., c. 39, §2; R.I. Gen. Laws, tit. 45, c. 3, §8.

[2] Conn. Gen. Stat., tit. 7, c. 90, §7-3; Vt. Stat. Ann., tit. 24, c. 31, §§703, 704.

[3] Me. Rev. Stat., c. 90-A, §31-I; Mass. Gen. Laws, c. 39, §10; N.H. Rev. Stat. Ann., c. 39, §2; R.I. Gen. Laws, tit. 45, c. 3, §8.

In Connecticut and Vermont it rightly appears to be considered superfluous to spell this out. Obviously a meeting is not "warned" if the time and place are omitted.

[4] Conn. Gen. Stat., tit. 7, c. 90, §7-3; Me. Rev. Stat., c. 90-A, §31-11; Mass. Gen. Laws, c. 39, §10; N.H. Rev. Stat. Ann., c. 39, §2; Vt. Stat. Ann., tit. 24, c. 31, §704.

In Rhode Island, this requirement applies to special meetings only. R.I. Gen. Laws, tit. 45, c. 3, §6. At annual meetings the warrant must contain notice of the business required by law to be transacted therein (this should be at least theoretically superfluous), tit. 45, c. 3, §8; and the annual meeting may pass any other lawful vote that it pleases, without regard to the warrant, Lonsdale Co. v. Taft, 34 R.I. 496, 84 Atl. 795 (1912), except for disposing of town land or making a tax, R.I. Gen. Laws, tit. 45, c. 3, §12.

[5] Haven v. Lowell, 5 Met. 35 (Mass. 1835); Marden v. Champlin, 17 R.I. 423, 22 Atl. 938 (1891); Walsh v. Farrington, 105 Vt. 269, 165 Atl. 914(1933).

[6] Woodward v. Reynolds, 58 Conn. 486 (1890); Austin v. York, 57 Me. 304 (1869); Woodlawn Cemetery v. Everett, 118 Mass. 354 (1875); Child v. Colburn, 54 N.H. 71 (1873); Atwood v. Lincoln, 44 Vt. 332 (1872).

[7] See §28 infra.

§4   1: THE TOWN MEETING   13

The warrant is usually issued by the selectmen,[8] and they insert articles either on their own motion or upon the written request of a specified minimum number of registered voters of the town,[9] filed before the selectmen "close" the warrant.[10]

The town officers have no authority to call a special meeting for an illegal purpose and no power to spend town funds for such a meeting, even upon petition.[11] They cannot be compelled to call such a meeting.[12] It would seem to follow that they cannot be compelled to insert an illegal article in their own warrant. On the other hand, they cannot be enjoined from calling the meeting[13] or compelled to delete an illegal article from the warrant for an otherwise legal meeting.[14]

Suppose the substance of the request is proper, but the form of it is improper. May the selectmen edit it, with the advice of town counsel? The Massachusetts and New Hampshire statutes merely require the selectmen to insert "the subjects" requested,[15] and it is arguable that this gives them some discretion in this respect. However, Massachusetts town counsel have expressed doubts on this point,[16] and Massachusetts moderators concurred.[17] Can it be done with

---

[8] Conn. Gen. Stat., tit. 7, c. 90, §§7-1-7-3; Me. Rev. Stat., c. 90-A, §30; Mass. Gen. Laws, c. 39, §10; N.H. Rev. Stat. Ann., c. 39, §2; Vt. Stat. Ann., tit. 24, c. 31, §703.
In Rhode Island, the warrant is issued by the town clerk, R.I. Gen. Laws, tit. 45, c. 3, §§G, 8; and for representative meetings in Connecticut it is usually issued by the moderator.

[9] Me. Rev. Stat., c. 90-A, §32 (10 percent of the voters - but not less than 10); Mass. Gen. Laws, c. 39, §10 (10 or more for the annual meeting; 10 percent of the voters or 100, whichever is less, for a special meeting); N.H. Rev. Stat. Ann., c. 39, §3 (10 or one sixth-whichever is greater, presumably); Vt. Stat. Ann., tit. 24, c. 31, §704 (5 percent).

[10] Tilden, *Town Government*, 38 B.U.L. Rev. 347 (1958).

[11] Opinion of the justices, 51 R.I. 322, 154 Atl. 647 (1931).

[12] State ex rel. Weisberg v. Board of Selectmen of North Haven, 16 Conn. Supp. 486 (1950); Willis v. Sauer, 19 Conn. Supp. 216 (1954); Curtis v. Berry, 68 N.H. 18, 40 Atl. 393 (1894).

[13] Rixford Manufacturing Co. v. Highgate, 102 Vt. 1, 144 Atl. 680 (1929).

[14] Jones v. Selectmen of Weston, 238 Mass. 218, 130 N.E. 271 (1921).

[15] Mass. Gen. Laws, c. 39, §10; N.H. Rev. Stat. Ann., c. 39, §3. Compare Me. Rev. Stat., c. 90-A §32 ("a particular article"), and Vt. Stat. Ann., tit. 24, c. 31, §704 ("any article or articles").

[16] At a meeting on October 18, 1961.

[17] At a meeting on November 3, 1961.

the consent of the petitioners? Only if all the petitioners appear and consult the town counsel before the petition is filed. After that it is a public document, and editing depends on a liberal construction of the statute. The safer course is to use the petitioners' language without change so that the selectmen may not be accused of changing the sense of it. If the selectmen approve the substance of the request, but not its precise language, the selectmen may insert their own article containing the substance properly worded, preferably just prior to the requested article, and in such event action (whether affirmative or negative) on the article inserted by the selectmen will make disposition of the requested article a mere formality.

Notice of the meeting must be given a required number of days[18] prior to the meeting in a manner provided by law — by statute or by-law or vote of the town or otherwise.[19] In the case of a representative town meeting the clerk also mails copies of the warrant to each town meeting member a required number of days prior to the meeting.[20]

---

[18] Conn. Gen. Stat., tit. 7, c. 90, §7-3 (at least 5 days, including the day of the notice and Sundays and holidays but not including the day of the meeting); Me. Rev. Stat., c. 90-A, §31-IV (7 days); Mass. Gen. Laws, c. 39, §10 (7 days); N.H. Rev. Stat. Ann., c. 39, §5 (14 days); R.I. Gen. Laws, tit. 45, c. 3, §8 (7 days); Vt. Stat. Ann., tit. 24, c. 31, §703 (at least 12 and not more than 20). The day of posting does not count. Drowne v. Lovering, 93 N.H. 195, 37 A.2d 190 (1944).

[19] Conn. Gen. Stat., tit. 7, c. 90, §7-3 (by posting upon the signposts of the town and such other places as the town may designate at an annual meeting and by publication in a newspaper published or circulated in the town); Me. Rev. Stat., c. 90-A, §31-IV (posting in some conspicuous public place in the town unless the town has adopted a different method); Mass. Gen. Laws, c. 39, §10 (in the manner prescribed by the by-laws, or if there are no by-laws, by a vote of the town, or in a manner approved by the attorney general); N.H. Rev. Stat. Ann., c. 39, §§4, 5 (posting at the place of meeting and at one other public place in the town and, for special meetings, publication in a newspaper of general circulation in the town or as otherwise prescribed by vote (§12)); R.I. Gen. Laws, tit. 45, c. 3, §8 (in 3 or more public places in the town); Vt. Stat. Ann., tit. 24, c. 31, §703 (posting in three public places in the town, and for special meetings, publication in a newspaper published or circulated in the town, designated by the selectmen).

In the Boston Town Records for 1635, we find that meetings were sometimes called "upon publique notice" (i.e., by posting, presumably) and sometimes "upon pryvate warning" (i.e., "from house to house").

[20] e.g. Mass. Gen. Laws, c. 43A, §5.

§4   1: THE TOWN MEETING   15

The period within which the annual meeting must be held is fixed by law.[21] The selectmen may at any time call a special town meeting, either on their own motion or upon a written request by a required minimum number of registered voters; in the latter case the meeting must usually be held within a specified number of days after receipt of the request.[22]

Massachusetts provides that two or more distinct town meetings for distinct purposes may be called by the same warrant.[23] This probably goes back to the time when different classes of voters were allowed to attend different kinds of meetings: voters at large to elect representatives to the General Court, and property owners to vote appropriations.[24] The only purpose for doing this today would seem to be the segregation of important business that must take effect promptly, free from the possibility of reconsideration, in a meeting that can be dissolved forthwith, while the other meeting carries on with other business.[25]

Two or more distinct meetings may also be called for distinct purposes at the same place, but at a somewhat

---

[21] Conn. Gen. Stat., tit. 7, c. 90, §7-1 (first Monday in October); Me. Rev. Stat., c. 90-A, §35 (in March); Mass. Gen. Laws, c. 39, §9 (February, March, April or May); N.H. Rev. Stat. Ann., c. 39, §1 (second Tuesday of March); R.I. Gen. Laws, tit. 45, c. 3, §1 (annually or biennially, as required by law in each town); Vt. Stat. Ann., tit. 34, c. 31, §702 (first Tuesday of March).

[22] Conn. Gen. Stat., tit. 7, c. 90, §7-1 (20 inhabitants; 21 days); Me. Rev. Stat., c. 90-A, §32 (10 percent but not less than 10 voters; no time specified); Mass. Gen. Laws, c. 39, §10 (20 percent or 200, whichever is less; 45 days); N.H. Rev. Stat. Ann., c. 39, §3 (50 or one fourth of the voters — no time specified, but the petition must be filed at least 60 days before the annual meeting); R.I. Gen. Laws, tit. 45, c. 3, §6 (10 percent; no time specified); Vt. Stat. Ann., tit. 24, c. 31, §§705, 708 (5 percent; 10 days).

In Maine the same number of petitioners may have the meeting called by a justice of the peace if the selectmen unreasonably refuse to call a meeting. In Rhode Island the clerk who neglects or refuses to issue a warrant forfeits $50. Massachusetts (Gen. Laws, c. 39, §§11, 12), New Hampshire (Rev. Stat. Ann., c. 39, §§9, 10) and Vermont (Stat. Ann., tit. 24, c. 31, §707) also provide remedies for failure of the selectmen. In Connecticut, mandamus is the remedy. Cummings v. Looney, 89 Conn. 557, 95 Atl. 19 (1915).

[23] Mass. Gen. Laws, c. 39, §10.
[24] Cragie v. Mellen, 6 Mass. 7 (1809).
[25] See §2 *supra* and §35 *infra*.

different time, by separate warrants.[26]

In Connecticut the voters prescribe the place for holding meetings.[27] Elsewhere it appears to be fixed by the authority that calls the meeting.[28] In Massachusetts the town may by by-law designate the hour for the annual meeting.[29] Town meetings in Massachusetts must be held within the geographical limits of the town unless a special law, charter, or town by-law provides otherwise.[30] Elections, however, must be held within the town's geographical limits.

---

[26] See §21 *infra*.
[27] Conn. Gen. Stat., tit. 7, c. 90, §7-5.
[28] Allen v. Hackett, 123 Me. 106, 121 Ad. 906 (1923). Mr. Hackett lost that round, and Mr. Allen won, but in New England these issues, though they are fought to the highest court, do not result in permanent animosities. Seventeen years later, Mr. Hackett was described as "perennial selectman" of Harpswell, and he got his picture in a book, listening carefully to...Mr. Allen. Gould 23.
[29] Mass. Gen. Laws, c. 39, §22.
[30] Mass. Gen. Laws, c. 39, §9.

Chapter 2

The Cast of Characters

§5. Quorum

Voters (or town meeting members) are one of the four indispensable elements of a town meeting. The other three are a moderator, a clerk, and a properly executed warrant with return of service. However, although the meeting may elect temporary substitutes for the official moderator[1] and for the official clerk[2] if they are absent, there is no substitute for the qualified voters. In Massachusetts, the by-laws of an open meeting usually,[3] and the acts establishing representative meetings always,[4] specify a minimum number of voters or members who must be present before the meeting can transact any business. In Rhode Island the number is fixed by statute at seven in towns not over 3,000 in population, and 15 in the rest.[5] This number is called the quorum.[6] When the quorum is not a fixed number but a fraction, the denominator of the fraction is not the number of places but the number of members elected whose membership has not been terminated by death or resignation[7] or moving away.

There was a time when voting at a town meeting was restricted to those who qualified by belonging to the right church and owning enough property.[8] The religious test vanished long ago, but property is still a factor in Connecticut.

---

§5 [1] Sprague v. Bailey, 19 Pick. 436 (Mass. 1837); Mass. Gen. Laws, c. 39, §14.
[2] School District in Stoughton v. Atherton, 12 Met. 105 (Mass. 1846); Mass. Gen. Laws, c. 41, §14.
[3] Mass. Gen. Laws, c. 39, §13. See Blackstone (50), Dover (15 percent), Essex (30), Groton (125), Groveland (annual 100, special 15), Hamilton (200), Hudson (100), Leicester (30), Manchester (100), Marion (50), Northboro (50), Randolph (330), Southbridge (150), Southwick (15), Stockbridge (50 for appropriating funds), Sudbury (5 percent), Tewksbury (5 percent), Upton (20), Weston (40), Wrentham (100).
[4] See Mass. Gen. Laws, c. 43A, §5; N.H. Rev. Stat. Ann., c. 40A, §6.
[5] R.I. Gen. Laws, tit. 45, c. 3, §14.
[6] "Quorum" is a Latin word meaning "of whom." When the King appointed a board, the document was written in Latin, and he was apt to name a group of people "of whom" a specified minimum had to be present.
[7] Deschler 20.
[8] See Tilden, Town Government, 38 B.U.L. Rev. 347, 356 (1958).

In Connecticut it is an enlarging factor; in addition to the electors, any non-resident citizen over 18 who is liable for a tax on an assessment of not less than $1,000 may vote at any open town meeting other than an election, unless restricted by a special statute.[9] Meetings at which taxes are imposed or money spent are called "financial town meetings" in Rhode Island.[10]

In Maine, each person qualified to vote for governor in the town may vote in the town election and in all town affairs.[11] In Massachusetts, the moderator of an open meeting shall receive the vote of any person whose name is on the voting list, or who presents a proper certificate from the registrars of voters.[12] In New Hampshire, every inhabitant who is a citizen over 18 may vote, except paupers and persons excused from paying taxes at their own request.[13] In Vermont, a citizen over 18 whose list is taken in the town and whose poll and old-age assistance taxes are paid may vote, but anyone who lives in a village in the town he may not vote for road commissioner in a town meeting unless 15 percent of the highway tax is spent on highways outside the village.[14]

Towns frequently change the number of voters necessary to constitute a quorum, and some towns have abolished quorum requirements completely.[15]

There are three advantages to abolishing quorum requirements. First, the problem of being unable to conduct a meeting, or of being forced to adjourn for lack of a quorum, is eliminated. Second, meetings may begin on time. Voters in towns with quorum requirements often assume that, although a meeting is scheduled for 7:30, no quorum will be present until substantially later and that therefore there is no reason to appear at 7:30.

The natural concern with respect to a zero quorum is that

---

[9] Conn. Gen. Stat., tit. 7, c. 90, §7-6.
[10] See, for example, Opinion of the justices, 51 R.I. 322, 154 Atl. 647 (1931).
[11] Me. Rev. Stat., c. 90-A, §341.
[12] Mass. Gen. Laws, c. 39, §18.
[13] N.H. Rev. Stat. Ann., tit. IV, c. 54, §1.
[14] Vt. Stat. Ann., tit. 24, c. 31, §701.
[15] Hull, for example.

a small number of voters may convene and conduct business without a broad consensus. This is understandable, but it should be noted that anecdotal evidence offered at meetings of the Massachusetts Moderators Association has more than once brought to light cases where attendance actually increased when quorum requirements were eliminated. However, no detailed study has been conducted.

If a quorum is required, moderators should ascertain (with the assistance of the town clerk) how matters stand on this point before they rap their gavels to open the meeting. Usually the sound of the gavel will bring scurrying in those voters who hang around gossiping just outside the door, so the moderator can count them as well as those inside and seated. If he or she doesn't rap, they will stay outside indefinitely.

If a quorum is not present, the meeting may do no business, but may adjourn to a later hour or day or (in the discretion of the moderator, when not prevented by a by-law) dissolve.[16] It may even adjourn if the moderator is not present, or not yet elected,[17] but there should be a clerk to record an adjournment.[18]

Even where a quorum is not specified by statute or by-law, meetings have sometimes adjourned voluntarily "upon account of the thinness of this Meeting."[19]

If a quorum is present (counting those just outside the door) the moderator should firmly declare the fact and proceed with the business of the meeting. Moderators are entitled thereafter to assume that a quorum is present unless and until the presence of a quorum is doubted.[20] When an action has been completed it is too late to make the point of order that a quorum was not present when it was done.[21]

If the yeas and nays on a counted vote fail to add up to a quorum; the vote is nevertheless valid if the record shows a quorum to have been present at the beginning of the meeting

---

[16] See §§59 and 61 infra.
[17] Attorney General v. Simonds, *111* Mass. *256 (1893)*.
[18] Taylor v. Henry, 2 Pick. *397* (Mass. *1824)*.
[19] Boston Town Records, Sept. *29, 1778.*
[20] Deschler *21;* Hackett 49.
[21] Deschler *21;* see *§59 infra.*

and the presence of a quorum was not thereafter challenged.[22] If, at any time, the point of no quorum should be raised and established, there is nothing further that the meeting can do but adjourn to a fixed time or (in the discretion of the moderator, if not prevented by a by-law) dissolve. An open town meeting can do effective business and then peter out, without theoretically impairing the business actually done before the quorum melts away (although the fear of reconsideration would make counsel for prospective purchasers of town bonds unhappy until the meeting was dissolved). However, in a representative town meeting the major actions taken are legally ineffective until a certain number of days after the meeting dissolves,[23] and in some of these towns a by-law forbids dissolution before all the articles have been acted upon. Consequently it behooves all town meeting members in such towns to stay and maintain a quorum until the warrant has been finished so the meeting may dissolve and give effect to the evening's business.

If a quorum is present, it doesn't matter, legally, how many people are absent.[24]

§6. The Moderator

From the very beginning, town meetings have had a presiding officer called the moderator, with power "to give liberty of speech, and silence unreasonable and disorderly speakings, to put all things to vote, and in case the vote be equal to have the casting voice."[1] Lest he attempt to exercise royal prerogatives, it was expressly provided that "non of these Courts shall be adjourned or dissolved without the

---

[22] Del Prete v. Board of Selectmen of Rockland, 351 Mass. 344, 220 N.E. 2d 912 (1966).
[23] See §2 *supra* and §61 *infra*.
[24] Smith v. Westerly, 19 R.I. 437, 35 Atl. 526 (1896). The fact that only 123 out of 600 voters attended was held not significant. "While it were well if this were otherwise and the people took a more general and active interest in public affairs, yet we must take things as we find them, and judge accordingly."

§6 [1] The Fundamental Orders of Connecticut §§6, 10 (1639). See also The Body of Liberties §§54, 71 (Massachusetts, 1641).

consent of the major parte of the Court."[2] Further, if he should refuse to put a vote, or pronounce a sentence, "The Major parte of the members of that Court or Assembly shall have power to appoint any other meete man of them to do it, And if there be just cause to punish him that should and would not."[3] One wonders what incident provoked this. Such an incident must also have occurred in New Hampshire, for that state now provides that any moderator who willfully neglects or refuses to make any vote certain by a poll, or who willfully violates or neglects to enforce any rule of proceeding which has been established by vote of the town *or otherwise,* shall be fined not more than $500 or imprisoned for not more than six months.[4] It takes a brave person to be a moderator in New Hampshire.[5]

"According to the authority of the 'Lex Parliamentaria,' the Speaker ought to be 'religious, honest, grave, wise, faithful, and secrete.' This is the reason why there is no lack of men ready to step into the office."[6]

The word "moderator" comes from the Latin word that is spelled the same and means the same: "one who regulates or governs."[7] It is used chiefly to describe the persons who preside in town meetings, in Presbyterian and Congregational assemblies, and in the examinations for honors and degrees at Oxford and Cambridge.[8] He is not a mere judge.[9]

In nuclear physics the term "moderator" is used to describe the substance which is mixed with uranium in a

---

[2] The Fundamental Orders of Connecticut §10 (1639).
[3] The Body of Liberties §54 (1641).
[4] N.H. Rev. Stat. Ann., c. 40, §6, See State v. Waterhouse, 71 N.H. 488, 53 Atl. 304 (1902).
[5] Some enjoy the challenge. See the 1845 letter quoted in Rawson, New Hampshire Borns a Town 67 (1942): "Father is as merry as possible. I wish they would have town meeting every week if it would always have such a good effect on his spirits. He is moderator."
[6] Hackett 53.
[7] Century Dictionary and Cyclopedia.
[8] Ibid.
[9] But compare Woodbury, C.J., in In re United States, 286 F.2d 556, 561 (1st Cit. 1961): ". . . the trial judge is not a mere moderator." Much depends on the point of view.

reactor to slow down the high-speed particles to the point where they can do some useful work.[10] This is not unlike the function of a moderator in a town meeting.

Voters addressing the moderator during a meeting typically refer to a man as "Mr. Moderator" and a woman as "Madam Moderator."

It seems clear that the moderator must be a registered voter of the town, although some of the statutes specify this[11] and some do not.[12]

1. *Election of the Moderator.* Traditionally, the first order of business at each meeting was the election of a moderator, by voice, hand or standing vote or ballot, to preside over that meeting. The moderator's term of office expired upon the dissolution of the meeting. This practice still prevails in Maine and parts of Connecticut[13] and Massachusetts. In Rhode Island and Vermont[14] the moderator's term continues until the next annual meeting, and in New Hampshire[15] and some Connecticut towns[16] he or she is elected biennially. In Massachusetts a town may vote to elect a moderator for a term of one or three years.[17] In Massachusetts the moderator of a representative town meeting is elected by all the voters by ballot, and not by the town meeting members only, except when there is a vacancy.[18] In

---

[10] Smyth, Atomic Energy 33, 34 (1954).
[11] Conn. Gen. Stat., tit. 7, c. 90, §7-7, and tit. 9, c. 146, §9-186; Vt. Stat. Ann., tit. 24, c. 31, §711. See Barre v. Greenwich, I Pick. 129 (Mass. 1822).
[12] Me. Rev. Stat., c. 90-A, §36 111; Mass. Gen. Laws, c. 41, §1; N.H. Rev. Stat. Ann., c. 40, §1; R.I. Gen. Laws, tit. 45, c. 3, §15.
[13] Conn. Gen. Stat., tit. 7, c. 90, §7-7; Me. Rev. Stat., c. 90-A, §34 II.
[14] R.I. Gen. Laws, tit. 45, c. 3, §15; Vt. Stat. Ann., tit. 24, c. 31, §711.
[15] N.H. Rev. Stat. Ann., c. 40, §1.
[16] Hamden, Wallingford, Groton and West Haven, for example.
[17] For some representative town meetings, see Mass. Gen. Laws, c. 43A, §8. The only authority we can find for this well-known fact, with respect to open meetings, is the implication contained in the very first sentence of Gen. Laws, c. 39, §14, entitled "Election of Moderator." One would expect to find the affirmative statement either here or in Gen. Laws, c. 41, §1, entitled "Officers to be Elected." Chapter 41, §7 authorizes a town to fix the term but does not specify "one or three years."
[18] See Mass. Gen. Laws, c. 43A, §8.

Connecticut he or she is usually elected by the meeting.[19]

At any town meeting at which a moderator is to be elected in the traditional way, the town clerk presides,[20] but if the clerk is absent or if there is no clerk, the chairman of the selectmen,[21] or senior selectman, or justice of the peace[22] calling the meeting (if the meeting is so called), or a constable[23] presides, in that order, until a moderator is chosen. The election is usually by ballot,[24] and a plurality is usually sufficient.[25]

If a vacancy in the office of moderator occurs during any term, the vacancy is filled by the voters of the town. If a moderator is absent at any town meeting, the town meeting may elect a temporary moderator. In towns that have representative town meetings, any vacancy in the office of moderator may be filled by the town meeting members at a meeting held for that purpose (and not by the registered voters of the town);[26] and at any such meeting at which the moderator is absent, a temporary moderator may be elected by the town meeting members.

Every moderator, however chosen, before entering upon his or her official duties is sworn to the faithful performance of those duties by the town clerk.[27]

In Massachusetts, if a town meeting is held in two or more separate places, the moderator may appoint an assistant moderator to preside at the place of meeting where the

---

[19] In Trumbull, Hamden, New Canaan, Wallingford, Southington, South Windsor, Darien, Westport, Waterford, West Haven, for example.
[20] Me. Rev. Stat., c. 90-A, §34 11; Mass. Gen. Laws, c. 39, §14.
[21] Me. Rev. Stat., c. 90-A, §34 11; Mass. Gen. Laws, c. 39, §14.
[22] Mass. Gen. Laws, c. 39, §14.
[23] Me. Rev. Stat., c. 90-A, §34 11.
[24] See Me. Rev. Stat., c. 90-A, §35; Mass. Gen. Laws, c. 39, §§14, 20, and c. 43A, §8; N.H. Rev. Stat. Ann., c. 40, §1; Vt. Stat. Ann., tit. 24, c. 31, §718. See §67 *infra.* Filling a vacancy is perhaps less formal.
[25] Conn. Gen. Stat., tit. 9, c. 146, §9-173; Mass. Gen. Laws, c. 50, §2; N.H. Rev. Stat. Ann., c. 40, §1. In Vermont a majority is required when the vote is by ballot. Vt. Stat. Ann., tit. 24, c. 31, §712. In Maine the election of a moderator is excepted (perhaps unintentionally) from the provision that election shall be by a plurality vote. Me. Rev. Stat., c. 90-A, §37. See §52 *infra.*
[26] See Mass. Gen. Laws, c. 43A, §8; N.H. Rev. Stat. Ann., c. 40A, §9.
[27] Mass. Gen. Laws, c. 41, §107.

moderator is not present, and the assistant has all the powers vested by law in the moderator to preside at and regulate the proceedings in the meeting at which he or she presides, except that the assistant may not recognize any citizen desiring to address the meeting without the permission of the moderator.[28]

2. *Powers and Duties of the Moderator.* The moderator presides and regulates the proceedings,[29] decides all questions of order[30] and makes public declaration of all votes.[31] No person addresses the meeting without leave of the moderator,[32] and if any person, after warning from the moderator, persists in disorderly conduct, the moderator may order the person to withdraw, and if he or she does not withdraw, may order a constable or any other person to remove the disrupter and confine him or her in some convenient place until the meeting is adjourned.[33]

If a vote declared by the moderator is immediately questioned by seven or more voters, the moderator verifies it by polling the voters or dividing the meeting unless the town has provided some other method.[34]

The moderator should encourage questions from the floor

---

[28] Mass. Gen. Laws, c. 39, §14.
[29] Conn. Gen. Stat., tit. 7, c. 90, §7-7; Me. Rev. Stat., c. 90-A, §34-111; Mass. Gen. Laws, c. 39, §15; N.H. Rev. Stat. Ann., c. 40, §4: R.I. Gen. Laws, tit. 15, c. 3, §§17, 18; Vt. Stat. Arm., tit. 24, c. 31, §§724, 725.
[30] Mass. Gen. Laws, c. 39, §15; N.H. Rev. Stat. Ann., c. 40, §4; Vt. Stat. Anti., tit. 24, c. 31, §724.
[31] Mass. Gen. Laws, c. 39, §15; N.H. Rev. Stat. Ann., c. 40, §4; Vt. Stat. Anti., tit. 24, c. 31, §724.
[32] Me. Rev. Stat., c. 90-A, §34 111 A; Mass. Gen. Laws, c. 39, §17; N.H. Rev. Stat. Ann., c. 40, §7. See also Conn. Gen. Stat., tit. 53, c. 943, §53-172.
[33] Conn. Gen. Stat., tit. 7, c. 90, §7-8; Me. Rev. Stat., c. 90-A, §34-111 A-1; Mass. Gen. Laws, c. 39, §17; N.H. Rev. Stat. Ann., c. 40, §8; R.I. Gen. Laws, tit. 45, c. 3, §19; Vt. Stat. Ann., tit. 24, c. 31, §725. See Doggett v. Hooper, 306 Mass. 129, 27 N.E.2d 737 (1940). Disturbing a town meeting is also an indictable offense at common law. Commonwealth v. Hoxie, 16 Mass. 385 (1820). In Massachusetts it is a crime to smoke or keep intoxicating liquor at a town meeting, and the moderator may cause the offender to be removed from the meeting, but not confined. Mass. Gen. Laws, c. 54, §73. See also §62 infra.
[34] Me. Rev. Stat., c. 90-A, §34 111 C; Mass. Gen. Laws, c. 39, §15; N.H. Rev. Stat. Ann., c. 40, §5; Vt. Stat. Ann., tit. 24, c. 31, §724. For an examination of the very slight differences in the wording of these statutes, see Chapter 11.

as to procedure. Even if all the rest of the meeting knows the answer, it does no harm to review and restate a principle from time to time. Furthermore, a voter who has taken time to inquire how to go about accomplishing a given purpose is less likely to present the moderator with an ill-considered motion to be untangled, if possible.[35]

The moderator may speak in the debate, but it is a great mistake to do so while presiding, unless it appears that the moderator alone is in possession of relevant and significant information of a thoroughly objective nature which ought to be imparted to the meeting. Otherwise, if the moderator must speak, he or she should step down and let someone else preside.[36]

Moderators may also vote in an open meeting,[37] or in a representative meeting if they are, ex officio or by independent election, members,[38] but it is never desirable and, except in two instances, never necessary for them to do so. They may vote to break a tie and, if a motion the moderator opposes would otherwise carry by one vote, he or she may vote against it, thus creating a tie and defeating it. In these two instances moderators who are voters or members in their own right must be prepared, with the spotlight full upon them, to decide the fate of the motion. Whether he or she votes or abstains, the moderator will be the deciding factor.[39] The moderator of a representative meeting who is not a member cannot vote.[40]

On the whole, it seems that a moderator of a representative meeting who is not a member ex officio should not stand for election as a member also. All that is gained is the dubious privilege of breaking a tie or creating a tie when one vote will do it (a situation which may never arise), and the

---

[35] There are limits, of course. See issue No. I of the Town Moderator (Massachusetts Moderators' Association, Sept. 1, 1960).
[36] Bolton 20; Hackett 169. See §65 *infra*.
[37] In the early days in Rhode Island, he had a double vote. Eaton, The Right to Local Self-government, 13 Harv. L. Rev. 441, 451 (1900).
[38] Demeter 43; Robert 238.
[39] House Rule 1, 6, requires the Speaker to vote where his vote would be decisive.
[40] Cushing 197; Robert 192, 238. *Contra:* Bolton 20.

practical effect for the moderator's precinct is to deprive it of one of its voices.

Although the town clerk is charged with the duty of recording all votes passed at town meetings,[41] it is wise for the moderator to keep reasonably complete personal and unofficial notes of the action taken, and particularly of the count on record votes. There is some question whether the statutes require the town clerk to record the votes on preliminary motions, and most do not do so. Accordingly, some moderators keep a running record of the various motions (whether preliminary or final) made under each article, including the action thereon, the names of the persons who speak on each motion and the time when each begins and ends his debate. In the event of litigation such a record might be of value.[42]

§7. The Town Clerk

Of the town clerk's many duties, the one that concerns us most here is the duty to record all votes passed at town meeting as declared by the moderator.[1] This makes the clerk or a substitute,[1a] together with the quorum, the warrant with a properly completed return of service, and the moderator, one of the four indispensable elements of the meeting. In Massachusetts clerks enter upon their duties seven days after their election.[2] They should be sworn, either by the moderator or by a justice of the peace,[3] at or before the first session of the first meeting at which they act as clerk. They can record

---

[41] Conn. Gen. Stat., tit. 7, c. 92, §7-23; Me. Rev. Stat., c. 90-A, §34 IV; Mass. Gen. Laws, c. 39, §15, and c. 41, §15; N.H. Rev. Stat. Ann., c. 41, §16; R.I. Gen. Laws, tit. 45, c. 3, §22; Vt. Stat. Ann., tit. 24, c. 35, §1152.
[42] See the cases cited infra §17, note 5.

§7 [1]Conn. Gen. Stat., tit. 7, c. 92, §7-23; Me. Rev. Stat., c. 90-A, §34 IV; Mass. Gen. Laws, c. 39, §15, and c. 41, §15; N.H. Rev. Stat. Ann., c. 41, §16; R.I. Gen. Laws, tit. 45, c. 3, §22; Vt. Stat. Ann., tit. 24, c. 35, §1152.
[1a] Mass. Gen. Laws, c.41, §19.
[2] Mass. Gen. Laws, c. 41, §107.
[3] Mass. Gen. Laws, c. 41, §107.

their own election and their own oath,[4] provided they do it at that session, but an adjourned session may be too late.[5] If a moderator is to be elected at the meeting, the town clerk calls the meeting to order and presides until the moderator is elected.[6] The clerk's responsibility for recording the votes of the meeting is a high one.[7] His or her record of a vote may not be attacked collaterally or varied by other evidence.[8] If a clerk makes a mistake,[9] he or she may correct it at any time before ceasing to be town clerk,[10] but not after.[11] The moderator cannot help the clerk. "We considered of that, but he is no more than any other witness."[12] Conversely, the clerk cannot correct the moderator's mistake.[13] He or she can help the moderator vastly by a timely nudge or whisper, however.

Since the voters can not amend the record, inquiries from

---

[4] Briggs v. Murdock, 13 Pick. 305 (Mass. 1832).
[5] Taylor v. Henry, 2 Pick. 397 (Mass. 1824). Compare Taylor v. Henry with Sprague v. Bailey, 19 Pick. 436 (Mass. 1837). But also see Bartlett v. Kinsley, 13 Conn. 327 (1843), in which the town clerk was sworn and made his record two months later, but the meeting and the record were held valid.
[6] Me. Rev. Stat., c. 90-A, §34 II; Mass. Gen. Laws, c. 39, §14.
[7] Mass. Gen. Laws, c. 39, §15, and c. 41, §15.
[8] Taylor v. Henry, 2 Pick. 397 (Mass. 1824); School District in Stoughton v. Atherton, 12 Met. 105 (Mass. 1846); Mayhew v. District of Gay Head, 13 Allen 129 (Mass. 1866); Suburban Land Co. v. Billerica, 314 Mass. 184, 49 N.E.2d 1012, 147 A.L.R. 660 (1943); Attorney General v. Ware, 328 Mass. 18, 101 N.E.2d 365 (1951); Franklin Falls Pulp Co. v. Franklin, 66 N.H. 274, 20 Atl. 333 (1890).
[9] Lincoln v. Chapin, 132 Mass. 470 (1882). See §17 infra, re mandamus.
[10] Boston Turnpike Co. v. Pomfret, 20 Conn. 590 (1850); Chamberlain v. Dover, 13 Me. 466 (1836); Welles v. Battelle, 11 Mass. 477 (1814); Sprague v. Bailey, 19 Pick. 436 (Mass. 1837); Halleck v. Boylston, 117 Mass. 469 (1875); Hoag v. Durfey, I Aik. 286 (Vt. 1826). See Boston Town Records, Sept. 27, 1643, where an omission on one page is corrected on the next, accompanied by "I humbly crave pardon for this error." There is a difference of opinion as to whether the record may be amended after others have acted in reliance on it. Compare Chamberlain v. Dover, *supra*, and Boston Turnpike Co. v. Pomfret, *supra*, with Sawyer v. Manchester & Keene R.R., 62 N.H. 135 (1882).
[11] Boston Turnpike Co. v. Pomfret, 20 Conn. 590 (1850); Hartwell v. Littleton, 13 Pick. 229 (Mass. 1832); School District in Stoughton v. Atherton, 12 Met. 105 (Mass. 1846). Except in Maine. Me. Rev. Stat., c. 90-A, §57 1.
[12] Parker, C.J., in Taylor v. Henry, 2 Pick. 397, 403 (Mass. 1824).
[13] Judd v. Thompson, 125 Mass. 553 (1878); Felker v. Chesley, 66 N.H. 381, 29 Atl. 540 (1891).

the floor of a town meeting concerning the record should only be allowed for informational purposes, when and if relevant to the pending action. Any wrangling over the content of the record should be promptly dispensed with by the moderator, who should advise the speaker(s) to visit the town hall and consult the town clerk in the morning.

If the meeting adopts, by a brief affirmative vote, a long set of new by-laws contained in a printed report of a committee, it is prudent for the town clerk to copy the whole pamphlet into the records to avoid any uncertainty as to the identity of the by-laws adopted.[14]

Town clerks are required, as soon as a vote appropriating money becomes effective, to certify each appropriation to the assessors and the town accountant or treasurer.[15] If the meeting is actually called and the vote actually passed, the clerk is not liable to one who is arrested by the tax collector, even if there is a defect in the calling or the conduct of the meeting, as these are matters for which he or she is not responsible.[16] But the clerk is not required to certify to bond counsel that the meeting was duly called and conducted, and he or she had better be sure of both the facts and the law if doing so voluntarily.

The clerk cannot usurp the function of the moderator by proclaiming his or her own rulings as to the validity of the proceedings.[17]

§8. The Selectmen

The particular distinctive part which the selectmen play in a town meeting comes at the very beginning: it is they who set the time and place for the meeting and prepare and issue

---

[14] See Smith v. Abington Savings Bank, 171 Mass. 178, 50 N.E. 545 (1898); Mayo v. West Springfield, 260 Mass. 594, 157 N.E. 700 (1927).
[15] Mass. Gen. Laws, c. 41, §15A.
[16] Allen v. Metcalf, 17 Pick. 208 (Mass. 1835).
[17] Hill v. Goodwin, 56 N.H. 441 (1876).

§8

the warrant pursuant to which it is called.¹ After that it is theoretically possible to dispense with them entirely. Actually, it is as difficult to imagine a town meeting without the selectmen as it is to imagine a Thanksgiving turkey without cranberry sauce. In Massachusetts towns that do not have finance committees, the selectmen are required to submit a budget at the annual town meeting.² Apart from this, the zeal and public spirit which carry them to their distinguished office would never let them be absent or indifferent. In many representative town meetings their special interest is recognized by their designation as members at large, ex officio.³

In many towns where the first order of business is to elect a moderator, it is traditional for the senior selectman to call the meeting to order and preside over the nomination and election of the moderator.⁴ In Massachusetts, by statute,⁵ the town clerk presides, in the absence of a moderator, until a moderator is elected, but if the town clerk is absent, the senior selectman presides until a moderator is elected. Then the selectmen receive and count the votes for a temporary clerk.⁶

---

§8 ¹Conn. Gen. Stat., tit. 7, c. 90, §§7-1, 7-2, 7-3; Me. Rev. Stat., c. 90-A, §30; Mass. Gen. Laws, c. 39, §§9-12; N.H. Rev. Stat. Ann., c. 39, §§l, 2; Vt. Stat. Ann., tit. 24, c. 31, §703.

In Rhode Island the meeting is called by the town clerk, R.I. Gen. Laws, tit. 45, c. 3, §§5, 8; and Connecticut representative town meetings are called by the moderator. Conn. Sp. Acts of 1957: No. 216, §55 (Darien); No. 251, §6 (Groton); No. 170, §10 (Southington); No. 215, §10 (South Windsor); No. 49, §5 (Wallingford); No. 504, §11 (Waterford); No. 533, §5 (West Haven); No. 348, §5 (Westport).

² Mass. Gen. Laws, c. 39, §16. Even in towns which do have finance committees, a by-law may authorize the selectmen to present the budget. Such a by-law is rare. See Comins, Bulletin F, Massachusetts Association of Town Finance Committees 7 (1959).

³ Fairfield, Conn., and Brookline, Lexington, and Milton, Mass., for example.
⁴ Westbrook, *Biography of an Island* 217 (1958) (Swan's Island, Me.).
⁵ Mass. Gen. Laws, c. 39, §14.
⁶ Mass. Gen. Laws, c. 41, §14.

§9. The Town Counsel

Around the time of the town meeting, the town counsel may have the impression that he or she is working double time.[1]

"...It is primarily the responsibility of the selectmen to prepare for the town meeting. However, they may delegate the actual preparation of the town meeting warrant to the town counsel, subject, of course, to their final approval of the form and content. If counsel is given this task, he must assemble the material, see to it that every article is in proper legal form and make sure that no vital article is omitted. (The General Laws require, for example, the inclusion of a separate article in the annual town meeting warrant to provide for the salaries of elected officers.)"[2]

No one should take this statement literally and assume that every article in the warrant is proper. Some articles may have been inserted on petition, and they may be of doubtful legality, either in substance or in form.[3]

If the town counsel is present at the meeting, the moderator will usually consult with him or her on difficult questions. Town counsel may state an opinion to the meeting, and the moderator will generally give town counsel's opinion substantial weight. However, procedural rulings at town meetings are made by the moderator, and the moderator is not bound by town counsel's opinion.

The moderator certainly should bear in mind that most articles sponsored by town boards and officers are drafted by the town counsel and that town counsel also usually drafts the motions presented,[4] frequently after careful consultation with the attorney general or bond counsel, so moderators should be very sure of themselves indeed before publicly expressing an adverse opinion. If a moderator is troubled by a motion prepared by town counsel he or she would do well to declare

---

§9 [1]Hardy, *The Role of the Town Counsel* I (Bureau of Government Research, University of Massachusetts, 1960). See also 38 B.U.L. Rev. 408 (1958).
[2] Hardy, op. cit. *supra* at 10, 11.
[3] See §4 *supra*.
[4] Hardy, op. cit. *supra* at 11.

a recess and consult the lawyer privately.

In addition to preparing articles and motions, town counsel must be prepared to answer every legal question that may be directed to him or her from the floor. This is a big assignment,[5] and the moderator should assist by seeing that town counsel has plenty of time to answer properly and by ruling out questions not relevant to the business before the meeting.

"The town counsel's work relating to the town meeting is not over when the bang of the moderator's gavel signals the end of the meeting. There is usually much clean-up work to be done — titles to be examined, orders for eminent domain takings to be prepared, deeds to be drawn, petitions to the General Court to be written and processed, contracts to be drawn or approved, meetings with state boards to be attended, and conferences with many special town committees to be arranged."[6]

§10. The Finance Committee

Towns in Connecticut, Massachusetts and New Hampshire may, and towns in Massachusetts whose valuation exceeds $1,000,000 must, establish a committee known as the board of finance in Connecticut, the appropriation, advisory, warrant or finance committee in Massachusetts, and the budget committee in New Hampshire.[1] Finance committee is the commonest usage in Massachusetts.

In Connecticut this committee is appointed by the selectmen in the first instance[2] and thereafter elected.[3] In New Hampshire it consists of a member of the school board, a member of each village board of commissioners, a selectman,

---

[5] Id. at 12.
[6] Ibid.

§10 [1]Conn. Gen. Stat., tit. 7, c. 106; Mass. Gen. Laws, c. 39, §16; N.H. Rev. Stat. Ann., c. 32; see Finance Committee of Falmouth v. Falmouth Board of Public Welfare, 1963 Mass. Adv. Sh. 351 (citing Town Meeting Time).
[2] Conn. Gen. Stat., tit. 7, c. 106, §7-340.
[3] Conn. Gen. Stat., tit. 9, c. 146, §9-202.

and three, six, nine, or twelve members at large (as the meeting adopting the statute may by vote determine), who are either appointed by the moderator or elected, as the town may choose from time to time.[4] In Massachusetts the election or appointment of the committee is determined by by-law.[5] The committee is elected in only about 27 Massachusetts towns; in a few of them it is appointed by other town officers, and in the great majority of them it is appointed by the moderators, "who with quasi judicial approach have given serious thought to their appointees."[6]

During the winter months there are no harder-working town officials than the members of the finance committee, as they study the requests of the department heads in accordance with their duty to prepare the budget for the following year. In addition, they study the other articles proposed and prepare recommendations on them also, although in some towns, by custom and not by any limit on their authority,[7] they do not consider articles that do not involve money.

In Connecticut the board of finance has substantial powers (and corresponding responsibilities). The town meeting may make no appropriation in excess of that recommended for the purpose by the board, and no appropriation not recommended by the board.[8] In New Hampshire, the total amount appropriated at any annual meeting may not exceed the recommended budget by more than 10 percent, and no appropriation may be made for any purpose not included in the budget, except that the committee may also submit items they do not recommend, and the voters may act on them but may not appropriate an amount that would increase the total over the 10 percent allowed.[9] At

---

[4] N.H. Rev. Stat. Ann., c. 32, §2.

[5] Mass. Gen. Laws, c. 39, §16.

[6] Comins, Bulletin F, Massachusetts Association of Town Finance Committees 6 (1959). See Model By-Laws for Massachusetts Towns 28 (1940).

[7] Comins, op. cit. *supra* at 8.

[8] Conn. Gen. Stat., tit. 7, §7-344.

[9] N.H. Rev. Stat. Ann., c. 32, §8. The last sentence of §8, as amended in 1961, reads, "The ten per cent increase herein allowable above the total amount specified in the budget for said meeting shall be computed on the total amount recommended less that part of any appropriation item which is to be raised by the issuance of bonds

special meetings no appropriation may be made for any purpose not approved, and no increase of more than 10 percent may be made.[10]

In Massachusetts, the finance committee's recommendations have no such force. They are purely advisory.[11] An occasional attempt has been made, by by-law, to restrict the meeting from altering the finance committee's recommendations. The General Court has blown hot and cold on this. In the same year it nullified a Danvers by-law that required a two-thirds vote to override the finance committee,[12] and presented to Ipswich for acceptance a statute which, among other things, provided that no recommendation of the finance committee relating to the appropriation of money should be increased or decreased except by a two-thirds vote.[13] A by-law that requires the finance committee to report is directory, but a by-law that provides that no appropriation may be made unless the financial committee has first made a recommendation is mandatory and an appropriation vote is not valid unless the recommendation has first been made.[14]

In many towns the report of the finance committee is distributed to the voters or members, and its recommendations are moved as main motions under each article.[15] This procedure has the advantage of clarity. While the motion may be amended (as to amounts, down in Connecticut, up or down in Massachusetts, and down or, within the 10 percent limit, up in New Hampshire), every voter may keep track of the amendments with a sharp pencil and a little attention. The use

---

and notes."
[10] N.H. Rev. Stat. Ann., c. 32, §9.
[11] Illig v. Plymouth, 337 Mass. 239, 149 N.E.2d 140 (1958); Mass. Gen. Laws, c. 44, §33B; Clinton Housing Authority v. Finance Committee of Clinton, 329 Mass. 495, 109 N.E.2d 449 (1952). However, a special meeting cannot transfer a previous appropriation without such a recommendation.
[12] Mass. Acts of 1949, c. 13, §39.
[13] Mass. Acts of 1949, c. 247, §38.
[14] Loring v. Westwood, 238 Mass. 9, 130 N.E. 85 (1921). Cf. Young v. Westport, 302 Mass. 597, 20 N.E.2d 404 (1939).
[15] See §§18 and 23 infra.

of illustrative graphs, charts and profiles is recommended.[16] The more the committee can set forth in its printed report its reasons for its recommendations, the more irrelevant debate can be eliminated and the time of the meeting saved. This is a counsel of perfection, however, which it is unreasonable to expect a hard-pressed volunteer committee to follow altogether. The existence of the finance committee does not relieve the rest of the meeting from thinking and asking questions for themselves.[17]

§11. The School Committee

The school committee plays a very important part in town meetings, if for no other reason than that its budget is so large a part of the budget of the town.

Each Massachusetts town has both a constitutional[1] and a statutory[2] obligation to support and maintain the public schools. Until the passage by the voters in Massachusetts in 1980 of the so-called Proposition 2 ½,[3] Massachusetts school committees were empowered to determine what amounts were necessary to carry out their duties and if the town meeting failed to appropriate the sum requested, a court could compel the town to appropriate the deficiency, together with a sum equal to 25 percent thereof. In 1980 the statute[4] was amended to continue the requirement that "every city and town shall appropriate a sum of money sufficient for the support of the public schools..." but with the added proviso that no town is required to provide more money for support of the public schools than is appropriated by vote of the town meeting. The statute further provides that in acting on appropriations for school purposes, the town meeting shall vote only on the total amount of the appropriation and shall not allocate

---

[16] Comins, op. cit. *supra* at 20.
[17] Choate v. Sharon, 259 Mass. 478, 156 N.E. 542 (1927).

§11 [1] Massachusetts, c. V, §11.
[2] Mass. Gen. Laws, c. 71, §34.
[3] Mass. Acts of 1980, c. 580.
[4] Mass. Gen. Laws, c. 71, §34.

appropriations among accounts, place any restriction on appropriations or otherwise limit the authority of the school committee to determine expenditures within the total appropriation. The town meeting may, however, make non-binding monetary recommendations to increase or decrease particular items.

The Massachusetts Education Reform Act of 1993[5] includes school finance provisions establishing a minimum amount that shall be appropriated by each town for the support of the schools.[6] If a town meeting fails to appropriate for the schools at least the minimum required amount, the commissioner of revenue may refuse to approve the tax rate for the next fiscal year.[7] In addition, state school aid may be reduced for the fiscal year following any year in which a town does not spend at least its minimum appropriation.[8] While it is probably beyond the power of the Moderator to rule out of order a main motion, or amendment, to appropriate a sum less than the statutory minimum, the Moderator should advise the meeting of the consequences of passing such a vote.

§12. Select Committees

"The authority of towns to choose special committees to perform municipal duties not vested by law in designated officers is beyond doubt."[1] The motion for the establishment of a committee may be either a main motion under an article or a subsidiary motion to refer the matter under discussion to a committee.[2]

---

[5] Mass. Acts of 1993, c. 71.
[6] Mass. Gen. Laws, c. 70, §6.
[7] Mass. Gen. Laws, c. 69, §1K.
[8] Mass. Gen. Laws, c. 70, §11.

§12 [1]Adams v. Plunkett, 274 Mass. 453, 462, 175 N.E. 60 (1931); Moulton v. Beals, 98 N.H. 461, 102 A.2d 489 (1954). See also Palmer v. Ferry, 6 Gray 420 (Mass. 1856). The New Hampshire Supreme Court in 1962 ruled that adoption of the proposal contained in an article "To see if the Town will vote to authorize the Town Manager to appoint a committee... " obliged the manager to appoint it. McMahon v. Town of Salem, 104 N.H. 219, 182 A.2d 463 (1962).
[2] See §41 infra.

Town meetings frequently establish committees either to investigate and report or to carry out substantive action. In the latter case particularly, the powers of the committee should be clear so as to avoid litigation.[3] The vote should, of course, set forth the duties of the committee and, in addition should include the how, the when and the where: How is the committee appointed, and when and where does it report? Experience has shown that it is wise as well to establish explicitly the name of the committee, the number of members, and the budget (if any) that the committee is to be granted. If there is to be a budget, there should be warning in the article under which the motion is made of the appropriation, borrowing, or transfer establishing the funding. There should also be an explicit understanding as to whether the committee is to be an ad hoc group, to function until the completion of some specific task and then dissolve, or whether it is to function as a standing committee for the foreseeable future, with or without a sunset clause to provide for a future review of the continued need for the group.

Frequently the moderator is directed to appoint the members of the committee. When this is the case, there are a number of considerations to keep in mind in making the appointments:

1. It is wise to appoint persons who have an unbiased interest in the subject matter to be considered by the committee. Furthermore, if the committee is to investigate a controversial question, it might well be advisable also to include a leading representative from the principal proponents and from the principal opponents. In the informality of committee procedure, under the influence of the unbiased members, these individuals would have an opportunity to see the other side's point of view and, with the aid of the unbiased members, it is likely that a fair compromise would be produced, which the town, knowing that all points of view have been represented, will accept.

---

[3] See the following cases where the authority of the committee was questioned: Damon v. Granby, 2 Pick. 345 (Mass. 1824); Marsh v. Dedham, 137 Mass. 235 (1884); Vinal v. Nahant, 232 Mass. 412, 122 N.E. 295 (1919); G. M. Bryne Co. v. Barnstable, 286 Mass. 544, 191 N.E. 45 (1934).

2. Committee members should be able to work together, and accordingly no one should be appointed who makes it difficult for the committee to accomplish its purposes because of his or her arbitrariness.

3. There should be some members of the committee who have a specialized knowledge of the subject matter to be considered by the committee. If, for example, the committee is to report on the advisability of building a new town hall, it would be helpful to have an engineer or a contractor on the committee. A professional would know best where to get the necessary information and would understand the problems involved. However, the issue of conflict of interest should be borne in mind. Wherever possible, the committee members and their families should not have any financial interest in the decisions of the committee, or if they do, those need to be handled consistent with the conflict of interest statute.[4] This problem should be squarely faced before the appointments are made.

4. Particular areas in the town or particular groups of inhabitants should in many cases be represented. Thus if a change in the zoning by-law would affect the north end of the town alone, certainly someone from that area should be on the committee. Or if a new school is being considered, a representative from the parent-teachers association should be appointed.

What about the appointment of a chairperson of the committee? It seems to be the custom in the appointment of legislative committees that the member first named chairs the group unless the committee decides to elect its own chairperson.[5] It is not clear whether a town moderator has the power to appoint a chair. Many do, and in any event the moderator may charge one of the members with the duty of bringing the committee together and organizing it. This may amount to a tactful way of designating the chairperson without causing the members of the committee to feel that they, have been deprived of the opportunity of choosing their own chair.

---

[4] Massachusetts General Laws, c. 268A, inserted by Acts of 1962, c. 779. Town counsel should be consulted if questions arise.
[5] Cushing 218; Demeter 195; Jefferson 139; Robert 131.

No doubt the vote instructing the moderator to appoint the committee could also instruct to appoint the chairman, but in practice it seldom does.

When the committee has been appointed, the moderator has no further power or duty with respect to it, except for the filling of vacancies.[6] Moderators have no legal obligation to see that the committees begin their work or report at the appointed time, but since the moderator appoints the committees, he or she may wish to see to it that they do.

Once the committee is appointed, the procedure by which it carries on its activities is usually informal,[7] but it must be in compliance with the applicable open meeting law.[8] There should be no limitation on debate or the number of times a member may speak. The chairman, instead of abstaining from speaking and voting, is usually the most active participant. A majority will be a quorum for any meeting and a committee may act by a majority of those present and voting at a duly called meeting at which a quorum is present.[9]

When the committee has completed its work, it should, of course, prepare its report and file it in accordance with the vote establishing the committee.[10] Frequently the town merely votes to accept the report, but the effect of such a vote may be uncertain. If the committee has taken action which it wishes the town to ratify, or proposes to take action which it wishes

---

[6] Lincoln by-laws provide that vacancies in any appointive office shall be filled by the person having the authority to make appointments to such office.

[7] Demeter 196; Robert 212.

[8] In Massachusetts, Massachusetts General Laws, Chapter 39, Section 23.

[9] Demeter 195. In Damon v. Granby, 2 Pick. 345 (Mass. 1824), the town voted to establish a committee of certain inhabitants to superintend the building of a meeting house, and a committee of three specified non-inhabitants to locate a place for the meeting house. The court held that the superintending committee had the authority to act by a majority but the locating committee required unanimous action. It was stated that the locating committee was not a committee of the town but that the members were commissioners and accordingly must act unanimously unless express authority to act by a majority had been given them. Regular committees "are a part of the whole body, representing the whole on the subject committed to them, and they therefore partake of the qualities and enjoy the power of the constituent." It appeared that the locating committee was not considered a part of the whole body because it was made up of nonresidents.

[10] See §18 *infra*.

the town to authorize, or if it wishes the town itself to act, it should see to it that an appropriate article is inserted in the warrant and that a motion is made from the floor.[11]

If, on the other hand, such a general article is inserted and the town wishes to avoid inadvertently committing itself with respect to the report, it would be advisable to have a motion "To receive and place the report on file without ratification of any action taken, or authorization of any action proposed," rather than a motion to accept. This is owing to the fact that an acceptance of the report may constitute an authorization of any future action recommended in the report or a ratification of past action described.[12] It is possible for an assembly to appoint itself a Committee of the Whole by a majority vote.[13] This procedure is rarely resorted to except in legislative assemblies, when the purpose of referring a question to the Committee of the Whole may be to obtain greater freedom of discussion. It is seldom appropriate for town meetings.[14]

---

[11] See McGovern v. Southbridge, 264 Mass. 578, 163 N.E. 175 (1928).

[12] Arlington v. Peirce, 122 Mass. 270 (1877); Corey v. Wrentham, 164 Mass. 18, 41 N.E. 101 (1895). See §18 *infra,* note 5.

In Fuller v. Groton, 11 Gray 340 (Mass. 1858), the question involved the validity of a vote indemnifying a school committee for expenses incurred in defending a libel suit against it. This vote was adopted under an article "To hear the report of any committee heretofore chosen, and pass any vote in relation to the same." The report of the committee was accepted and the vote included the authority to pay the expenses of the libel defense. It was held that this vote was authorized under the article. The court stated, "It is not necessary to state that the town will be called upon to grant money, if the subject is one which is likely to require money. This form of notice for action on reports of committees is of common use and sanctioned by authority." P. 342.

Compare Bickford v. Hyde Park, 173 Mass. 536, 54 N.E. 250 (1899), in which the report contained no recommendation, and acceptance was held to constitute no substantive action.

In Sugar Hill Improvement Association v. Town of Lisbon, 104 N.H. 40, 178 A.2d 512 (1962), the court made use of a committee report to construe confusing articles and votes.

[13] Cushing §§297 et seq.; Demeter 204 et seq.; Robert 229 et seq.

[14] The town of Saugus resorted to this procedure at a meeting held on July 10, 1961, apparently for the purpose of enabling a voter who had been removed from the meeting by the moderator to return to it when it was sitting as a Committee of the Whole.

§13. Constables, Checkers, Tellers and Pages

The first duty of a constable in connection with town meetings is the service of the warrant and the giving of the prescribed notice.[1] The constable's return of service is ordinarily read by the moderator or the town clerk when the meeting is opened. During the meeting the constable may be called upon by the moderator to remove unruly citizens.[2]

Checkers are appointed by the selectmen or the town clerk to screen all persons who wish to enter the meeting place and to ensure that only voters have access to the voting area.[3] In order to facilitate the admission of the voters, particularly in open town meetings where they may be numerous and where a crush may develop at the opening hour, separate voting lists for those with names beginning with A-M and N-Z are frequently used, with two checkers for each list. Since controversial matters are frequently carried or lost on a close vote, it is of great importance that the moderator be certain that only voters are voting.[4]

Tellers are appointed by the moderator to assist in taking a counted vote,[5] and in some towns are sworn. There should

---

§13 [1] Me. Rev. Stat., c. 90-A, §31 111; Mass. Gen. Laws, c. 39, §10, and c. 41, §94; N.H. Rev. Stat. Ann., c. 39, §6; R.I. Gen. Laws, tit. 45, c. 3, §8.

[2] Conn. Gen. Stat., tit. 7, c. 90, §7-8; Me. Rev. Stat., c. 90-A, §III Al; Mass. Gen. Laws, c. 39, §17, and c. 54, §73; N.H. Rev. Stat. Ann., c. 40, §8; R.I. Gen. Laws, tit. 45, c. 3, §19; Vt. Stat. Ann., tit. 24, c. 31, §725. Once upon a time the moderator had to turn the constable out for disorderly behavior. Boston Town Records, Oct. 1, 1779.

[3] See Boston Town Records, May 8, 1780. "On a Motion made, Voted that twelve Persons be appointed Monitors." They must have been either checkers or tellers, or both.

[4] See Chapter 11.

[5] Bolton 17; Tilden, *Town Government*, 38 B.U.L. Rev. 347, 361 (1958). There seems to be no statutory basis now for this widespread custom. Massachusetts once had a statute expressly authorizing the appointment of tellers in town meetings generally. Mass. Acts of 1883, c. 229. This statute appears to have merely formalized the existing practice. See note 3 *supra*. In 1893 this was limited to elections. Mass. Acts of 1893, c. 417, §116. See now Mass. Gen. Laws, c. 54, §21. Apparently it was universally assumed that the Legislature did not intend to exclude the use of tellers in other cases. Attorney General v. Crocker, 138 Mass. 214 (1885), cited by Tilden for the proposition that the office of teller is well recognized in the case law of the Commonwealth (op. cit. *supra* at 361), was an election case, and was based upon the 1883 statute. For two reasons, therefore, we cannot count it as now supporting the use

be a sufficient number to provide two tellers for each section of the auditorium, one to check the other as each row of voters is counted. Some moderators make these appointments prior to the meeting in order to ascertain whether or not a teller may be actively involved in a controversial matter. If a teller indicates the likelihood of speaking on such a matter, he or she should not be appointed, since there should be no possibility of any partiality in taking a counted vote.

High school students or Boy or Girl Scouts are often requested to act as pages. They may perform such miscellaneous duties as delivering messages, obtaining additional chairs, and carrying hand microphones to the speakers.

§14. Strangers

There is a school which believes that one not registered to vote in the town may not address the meeting without unanimous consent; that if the President or the Chief Justice of the Supreme Court were available and prepared to say a few words, one cantankerous individual could prevent the meeting from hearing either of them.

The basis for this notion is historical and not relevant to a New England town meeting. In the early 17th century, when the English House of Commons was struggling, at great individual risk, to establish the principles of parliamentary democracy against the power of the throne, they were very cautious about admitting strangers, and any member had the right to have the House or gallery cleared,[1] because strangers were apt to be spies who would report to King James or King Charles the names of those who spoke against the royal

---

of tellers outside of elections. Nevertheless, the foundation of the use in custom is firm. Since the 1883 statute required tellers to be sworn, and since its remains in Mass. Gen. Laws, c. 54, §21 are the nearest thing to statutory authority that we have, it would seem advisable in all cases that tellers be sworn.
§14 [1]Jefferson 173.

interests.[2]

On this side of the Atlantic, however, the colonists felt more safely independent. They kept a wary eye on "commanders, soldiers and other strangers,"[3] but one of the first laws enacted in the Bay Colony, in 1641, provided:

"Every man whether Inhabitant or foreigner, free or not free shall have libertie to come to any publique Court, Council, or Towne meeting, and either by speech or writing to move any lawful, reasonable, and material question, or to present any necessary motion, complaint, petition, Bill or information whereof that meeting hath proper cognizance, so it be done in convenient time, due order, and respective manner."[4]

Furthermore, since 1789, no individual member of Congress has had any right to have the gallery cleared. That power is vested in the Speaker, in case of disturbance or disorderly conduct.[5]

Some town by-laws expressly permit nonvoters to attend at the discretion of the moderator[6] or of the meeting.[7]

Note that our ancestors, in enacting the Body of Liberties, were concerned with the rights of individuals, and they provided that an individual had a right to address a town meeting, even if the person was a foreigner. They would have been astonished to learn that anyone could think that a meeting did not have the right to hear an individual.

While the voters in the town may be more familiar with local matters, it is unlikely that they have a monopoly of wisdom, and frequently there is much that an out-of-towner can impart to them.

It seems clear that a majority of the meeting should have

---

[2] See Bowen, *The Lion and the Throne* 36-37 (1957), for an account of the excitement when a stranger was discovered in the House during the speakership of Sir Edward Coke.

[3] Massachusetts Colony Laws, c. 92.

[4] The Body of Liberties, c. 54 (1641). See also Boston Town Records, May 8, 1780: "The left Quarter of the upper Galary was Assigned by the Moderator for Strangers, and Persons under twenty One years of Age."

[5] House Rule I, 2.

[6] Bedford, Manchester, and Shirley.

[7] Westborough.

the right to hear any person they wish to hear, "so it be done in convenient time, due order, and respective manner."[8]

Notwithstanding the Body of Liberties on the subject, in modern practice the substance of the meeting, in particular the making of motions, must be left to the registered voters.

If a cantankerous individual takes advantage of a by-law to prevent the meeting from hearing a nonvoter it wishes to hear, the meeting has a remedy: It may simply recess. The cantankerous individual may leave if he or she wishes; the others may remain in the hall and listen to the speaker.

On the other hand, there seems to be no doubt that a meeting may, by majority vote, exclude strangers if it is so minded,[9] and, by statute, no one may speak without permission from the moderator.[10] This obviously applies to strangers as well as to voters.

In a representative town meeting a registered voter has a right to speak, subject to conditions prescribed by the meeting, even though she or he may not be a town meeting member. The standard form statutes so provide,[11] and the special statutes are alike in this respect.[12] It is clear, however, that this right to speak must also be subject to the power of the moderator to preserve order, regulate the proceedings and determine who shall speak, although the standard and special statutes do not expressly so provide.

---

[8] The Body of Liberties, c. 54 (1641).
[9] Mass. Gen. Laws, c. 39, §17.
[10] See Brooklyn Trust Co. v. Town of Hebron, 51 Conn. 22 (1883), in which the town voted "That no Middletown man be allowed to address this meeting."
[11] Mass. Gen. Laws, c. 43A, §5; N.H. Rev. Stat. Ann., c. 40A, §6.
[12] For example, Fairfield, Conn. (Conn. Pub. Acts 1947, c. 527, §4); Sanford, Me. (Me. Pub. Laws of 1935, c. 72, §6); Milton, Mass. (Mass. Acts of 1927, c. 27, §2); Randolph, Mass. (Mass. Acts of 1947, c. 324, §5); Shrewsbury, Mass. (Mass. Acts of 1953, c. 553, §14); Swampscott, Mass. (Mass. Acts of 1927, c. 300, §3).

Chapter 3

Preliminary Considerations

§15. Preparation for the Meeting

The smoothness and efficiency with which a town meeting is run may well depend on the moderator's thoroughness in preparation. The suggestions given below may be helpful.

    1. *The Warrant.* The selectmen, who are responsible for setting the date of the meeting, should ascertain whether the moderator will be available for the desired date and should provide a copy of the warrant as soon as possible, to enable the moderator to study it with care and become familiar with the articles. The moderator should confer with the selectmen, the town counsel, the town clerk, the chairman of the finance committee and others to discuss the subject matter of the articles so as to be well informed on all matters to be presented to the meeting.[1] He or she might also plan to attend any hearings that may be involved, although it is important at all times to avoid giving any impression of partiality or personal interest in the outcome of any article. It is particularly advisable to discuss the articles with the town counsel and thus ascertain whether any legal questions or procedural problems may arise. This is also the time to review carefully any possible conflicts of interest on the moderator's part, and take appropriate steps. (See Chapter 10, §65.)

The moderator should make conspicuous notes in the margin beside each article as reminders of special procedural requirements, such as reports by the planning board, which are conditions precedent to zoning amendments, and of the quantum of any vote required in excess of a majority. Appropriate notations as to statutes and other references

---

§15 [1]In New Hampshire towns which have accepted the Municipal Budget Law (N.H. Rev. Stat. Ann., c. 32), the voters may not make appropriations which exceed, in the aggregate, the budget recommended by the budget committee by more than 10 percent. It would appear that the moderator must compute this overall limit and be prepared to keep, or have kept, a running tally of the appropriations so as not to exceed it.

should also be recorded so that the moderator can call them to the attention of the meeting if challenged on a ruling.

Some moderators go so far as to prepare a loose-leaf notebook with at least one page per article, for recording just such details. If this is done, it makes a handy place to store motions prepared in advance, and other pertinent written material. A page may also be prepared for each article on which the moderator may, during the meeting, note when debate began and ended, and the outcome of the vote(s) on the article.

It is not the moderator's responsibility prior to the meeting to investigate personally whether or not all conditions precedent to the validity of a vote have been satisfied. For example, the moderator need not personally compute the town's debt limit before entertaining a motion to borrow money, or personally see to it, before entertaining a motion to accept a town way, that the selectmen filed the layout with the town clerk. However, if a statute or a by-law requires that a recommendation be made to the meeting itself, as a condition,[2] the moderator should call for the recommendation before proceeding. (See also Section 25 below, which deals with situations where required conditions precedent have not been met.)

2. *Motions.* It will be helpful to the smooth running of the meeting for the moderator to examine the main motions that are to be presented under the articles to see that they are in properly prepared written form. If the proponents of any article are not familiar with town meeting procedure, they will undoubtedly be grateful for any suggestions that the moderator can give them. Here again it is of importance for the moderator to avoid any impression of partiality and explain that his or her interest is merely in seeing that

---

[2] Massachusetts examples: a recommendation of the planning board on an amendment to the zoning by-law, Mass. Gen. Laws, c. 40A, §6, Whittemore v. Town Clerk of Falmouth, 299 Mass. 64, 12 N.E.2d 187 (1937); a recommendation of the appointing board for indemnity to an injured fireman or policeman, Mass. Gen. Laws, c. 41, §100, Berube v. Selectmen of Edgartown, 336 Mass. 634, 147 N.E.2d 180 (1958); a recommendation of the finance committee for a transfer of funds at a special meeting, Mass. Gen. Laws, c. 44, §33B. See §54 infra.

questions are properly placed before the meeting and that procedural entanglements are avoided.

3. *Procedural Questions.* It is wise for the moderator to establish a reputation for being available for consultations in connection with procedural questions that may be anticipated for the meeting. A moderator who establishes this reputation will frequently receive information as to procedural moves, and thus will be able to be fully prepared for them at the meeting and not taken by surprise. Any information given in this connection should, of course, be received in confidence so that the moderator will maintain a reputation for judicious impartiality.

4. *Officials.* The moderator should see that all officials necessary for the conduct of the meeting have been appointed and are informed of the date and place of the meeting. Such officials include checkers and pages.[3] If an invocation is to be given by a member of the clergy, the moderator should be certain that he or she has been seasonably invited and is able to appear. It is customary to rotate the invitation among the clergy of the various places of worship so that they have an equal opportunity to open the meeting.

It might well be advisable to confer with the selectmen or chief of police as to the disposition of the police or constables, in order to be certain that the meeting is carried on in an orderly fashion and that assistance is available if anything gets out of hand.

5. *Physical Equipment.* The selectmen are required to designate the place of the meeting and therefore to provide adequate space and equipment. The moderator's own desires as to the arrangement of tables and seats (having in mind divisions by aisles to facilitate counting by tellers), the podium, the public address system, projection equipment and the like should be carried out. It is customary for the clerk to bring the gavel, ballots and ballot boxes (where secret voting is in order), and the original warrant bearing the return of service.

It should be kept in mind that if the physical preparations

---

[3] See §13 *supra.*

§15   3: PRELIMINARY CONSIDERATIONS   47

are not adequate, it is probable that the moderator will be blamed. In an open meeting, for example, the moderator should make sure that space is prepared in such other meeting places as may be deemed necessary for an overflow crowd, with the necessary public address systems installed and assistant moderators appointed.[4] Frequently the public address system fails to work in some particular, and it is wise, therefore, to see that the technician in charge of the system is close at hand so that any difficulty may be corrected on short notice. Some towns have adopted the technique of using portable microphones and having these handed by pages to the speakers. This method not only is convenient for the speaker, who is thus spared the sometimes awkward journey past other people's knees to the stationary microphone, but also has the advantage of saving considerable time. Some moderators may use an electronic device that controls the microphones and can cut off debate, if necessary, to maintain order.

In most towns visitors are allowed to attend the town meeting although, of course, not to vote.[5] This is a practice that should not be discouraged, since it enables such nonvoters as high-school students and visitors from foreign countries to learn how a New England town meeting is conducted. From the moderator's point of view, it is important that a segregated area is provided for the visitors and thereby ensure that they will not improperly participate in the debate or voting. This should be arranged in advance and the checkers notified, to enable them to direct the visitors properly when they request entrance into the meeting hall. If it is a large open meeting, the problem will be considerably simplified by providing separate access to the visitors' area, and frequently a balcony or the stage behind the moderator is available for this purpose. If separate access is not possible, the moderator should see that someone is in charge of seating the visitors, not only to direct them to their seats but also to be certain that they do not subsequently move into the voting

---

[4] Mass. Gen. Laws, c. 39, §§10, 14. See N.H. Rev. Stat. Ann., c. 40, §3a; R.I. Gen. Laws, tit. 45, c.4, §3.
[5] See §14 supra.

area.[6]

§16. Opening the Meeting[1]

Upon ascertaining that a quorum is within sound of the gavel, the moderator should declare that a quorum is present and call the meeting to order,[2] by stating: "A quorum being present, the meeting will come to order."

If the town clerk is absent or the office of clerk is vacant and no assistant clerk is present,[3] the first business in order is the election by ballot of a temporary clerk.[4] Obviously, this is not done by official ballot, even though these are used at the annual election. The ballots are received and counted by the selectmen, if present; otherwise by three persons then chosen in a manner determined by the voters.[5]

The temporary clerk should be sworn by the moderator immediately, as follows: "Do you swear that you will faithfully and impartially perform the duties of temporary clerk?"[6]

If a clerk is not sworn before the meeting adjourns, there may be no way to prove the legal organization of the meeting.[7] The clerk's record of his or her own election is valid, provided the person is sworn that day.[8]

1. *The Return of the Warrant.* The moderator, upon opening the meeting, should inform the voters that the return

---

[6] Nonvoters of tender age may spend the evening on their mother's lap. See Gould 26.

§16 [1] In Hill v. Goodwin, 56 N.H. 441 (1876), opening the meeting included climbing through a window to open the door, which had been locked by an unfriendly town clerk.
[2] Bolton 6.
[3] See Mass. Gen. Laws, c. 41, §19.
[4] See Mass. Gen. Laws, c. 41, §14.
[5] See Mass. Gen. Laws, c. 41, §14.
[6] For the New Hampshire form, see N.H. Rev. Stat. Ann., c. 42, §2. For Rhode Island, see R.I. Gen. Laws, tit. 45, c. 4, §11.
[7] Taylor v. Henry, 2 Pick. 397 (Mass. 1824).
[8] Briggs v. Murdock, 13 Pick. 305 (Mass. 1832).

of the warrant shows that it has been properly served.[9] This can be accomplished by reading or by having the town clerk read the return of the constable who published the warrant, although it is not necessary.

It is also unnecessary to read the warrant itself at this time, but it and the return must become part of the record of the meeting.

2. *Swearing in Newly Elected Officers.* A moderator, or a clerk, who has just been elected should be sworn before the meeting. The clerk must swear in the moderator, but the clerk may be sworn in either by the moderator or, if the moderator is newly elected also, by a justice of the peace.[10] Representative town meeting members hold office, and it has been said that whether they shall be sworn is a serious question.[11] They need not be,[12] but it is often customary. A proper form of oath is: "Do you swear that you will faithfully and impartially perform the duties of _____?"

3. *The Anthem and the Prayer.* It is customary in many towns to open the town meeting with the singing of the national anthem (or salute to the flag) and a prayer, while other towns strictly avoid the practice. This is a matter for local decision.

While the Supreme Court has forbidden public schools to sponsor prayer,[13] Justice Brennan, concurring, distinguished prayers in legislative chambers on the ground that legislators

---

[9] In the Boston Town Records for February 1, 1780, we find that "on reading the Warrant it appeared by the Return made by the Constables that they had neglected to Warn one of the Wards, so it was Voted that the Selectmen be desired to issue another warrant, and the meeting dissolved."

[10] Conn. Gen. Stat., tit. 7, c. 92, §7-17; Me. Rev. Stat., c. 90-A, §§34 11, 36VII; Mass. Gen. Laws, c. 41, §107; N.H. Rev. Stat. Ann., c. 42, §1; R.I. Gen. Laws, tit. 45, c. 4, §11; Vt. Stat. Ann., tit. 24, c. 33, §831 (clerk).

[11] Lincoln, Some Notes on Representative Town Meetings, 33 Mass. L.Q. 31, 32 (April, 1948). See also §66 infra.

[12] Mass. Gen. Laws, c. 41, §107, specifies that the moderator and every person elected to any other town office designated by name in §1 shall be sworn, and the office of town meeting member is not designated by name in §1.

[13] School District of Abington Township, Pa. v. Schempp, 374 U.S. 203, 83 Sup. Ct. 1560 (1963).

"are mature adults who may presumably absent themselves . . . without incurring any penalty."[14] So are voters.

In some towns the anthem and prayer are used only at annual meetings and not at special meetings. There would seem to be no sound basis for such a distinction.

Many moderators adopt the diplomatic practice of rotating the choice of clergy among the various religious denominations represented in the town.

4. *Distinguished Visitors.* Now and then the moderator may learn of the presence of a distinguished visitor in the gallery and may wish to make such guests known to the meeting. An appropriate time for this is following the prayer. Our schools and colleges bring an ever-increasing number of foreign students to our towns, and the pleasant custom of inviting them to observe democracy at work is spreading. A few words of introduction and welcome are in order.[15]

5. *Complimentary Resolutions.* Sometimes the town wishes to express its appreciation of some achievement or service on the part of a citizen, or sympathy on an illness or death. The opening of the meeting is the time for such expressions. No article is necessary.

6. *Introductory Comments.* After completing these formalities, many moderators take a few minutes to explain some basic procedural rules. For example, the moderator might explain what an article is, what a motion is, what a person wishing to speak should do (line up at the microphone, or stand and remain standing, or whatever the local practice is), that when recognized a speaker should begin by stating his or her name and address and that all remarks should be addressed to the moderator. The moderator might also inform the meeting about any by-laws regarding time limits for speakers. In some towns where there is no such by-law the moderator asks the meeting if it wishes to impose a time limit — e.g. 10 minutes — on all speakers.

Finally, the moderator might explain the meaning of a call

---

[14] 374 U.S. at 203, 83 Sup. Ct. at 1612. Any doubt can be avoided by holding the prayer before the meeting is officially called to order.

[15] See the article by Tavares de Sá cited *supra* §1, note 8. See also §14 *supra*.

for the question.

Some moderators also make available prior to the meeting a short publication which covers these and other fundamental procedural matters. Another approach is to include such material in the Finance Committee's report, along with the warrant and the Committee's recommendations. If this is done, the moderator need mention only those matters needing special emphasis, and otherwise simply allude to the availability of the procedural information. Care should be taken to point out that it is a summary prepared for the convenience of voters, and that the full text of the rules of order, whatever that might be, is the binding authority.

§17. Reports of Committees[1]

Annual reports of town officers, boards and standing committees are ordinarily printed in the town report, where they are available to any voter. In many towns it is traditional to insert in the warrant an article "to hear and act on the reports of the town officers, boards, and committees."

This language can create problems. For example, suppose the school committee in its report, part of the town's annual report, recommends building a new school for $20,000,000. Suppose further that the town votes yes on the traditional article. Would a motion then be in order to appropriate $20,000,000 for the construction of a new school.

While there is some support for the proposition that the motion would be in order[2] the better view is that the town was not properly notified that it would be asked to appropriate $20,000,000 for a new school, and that therefore the motion is beyond the scope of the article.

Many towns[3] expressly provide, by by-law, that no action shall be taken on any committee report unless there is an

---

§17 [1]See Sections 10 and 12 *supra*.
[2] For example, in Benham v. Potter, 77 Conn. 186, 58 Atl. 735 (1904), the court held that an article "to take action upon the report of the finance committee" authorized a vote to appropriate $9,000 for a school house.
[3] Arlington, Bedford, Danvers, Framingham, Hamilton and Wakefield, for example.

article in the warrant expressly covering the action, and this is good practice.

Bolton criticized the standard article as "a completely useless procedure."[4] Town meetings would function perfectly well if it were eliminated entirely. As an alternative, an article "to receive the reports of town officers, boards and committees" is preferable to the standard article.

§18. The Order of Consideration of the Articles

The warrant is prepared by the selectmen; they determine the order of the articles in the warrant, and normally, of course, the articles will be considered and acted upon in the order in which they appear. In the absence of a by-law to the contrary, however, the moderator has the power to change the order of the articles without the voters' approval, but should exercise the power sparingly and only for good cause, stating the reasons clearly and convincingly. The impression certainly should be avoided that the moderator thinks he or she has more common sense on this subject than the selectmen. A moderator should also avoid any alteration of order that would affect the vote on an article, since the losers may think they would have won if the original order had been retained.

There are occasions when common sense or expediency dictates that articles should be considered in a different order from that specified by the selectmen. For example, action under a special statute obviously should not be taken until after the statute has been accepted by the town, and if the action article precedes the acceptance article, the order should clearly be reversed. Sometimes a relationship between articles unperceived by the selectmen when they put the warrant together suggests a better sequence by the time of the meeting. Other times courtesy to nonresidents who have traveled some distance, by invitation, to attend the consideration of a particular article will justify taking it up out of order.

In the absence of a by-law to the contrary, the meeting itself always has the power to change the order of articles, and

---

[4] Bolton, p. 7.

the moderator should entertain motions from the floor for this purpose.

If the desired change is deferment of an article, it may be accomplished by a motion to postpone until after a specified subsequent article. If this motion is made before any other motion is offered under the current article, it is a main motion; if made while another motion under the article is pending, it is a subsidiary motion.[1] If the desired change is advancement of a later article, it may be presented as a main motion if no other business is pending; however, if other business is pending, the other business must be disposed of or postponed to a time certain before the motion to advance may be made.

If the motion to change the order is supported by reasons which reasonable people would entertain, though they fall short of persuading the moderator to take the action on his or her own motion, it requires only a majority vote. If the motion is mere jockeying for position, the moderator may, under the power to regulate the proceedings, require a two-thirds vote,[2] but should be prepared to give clear and convincing reasons for doing so, to avoid any implication of partiality.

When articles are considered in their numerical order, "stacking the hall" for a particular article is a rather simple matter. For example, a group interested in a particular article need not appear at the meeting until just before that article comes up, and can leave as soon as it is completed, including any possible reconsideration.

As a partial remedy, and perhaps also to add a little excitement to the proceedings, some towns have adopted a by-law providing that the order of consideration of articles shall be determined by lottery.[3] In these towns the town clerk places numbered slips of paper in a box or a drum and draws them out one at a time. After an article has been drawn, no other article may be taken up until the meeting has completed action on the drawn article.

Where a lottery system is used, the moderator should not entertain a motion to table an article, since a motion to remove

---

§18 [1] See §42 infra.
  [2] Bolton 9.
  [3] Hull and Shrewsbury, for examples.

the article from the table could be made at any time, thus defeating the purpose of the lottery by-law.

A by-law establishing a lottery system should authorize the moderator to declare that, because of legal requirements, certain articles must be considered before or after other articles. When invoking this provision, the moderator should clearly explain the reasons for doing so.

In the absence of any evidence to the contrary, it will be presumed that the articles were acted on in order.[4]

§19. The Reading of the Articles

In many towns, the moderator reads each article verbatim as it is reached. With the shorter articles this is easier than attempting to summarize accurately. With long articles, such as proposals to amend the zoning applicable to a tract of land described by metes and bounds, it is usually appropriate to skip the metes and bounds and state briefly the location of the land in general terms, followed by "as described in the article." A number of towns have adopted the practice of omitting the reading of the articles, either with the consent of the meeting or by tradition, with the moderator or town clerk reading only the caption and close of the warrant and the return of posting. If the reading of the articles is to be omitted, the warrant should be printed and in the hands of, or available to, every voter.

§20. Handling the Budget

The budget article is treated differently from town to town. There appear to be three general methods of dealing with it. First, in some towns the moderator reads the whole budget, item by item, and calls for a recommendation by the finance committee, debate and a vote on each item. This, of course, is time-consuming. In the alternative, the chair of the finance committee may read the budget, as the finance committee's recommendation and motion, before debate and

---

[4] Berger v. Wellesley, 334 Mass. 193, 134 N.E.2d 436 (1956).

the vote on each item.

Second, in other towns, the moderator reads the whole budget, item by item, or by groups of items, stating the dollar amounts recommended by the finance committee for each, but does not stop for debate. He or she merely pauses long enough after each item for any voter to call "Hold" or some other word of similar import,[1] and if one does, the item is laid aside for further consideration. At the end of the article the moderator entertains a motion to appropriate the amounts recommended by the finance committee for all the items not set aside. After that, the meeting reverts to the items set aside and takes them up in order for discussion and possible amendment, rejection or other disposition.

A third approach to the problem is even more timesaving. The moderator states the article in general terms, and the chairman of the finance committee moves, in brief terms, "That the amounts of money set forth in the printed report of the finance committee be appropriated, for the several purposes therein itemized, each numbered item being considered as a separate appropriation, and that the same be expended only for such purposes." The moderator then waits to see if there will be any motions to amend any of the items. (Almost invariably there will be a few, but not many, as a rule.) After the discussion and any motions to amend have been dealt with, the moderator calls for a vote on the main motion (the motion of the finance committee) as amended. This method is not recommended unless the finance committee's report has been published several days before the meeting, to allow time for study.

The first method is the equivalent of a complete division of the article;[2] the second is a partial division; and the third is a main motion with amendments.

Consideration of the budget (and other appropriations) has become complicated by the enactment of tax levy limits such as "Proposition 2 1/2"[3] enacted on initiative petition by vote of the people of Massachusetts at the 1980 state election.

---

§20. [1] "Pass" is ambiguous and should be avoided. See §30 *infra*.
[2] See §49 *infra*.
[3] Mass. Gen. Laws, c. 59, §21C.

The law imposes an annual levy limit and includes provisions for the selectmen to include on the ballot for a regular or special election one or more questions to allow the levy limit to be increased by a so-called "override" vote.

The tax limit creates the concern that the town meeting must, at some point, determine appropriations in an aggregate amount that will not cause the limit to be exceeded. Some town meetings, or their moderators, have taken the position that amendments to increase an item in the budget recommended by the finance committee will not be allowed unless accompanied by an equivalent reduction in some other appropriation, if the increase would be likely to cause the total to exceed the estimated tax levy limit. This procedure has most often been adopted at the beginning of an annual town meeting as a "rule of the meeting." In at least one case the moderator announced in a "Statement of Practice" that he would use this rule to govern future town meetings. The Superior Court held such a rule so imposed would be invalid.[4] The court did not indicate whether such a rule could be imposed by the town meeting upon itself. Other towns do not impose such a rule and, when final revenue information is available, call a special town meeting if necessary to make any reductions then needed to permit the tax levy to be set within the limits.

In some towns, the meeting adopts two sets of appropriations, one amount within the anticipated levy limit and a higher amount with respect to certain items, contingent upon approval by the voters at a special election of an increase in the levy limit. If the increase is approved by the voters, the higher amount becomes the approved appropriation. If the vote on the increase is in the negative, the smaller amount stands as the approved appropriation.

It is considered the better practice for the moderator to allow motions or amendments to be made, whether or not they might cause the levy limit to be exceeded. This gives the selectmen the option to call a special election to consider

---

[4] School Committee of the Town of Hanson v. Moderator, Mass. Sup. Ct. (Plymouth, C.A. 90-092A) September 4, 1991, Hely, J.

whether to increase the levy limit to balance the budget. In such event, the moderator should always call upon the finance committee or other appropriate town official to advise the meeting of the potential effect of a motion that might cause the levy limit to be exceeded.

§21. Two Meetings in One Night

There is no reason why a town should not, and there are often good reasons why a town should, schedule two meetings in one night. Sometimes this is because a matter of some urgency comes to the attention of the selectmen after they have closed one warrant but before it is too late to post another for the same night. Sometimes a meeting begun at an earlier date will vote to adjourn to the night of the later meeting. Doubling up saves time and expense. In either case, the second meeting will usually be scheduled to precede or follow the other so that the meeting expected to be the shorter will be held first, with the other following at an interval designed to reduce overlap or gap to a minimum.

The moderator conducts each meeting just as if it were the only one held that evening, except that prayers and ceremonies usually are held at the beginning of the first and omitted from the second.

If, when the time set for the second meeting arrives, it appears that the first still has some time to run, the first meeting has several choices open to it. It may recess "until the second meeting is recessed or dissolved"; it may recess just long enough for the moderator to call the second meeting to order for a vote by the second meeting to recess "until the first meeting is again recessed or dissolved"; or it may vote to recess until a particular article in the warrant for the second meeting has been acted upon. At that time, a vote by the second meeting to recess "until the first meeting has been recessed or dissolved" would be in order.[1] In other words, with a little attention to order, the two meetings can combine

---

§21 [1] If one meeting recesses until the other "dissolves," the first cannot reconvene if the second merely recesses.

themselves for all practical purposes. The moderator must see to it, however, that each meeting completes the business of its warrant (and not of the other warrant) and that each meeting eventually dissolves. The town clerk must make sure that the moderator keeps the two meetings separate in form, and that the record of one meeting is not confused with the record of the other.

Some towns hold an embedded special town meeting around the time of the annual meeting, in the belief that the annual meeting may only deal with appropriations for the fiscal year ahead, and that the special meeting is required in order to take up current-year matters. This is not the case; the annual meeting's primary purpose is to deal with the fiscal year ahead, but it is not limited in this respect, and actions on current matters may be taken.

§22. Broadcasting and Recording

In some towns, televising or videotaping the town meeting is routine, either for simultaneous or delayed broadcast. In others, the practice is strictly avoided.

It is a matter for local decision; the Massachusetts Open Meeting Law,[1] which provides for recording of meetings of governmental bodies by attendees under certain circumstances, does not apply to a town meeting.[2] In the absence of a by-law, it falls within the scope of the moderator's power to regulate the proceedings in his or her sound discretion, and moderators may well differ in their judgement. Local practice and tradition will often be the determining factor.

If a very controversial matter is to be debated and feelings are sure to run high, the introduction of broadcasting or televising equipment to which meeting — goers are unaccustomed might well discourage some from speaking, or encourage others. In either event a different outcome could result than would normally have occurred. On the other hand, broadcasting of the town meeting can have positive effects

---

§22 [1] Mass. General Laws Chapter 39, Section 23B.
[2] Mass. General Laws Chapter 39, Section 23A.

including encouragement of attendance and sharing of the proceedings with those unavoidably unable to attend (shut-ins and business travelers, for example).

A 1985 ruling by the Moderator of Needham[3] has for years provided helpful guidance in this area to members of the Massachusetts Moderators Association facing the issue for the first time. Although the development of technology has rendered some of the cautions unnecessary, a number of the key points are worthy of consideration by anyone charged with establishment of ground rules for television or videotaping during a town meeting. Here are the points deemed potentially most useful:

1. Generally, all recording activities shall be conducted in an orderly, unintimidating, unobtrusive manner and in accordance with standards of propriety, courtesy and decorum to the end that the dignity of the proceedings shall be preserved.

2. The moderator, having in mind that such recording is a privilege rather than a right, may at any time terminate recording in whole or in part, or take such other action to control the recording as the circumstances warrant.

3. The "recordings" referred to herein include in whole or in part television broadcast, radio broadcast, still photography or otherwise, whether for live or delayed broadcast.

4. Any person so requesting of the moderator shall not have a camera or lights directed at said person.

5. Mechanical recording, filming or broadcasting devices shall:

(a) not be positioned so as to interfere with seating, vision, or hearing of any persons within the hall or with the orderly process of the meeting.

(b) not be installed in, or removed from, the hall while the meeting is in session; excepting such devices which are totally portable and are customarily carried by one person.

(c) be placed, whether cameras, wires, tripods, terminals or other equipment, subject to the approval of the

---

[3] *Moderator's Ruling re Use of Television Equipment at Town Meeting*, Richard P. Melick, Moderator of Needham, May 6, 1985.

moderator; which will usually mean that cameras shall be stationary, although portable or mobile units shall be permitted within the discretion of the moderator.

(d) not be used to interview or communicate with any persons, whether within the hall or outside the hall, while the meeting is in session.

The recording of the proceedings, either electronically or by a stenographer or stenotypist, for the town records as distinguished from public broadcasting purposes, is a different matter. The town clerk has the duty of recording all votes and is probably entitled to use any aids deemed appropriate for that purpose, whether the meeting likes it or not, and many towns make an audio recording of their proceedings for this reason.

Chapter 4

Motions

§23. In General

All action taken by a town meeting is taken by votes upon motions. It is sometimes supposed, even by writers on the subject,[1] that an article in the warrant is a motion, and that the meeting votes directly on the article, but such is not the case. An article is not self-starting; it merely stakes out the limits of the area within which the meeting may act. Nothing affirmative may happen, and the moderator may not take a vote, unless someone makes a motion.

"The right to submit a proposition belongs to all members alike. There can be no monopoly of motion-making. On the opening day of the session, however, one or two gentlemen, of apparent consequence, are apt so far to forget this truth as to take upon themselves the entire burden of starting the public business. The delusion they are under seldom lasts longer than twenty-four hours."[2]

In some towns it is customary to recognize the sponsor of the article at the outset, and let that person make the first motion. In other towns it is customary to recognize the chairman of the finance committee, sometimes called the advisory or budget committee, and let him or her make the first motion. If the motion is more than a few words long, it is good practice, and a great help to the town clerk, to require that the mover submit the motion in writing. Many by-laws require certain motions, such as those involving money, to be in writing. In towns where the finance committee publishes its recommendations or suggested votes in a printed report distributed at or prior to the meeting, using its recommendations or suggested votes as main motions enables everyone to keep better track of the proceedings. If the

---

§23 [1] Demeter 232.
[2] Hackett 67. In a representative town meeting, any voter may speak, even though such an individual may not vote. As to making and seconding motions, the safer course would be to suggest that members handle these matters. If two members cannot be found to do these two things, the voter should be advised to withdraw the proposition. It could not carry under such circumstances.

committee is respected and followed, this procedure also saves much time.

In all cases, the first motion, by whomever made, will take the form of (1) an affirmative motion that the meeting take some specified action, (2) a negative motion that it take no action, or (3) a motion to refer the matter to a committee. The first two are obviously main motions and, in this instance, the third is also. It may also be made as a subsidiary motion after main and other motions have been made.

Sometimes the main motion is a motion, under an appropriate article, to amend an existing by-law. It is still a main motion in such a case, and is not to be confused with the subsidiary motion to amend a main motion.

A main motion presents the meeting with a simple choice: Yes or No. The meeting may, and frequently does, dispose of the proposition very summarily on this one motion, but it is not obligated to submit to such a cut-and-dried single choice. It has the right to debate the issue, amend it, defer it or dispose of it in some other fashion, and to do all this in a civilized way. To this end, other motions are available, usually classified, after the main motions, as subsidiary motions (which deal directly with the business of the main motion), incidental motions (which deal with the conduct of the meeting as it relates to the pending business) and privileged motions (which deal with the conduct of the meeting generally).

This being the case, the questions naturally arise: When may these subsidiary and other motions be made, and when may they be acted on? Not, obviously, in the chronological order in which they are made, and not, on the other hand, in any order in which the moderator may capriciously choose to put them. Instead, they are acted on in a sequence fixed by rules. The rules are not difficult and can be mastered by anyone who can master the rules of baseball. Many of them amount to no more than the application of common sense. For example, when there is a motion to amend, the main motion is not acted upon until it is known, by action on the motion to amend, whether it is in the shape the meeting wants it in. The motion to amend gives way to a point of order that the speaker cannot be heard at the back of the hall. Others are more arbitrary and must be memorized, not reasoned out. Of these it can only be said that a page of history is worth a volume of logic.

The hierarchy of motions appropriate in our view to a town meeting will be found on the inside of the front cover. The rules that fix the order in which motions may be made and acted on are often phrased in terms of the "rank" of the motion. Thus a low-ranking motion gives way to a motion of higher rank. The motion of higher rank may almost always be made notwithstanding the pendency of one or more motions of lower rank, and it temporarily, and sometimes permanently, supersedes the lower.[3] The motion of lower rank may never be applied to the main motion while a motion of higher rank affecting the main motion is pending. (But the motion of lower rank may sometimes be applied to a higher-ranking motion. For example, a motion to commit may be amended.) We shall take up each type of motion in order, beginning with the lowest ranking (the main motions) and ending with the highest (to dissolve). It will be noticed, from a glance at the aforementioned table, that the order of rank is in fact an approximate inversion of the order of importance. When the meeting is over, it is the main motions adopted that will count, and not the privileged motions.

No more than one motion of the same rank may be pending at one time. Thus two main motions may not be pending at one time.

§24. Seconding and Stating the Motion

"After a motion has been read, it should be seconded with promptitude. By this is meant that a member, other than the mover, should address the chair with the phrase 'I second the motion,' or its equivalent. No mystery about it. A newcomer can acquire in twenty-four hours the art of seconding

---

[3] If action on a lower-ranking motion has disposed of the matter (such as a motion for indefinite postponement or to commit), a higher ranking motion may not thereafter be offered unless the meeting votes to reconsider.

motions."[1]

The origin of the custom of seconding a motion is obscure, and the reason, if any, why it should be deemed necessary is equally so. One suspects that the world would not come to an end if it were abolished. Indeed, some towns do dispense with it entirely. However, it does no harm, takes very little time and affords an opportunity to participate, if in a small way, to those who are diffident about making longer speeches.

Where seconding is normally required, no action may be taken on a motion that fails to gain a second.

It is indisputably the fact that all the manuals prescribe that when the motion has been made and seconded, the chair must repeat it, word for word.[2] There is a sound basis for this rule if the motion has been made from the mover's place on the floor and is not printed in a report. It ensures that everyone hears it. Where the hall is equipped with a public address system and the mover makes use of the microphone, or where a printed motion is distributed at or shortly prior to the meeting, there is no need to waste the time of the meeting by immediately repeating the motion, and accordingly the rule should be tempered by a little common sense. On the other hand, a repetition of the motion during the debate may serve to keep the discussion from drifting into irrelevancies, and a restatement of the motion at the end of debate is frequently desirable to make sure that everyone understands what he or she is voting on.

§25. Motions of Doubtful Legality

There are three different types of motions of doubtful legality: first, where the motion seeks to do something illegal, such as spot zoning; second, where the motion seeks to do something which exceeds the authority of the meeting, such as fire the chief of police; third, where mandatory conditions precedent to town meeting action, such as the holding of a

---

§24 [1] Hackett 70.
[2] Bolton 13; Cushing 72; Demeter 27; Hackett 81; Jefferson 178; Robert 38; House Rule XVI, 2.

hearing, have not been met.

Since the moderator's authority is limited to ruling on procedural matters, the moderator does not have the power to rule on the legality of motions. Thus, in the first instance the moderator, and if possible town counsel, should advise the meeting of the possible consequences of an affirmative vote and should then let the chips fall where they may.

In the second instance, the meeting should be told that it lacks the power to fire the police chief and that any vote will simply express the sense of the meeting and will be non-binding.

The one instance where the moderator may rule the motion out of order occurs when the moderator is aware that mandatory conditions precedent have not been met. For example, M.G.L. c.40A, Section 5 requires that the Planning Board conduct public hearings prior to town meeting consideration of zoning articles. If the required hearings have not been held, the moderator should rule that as a procedural matter, the motion in question is not properly before the meeting and no vote should be taken.

§26. Withdrawal[1]

Once a motion is in the possession of the meeting, whether by a formal statement from the chair or informally by the commencement of debate, it may not be withdrawn without a majority vote or unanimous consent. There is no reason, however, why the chair should be reluctant to discover unanimous consent. After the motion has been voted on, it may not be withdrawn.

---

§26 [1] See §53 infra.

Chapter 5

Main Motions

§27. In General

There are three kinds of main motions: detailed affirmative main motions, brief affirmative main motions and negative main motions. In addition, there are three procedural motions which are treated as main motions: reconsideration (or rescission), take from the table (discussed in Section 45), and a motion to advance an article (discussed in Section 18).

Main motions may be made only when no other business is pending. They must be seconded unless a by-law or local practice provides otherwise and may always be debated and amended. They have no rank and therefore yield to all relevant subsidiary and incidental motions, and to all privileged motions, whether or not relevant.

The vote required to pass a main motion depends on substantive law.[1] As a rule it is a majority of those present and voting,[2] but there are many instances in which a statute requires some other proportion, such as two thirds[3] or even four fifths.[4] (See the Appendix for a summary.) This is a question that the moderator and the town counsel must annually check carefully, because statutes may change from year to year.

§28. Detailed Affirmative Main Motions — Scope

Main motions are frequently given in the precise words of the article, but they need not be. Although the article may not be amended, the main motion may differ somewhat from it and sometimes it must differ.

How far may the main motion differ from the article? This is a question of great practical importance, since it is constantly arising in town meetings. A motion may not exceed

---

§27 [1] See Blomquist v. Arlington, 338 Mass. 594, 156 N.E.2d 416 (1959).
[2] Conn. Gen. Stat., tit. 7, c. 91, §7-7; R.I. Gen. Laws, tit. 45, c. 3. §21.
[3] Mass. Gen Laws, c. 44, §§7, 8.
[4] Mass. Gen. Laws, c. 44, §64 (nine tenths at a special meeting).

the scope of the article and those who draft articles and motions, as well as the moderator, should be familiar with the rules relating to scope, which are discussed below.

The basic rule may be stated as follows: Since the purpose of the warrant is to apprise the voters of the subject matter to be considered at the meeting, all that is necessary is for the article to include a sufficient description of the subject matter to provide the voters with substantial and intelligent notice of the nature of the business to be acted upon.[1] The article need not contain details or "an accurate forecast of the precise action which the meeting will take . . ."[2] Matters incidental to and connected with the article are proper for consideration and action.[3]

Articles should be interpreted in a liberal manner and not with strictness or rigidity.[4] There are limits, however, to the scope that may be given an article. Thus a motion to amend the zoning by-law of the town is not permissible under an article to repeal the zoning by-law.[5] Nor is a motion to abolish the school districts in a town within the scope of an article to redistrict the school districts.[6] A contract already made by the selectmen for the purchase of a water plant may not be ratified under an article presenting only the general

---

§28 [1] Fish v. Canton, 322 Mass. 219, 77 N.E.2d 231 (1948); Tuckerman v. Moynihan, 282 Mass. 562, 185 N.E. 2 (1933); Coffin v. Lawrence, 143 Mass. 110 (1886); Reed v. Acton, 117 Mass. 384 (1875).

[2] Burlington v. Dunn, 318 Mass. 216, 61 N.E.2d 243 (1945).

[3] Haven v. Lowell, 5 Met. 35 (Mass. 1842).

[4] Tuckerman v. Moynihan, *supra*; Nelson v. Belmont. 274 Mass. 35, 174 N.E. 320 (1931); Coffin v. Lawrence, *supra*; Wood v. Jewell, 130 Mass. 270 (1881). Even if the article does not contain the word "appropriate," it is proper to vote an appropriation if the article calls for action which will obviously require money. For example: "To see if the Town will vote to repair Salem Street." Blackburn v. Walpole, 9 Pick. 97 (Mass. 1829); 5 Ops. Mass. Atty. Gen. 519 (1920). The word "raise" has been held to include "borrow." Whitney v. Stow, 111 Mass. 368 (1873). A motion to appropriate $200,000 by transfer from unexpended funds to purchase a parcel of land was held to be within the scope of an article to appropriate $200,000 to acquire the same parcel, but with the appropriation to be raised by borrowing subject to a debt exclusion under Proposition 2 ½. Carter v. Town of Douglas, Mass. Sup. Ct. (Worcester, No 00-011A) Jan. 9, 2001, Butler, J.

[5] Fish v. Canton, *supra*.

[6] Child v. Colburn, 54 N.H. 71 (1873).

proposition as to whether the town shall purchase the water plant.[7]

The words "or take any other action in relation thereto," or a similar phrase, may allow a more liberal interpretation of the article,[8] but they should not be relied upon to justify any action that is not reasonably relevant.[9]

When the article refers to specific amounts or measurements, unqualified by such words as "not in excess of," the general rules are more difficult to apply. Theoretically, in these cases the figures should be incidental to the subject matter of the article and should not limit the amounts or measurements that may be voted. Thus, where the warrant for the town meeting stated that an appropriation of $15,000 for the construction of a dock would be brought up for consideration, a vote appropriating $20,000 was upheld by the court. "The warrant here sufficiently apprised the electors of the fact that the subject of the construction of a dock at the expense of the town would be brought up for consideration. That was the primary question. The amount of money which should be appropriated for the project if it were approved was a mere incident."[10]

There is a school which believes that unqualified figures in the article do limit the action that may be taken.[11] Any

---

[7] Revere Water Co. v. Winthrop, 192 Mass. 455, 78 N.E. 497 (1906).

[8] Wood v. Jewell, *supra*; Grover v. Pembroke, 11 Allen 88 (Mass. 1865).

[9] Fish v. Canton, *supra*.

[10] Capone v. Nunes, 85 R.I. 392, 132 A.2d 80 (1957). It is, of course, possible to have a variance so great that the motion differs in kind and not merely in degree (or may be regarded as frivolous). If, for example, the article called for $10,000 to build a first aid station, a motion to appropriate $1,000,000 would presumably be a motion to build a hospital and should be rejected. In New Hampshire, appropriations in excess of the figure in the warrant are authorized by statute. N.H. Laws 1957, c. 239, §1, amending N.H. Rev. Stat. Ann., c. 39, §2. See Opinion of the justices, 101 N.H. 544, 134 A.2d 281 (1957), holding the proposed statute constitutional. But in New Hampshire towns which have accepted the Municipal Budget Law (N.H. Rev. Stat. Ann., c. 32) the total appropriations may not exceed the budget recommended by the budget committee by more than 10 per cent. §8. Connecticut towns which have boards of finance may not make any appropriation in excess of the amount recommended by the board. Conn. Gen. Stat., tit. 7, §7-344.

[11] Austin v. York, 57 Me. 304 (1869); 5 Ops. Mass. Atty. Gen. 519 (1920); Comins Bulletin F, Massachusetts Association of Town Finance Committees 15 (1959).

controversy may easily be avoided if the sponsor of the article will exercise care in drafting it and refrain from using unqualified figures. If no limit is intended, the proponent should use some such expression as "and appropriate a sum of money therefor" not mentioning any figure or "and appropriate the sum of $____ or any other sum". If the sponsor intends to impose a limit, such words as "not in excess of" or "not more than" should be inserted in front of the specific figure.

When they are perfecting amendments, deviations from zoning articles have been upheld on the question of scope, with the indication that the changes should not be of a fundamental character.[12]

If the article is "To see if the Town will do A and B," the two parts of the article may be so interdependent as to require that both parts be adopted, or neither, but they may also be so independent that the "and" may properly be construed to include "or." Thus, where the article read: "To see if the Town will accept Section 25 of Chapter 41 of the General Laws as amended, relating to the appointment of the Assessors, and will determine that the number of Assessors to be appointed by the Selectmen be one," a vote "That the Town accept Section 25 of Chapter 41 of the General Laws, as amended, relating to the appointment of assessors" was held to be within the scope of the article, though it did not deal with the number of assessors.[13] Presumably a motion would have been in order to divide the question and vote on the two parts separately.[14]

May we look to two or more articles to find authority for a single vote? If there are separate articles: "To see if the Town will buy a new car for the police chief and appropriate the money therefor" and "To see if the Town will buy a new car for the fire chief and appropriate the money therefor," one vote "To buy a new car for the police chief and a new car for the fire chief and appropriate $50,000 therefor" would be in

---

[12] Burlington v. Dunn, *supra;* Doliner v. Town Clerk of Millis, 1961 Mass. Adv. Sh. 1049, 175 N.E.2d 925.

[13] Noonan v. Selectmen of Brookline, 1962 Mass. Adv. Sh. 45, 179 N.E.2d 332 upholding a moderator's ruling by one of the co-authors.

[14] See §49 *infra.*

order. However, votes on combined articles should never be permitted if the effect would be to violate any limits or conditions contained in either article. Thus, if the two articles given above contained effective mandatory dollar limits of $25,000 each, the combined vote given above would be bad, because it might lead to an inadvertent illegal expenditure of more than $25,000 for one of them.[15]

Sometimes it happens that two or more articles deal with the same subject, for example, the construction of a school. One article may read "To see if the Town will appropriate not over $10,000,000 to build a school on X Site," and the other "To see if the Town will build a school for not over 200 pupils on X Site and appropriate the necessary money therefor." These articles clearly should be combined for discussion, as only one school can be built on X Site. A motion "To appropriate $10,000,000 (or less) to build a school for 200 pupils (or less)" would clearly be in order under either article.

A motion "To appropriate $10,000,000 (or less) to build a school for 250 pupils" would be in order under the first article only, and a motion "To appropriate $15,000,000 to build a school for 200 pupils (or less)" would be in order under the second article only. In either case, the moderator should make it clear that he or she is accepting the motion under the proper article.

Frequently the motion must be more detailed than the article. If the article is "To see if the Town will vote to buy a new fire engine and appropriate the necessary money therefor," the motion may contain specifications as to the type of engine or leave that to the department head, but it must contain a specific dollar amount.[16]

---

[15] See Twombly v. Selectmen of Billerica, 262 Mass. 214, 159 N.E. 630 (1928), in which the selectmen let one contract for the construction of three different pieces of road for a gross price, without regard to the fact that each piece of road had a separate appropriation separately voted for it. The court limited the amount that could be spent on each piece to that set forth in the vote relating to it. The same principle would seem to apply to a single vote based upon three articles.

[16] Conn. Gen. Stat., tit. 7, c. 97, §7-121; Vt. Stat. Ann., tit. 24, c. 31, §717 (specific sum or rate per cent on a dollar of the grand list).

Parole evidence is admissible to explain an ambiguous vote,[17] but the courts have better things to do than to clarify badly worded votes. Thus, instead of accepting a motion "That the selectmen be authorized to execute the contract with Dr. W," the moderator should require the mover to state at least the basic terms of the contract (perhaps leaving some terms to the discretion of the selectmen),[18] or identify a particular existing document.

§29. Brief Affirmative Main Motions

If the article is sufficiently clear and detailed, it may suffice to move "That the meeting accept (or adopt, or act favorably on) this article." Such a motion may be a great timesaver, and is widely used.[1] Probably this is what makes people think that articles are self-starting main motions that can be voted on directly. They remember voting favorably on the article and forget that a short motion preceded the vote.

The brief affirmative is out of order if the article lacks an essential detail, such as a dollar amount (although this can be covered by a motion "To adopt the article and appropriate $1,000"). Nonessential details are, by implication, left to the discretion of the board or officer whose function it is to carry out the vote,[2] but the power to determine the principal amount of an appropriation cannot be delegated.[3] The moderator should consult with town counsel before the meeting as to what details are essential.

The brief affirmative is also out of order if the article leaves any alternatives that should be specified in the motion. The common appendage "or take any other action relative

---

[17] Smith v. Abington Savings Bank, 171 Mass. 178, 50 N.E. 545 (1898); Mayo v. West Springfield, 260 Mass. 594, 157 N.E. 700 (1927); Walsh v. Farrington, 105 Vt. 269, 165 Atl. 914 (1933).
[18] Drury v. Butler, 171 Mass. 171, 50 N.E. 527 (1898).

§29 [1] At its annual town meeting in 1960, Tewksbury voted to "adopt" seventeen articles. See Suburban Land Co., Inc. v. Billerica, 314 Mass. 184, 49 N.E.2d 1012, 147 A.L.R. 660 (1943).
[2] Amey v. Pittsburg School District, 95 N.H. 386, 64 A.2d 1 (1949).
[3] Gove v. Lovering, 3 N.H. 292.

thereto" is not a real alternative, and a vote "To take favorable action on the article" is clear enough, notwithstanding those words.[4]

The brief affirmative may be amended just as well as a detailed affirmative.[5] But remember, it is the short main motion, not the article, that is amended.

§30. Negative Main Motions

When the finance committee has the floor first, it frequently has occasion to recommend that no action be taken under the article. This may be by motion to dismiss the article,[1] by motion that action be indefinitely postponed, or by motion to take no action. All of these mean the same thing and have the same effect. The motion to postpone indefinitely is, in general parliamentary practice, a subsidiary motion, to be applied only to a pending main motion, and is so described in all the manuals, but in town meetings it can be a main motion itself, if no other motion is pending, and has been judicially recognized as such and as the equivalent of a negative vote.[2] All suitable subsidiary and incidental, and all privileged, motions apply to this motion to postpone indefinitely, but see the following discussion as to amendments of a negative motion.

The sponsors of the article are, of course, not bound by the recommendation of the finance committee. The negative main motion is debatable, and the sponsors may speak against dismissal or postponement and in favor of action. They may persuade the meeting to defeat the negative motion. However,

---

[4] Suburban Land Co., Inc. v. Billerica, 314 Mass. 184, 49 N.E.2d 1012, 147 A.L.R. 660 (1943).

[5] Of those seventeen articles adopted by Tewksbury, three were with amendments.

§30.[1] Adams v. Crooks, 7 Gray 411 (Mass. 1856).

[2] Wood v. Milton, 197 Mass. 531, 84 N.E. 332 (1908); Manual for the Massachusetts General Court Note to Senate Rule 54.

An old-fashioned way of recording a negative vote was "Passed in the negative." Boston Town Records, March 9, 1778. The form of the motion that produced the vote thus recorded does not appear. On May 25, 1778, Boston voted "that the Matter ... Subside, which passed in the Affirmative."

it should be borne in mind that defeating the negative is not alone sufficient to establish affirmative action on the article. After defeating the negative, the sponsors should make an affirmative motion, and, since such is the obvious wish of the meeting, the moderator should see to it that someone does make such a motion. Moderators should never request that a motion be made, but they may say, "No affirmative action has yet been taken. Unless an affirmative motion is made, we shall proceed to the next article, and the record will show that no affirmative action was taken on this one."

Another method sometimes used by the sponsors of an article to overcome a pending motion to dismiss, postpone indefinitely or take no action is to offer a motion to amend such a pending motion by substituting therefor words calling for the affirmative action desired.[3]

To turn a negative into an affirmative by amendment seems to involve some risk of confusing the voters. If local tradition has always permitted amendment of a motion to dismiss, postpone indefinitely or take no action, it is reasonable to suppose that most of the voters will have no difficulty in following what is happening. If local tradition has not permitted such a motion in the past, there is no reason to encourage an innovation in this respect. It is sufficient to advise the mover that if the negative motion is defeated, he or she will have another chance later. It should be remembered that if the amendment is adopted, the main motion, as amended, must then be voted on, although this is, under the circumstances, a mere formality, except in those instances where the main motion is one which requires a two-thirds vote.

A motion to postpone "to the next annual town meeting" is not in order, since the next meeting cannot take it up without an appropriate article in its warrant, and this meeting cannot dictate the agenda for the next. The nearest to this that

---

[3] The manuals do not deal with a motion to postpone indefinitely as a main motion, but only as a subsidiary motion, and they are not unanimous on whether amendment of it is permissible. Robert (p. 152) and Demeter (p. 62) say that a motion to postpone indefinitely is not amendable. Hackett (p. 88) says it is, and Cushing says it is (p. 142) and it is not (p. 85). See §39 infra, note 5.

can be done is to postpone indefinitely and request (not instruct) the selectmen to insert a similar article in the warrant for the next meeting.

While defeating the negative cannot establish the affirmative, defeating an affirmative motion can, as a practical matter, frequently be taken as a sufficient negative. Theoretically anyone may make another and different affirmative motion, and this is sometimes done, but more often the declaration of the vote on the affirmative motion is followed by silence, and the moderator may properly proceed to the next article.

A motion "to pass the article" is ambiguous, since it may mean "pass over" to some voters and "adopt" to others. It should be avoided here. Furthermore, when the article was "To see what action the Town will take relative to leasing the town hall," and the selectmen stated that they had already leased it, a vote "to pass the article" was held to be an implied ratification.[4] (So, perhaps, would be a vote to dismiss, to take no action, or to postpone indefinitely.) The moderator should require the mover to state what action is intended, so that nothing will be left to implication, and the meeting will fully understand.

The most negative of all negative main motions is sometimes expressed by an eloquent silence after the reading of the article. In such cases, the moderator may declare that the meeting is taking no action, and proceed to the next article.[5] In some towns, in this situation, the action of the town meeting will be made explicit by a motion from a selectman or the finance committee chair that no action be taken on the article. This would seem to be good practice in order to avoid any ambiguity, and to define the situation if a proponent, arriving late, urges reconsideration and a return to the issue.

Be sure to distinguish an affirmative vote on a negative motion from a negative vote on an affirmative motion. The difference can be important. If the water board has the power to buy land unless the town instructs it not to, a negative vote

---

[4] Meredith v. Fullerton, 83 N.H. 124, 139 Atl. 359 (1927).
[5] Town Government (League of Women Voters of Concord, Mass., 1958).

on a motion to instruct it to buy a specified parcel is not a vote to instruct the board not to buy it, and the board may still buy the parcel.[6]

Another instance in which the difference is important appears in representative town meetings. The statutes establishing them provide for referenda, on petition, to review some of the important kinds of votes "passed" at the meeting.[7] In some, this applies only to affirmative votes of a few special categories,[8] but in others it applies to all votes with a few specified exceptions, such as "to adjourn,"[9] and to negative decisions as well as to affirmative.[10] Since the only effect a referendum can have is to reverse the action of the meeting, a referendum on a brief negative can only produce a brief affirmative, and the brief affirmative, as discussed above,[11] may be so incomplete as to be useless; as, for example, where the article lacks an essential detail, such as a dollar amount, or is in the alternative. For this reason, presumably, some special acts establishing representative town meetings provide that "No article in the warrant shall be finally disposed of by a vote

---

[6] Stoughton v. Paul, 173 Mass. 148, 53 N.E. 272 (1899). The court intimated that it would have had more trouble if the motion had been "To authorize the commissioners to buy." The article read "To see if the town will authorize and instruct..." See also §12 *supra*, note 1.

[7] See §2 *supra*.

[8] Darien (Conn. Sp. Acts of 1957, No. 216, §57); Southington (Conn. Sp. Acts of 1957, No. 170, §12); South Windsor (Conn. Sp. Acts of 1957, No. 215, §12); Wallingford (Conn. Sp. Acts of 1957, No. 49, §10); Waterford (Conn. Sp. Acts of 1957, No. 504, §13); West Haven (Conn. Sp. Acts of 1957, No. 533, §11); Westport (Conn. Sp. Acts of 1957, No. 348, §8); Mass. Gen. Laws, c. 43A, §10; Dartmouth (Mass. Acts of 1927, c. 26, §8); Falmouth (Mass. Acts of 1935, c. 349, §8); Randolph (Mass. Acts of 1947, c. 324, §10); Reading (Mass. Acts of 1943, c. 7, §9), for example.

[9] Swampscott (Mass. Acts of 1927, c. 300, §8); Winchester (Mass. Acts of 1928, c. 167, §8), for example.

[10] The wording of the representative Town Meeting Act is critical. In Opinion of the Justices, 370 Mass. 879, 352 N.E. 2d 678 (1976), the Court held that an act providing for a referendum on any "vote...passed" limits the referendum to affirmative town meeting action and does not allow a referendum on a negative town meeting vote. (Mass. Acts of 1954, c. 660 - Hopkinton). The Court noted that other representative Town Meeting Acts expressly allow a referendum on a "final vote... passing or rejecting a measure". See 370 Mass. 879, 883, 884.

[11] See §29 *supra*.

to lay upon the table, to indefinitely postpone, or to take no action."[12] In other words, the legislation requires that the article be disposed of by a negative vote on a detailed affirmative motion, not by an affirmative vote on a brief negative motion.

Should the moderators of other representative town meetings not subject to the same explicit statutory requirement attempt to impose the same rule? It would seem not. For one thing, there is the usual principle of statutory construction that where the legislature has spelled it out in one case, its omission to spell it out in another indicates a deliberate intention to omit the requirement in the latter case. For another, a ban on brief negatives falls far short of ensuring that the voters at large will have the final word on a controversial issue. At least half the time the controversy rages over a detail of a subject on the substance of which there is general agreement, and the issue is raised by a subsidiary motion to amend. For example, everyone will agree that the town will pay its policemen something. The question will sometimes be: How much? After this has been fought out on a motion to amend the finance committee's recommendation, the final vote is usually an anticlimax, and it would require considerable ingenuity for anyone to reach the heart of the question with a petition for a referendum, because it seems clear that the referendum cannot apply to a vote on a subsidiary motion. If the vote on the motion to amend is reversed, the vote on the main motion has got to be reconsidered, and the referendum machinery does not provide for that.

Where an article is so clear and specific that a brief affirmative would be in order,[13] there is no reason to strive to avoid a brief negative since a reversal of the negative by a referendum will produce a workable affirmative, at least in those towns that allow a referendum on a negative vote.

In any event, however, the moderator should be aware of

---

[12] Milton (Mass. Acts of 1927, c. 27, §7); Shrewsbury (Mass. Acts of 1953, c. 553, §16); Brattleboro (Vt. Acts of 1959, c. 302, §8), for example.

[13] See §29 *supra*.

the problem and should not frustrate, through mere inadvertence, a legitimate attempt to frame the principal issue in an affirmative main motion.

§31. Reconsideration and Rescission in General

Reconsideration and rescission differ from each other in that reconsideration alone is not final, but is merely a vote to give "further reflection, renewed attention, and more careful deliberation" to the action to be reconsidered. "It involves temporary postponement of final action" and "a new vote on the original question after more mature deliberation. What may be the result of that new vote, whether affirmative, negative, or different, as compared with the earlier vote, depends upon the judgment of the members of the assembly when it is taken."[1] The original motion is still pending and awaiting a new vote.

Rescission, on the other hand, is in effect a combination of a vote to reconsider and a vote to annul the previous action. The original motion has been disposed of and is no longer pending. If the mover wishes only to nullify the affirmative action, there is no reason why the meeting is compelled to vote twice. It will save the time of the meeting to combine both votes in one short motion to rescind. Since it incorporates a motion to reconsider, it is subject to the same rules that apply to reconsideration, and is therefore treated here.

Motions to reconsider or rescind have the rank of the motion to be reconsidered or rescinded. This need not be a main motion. However, it often is, and therefore reconsideration is grouped with the main motions for this discussion.

Reconsideration is sometimes brought about without the formality of a vote incorporating the word "reconsider," or any synonym for it, by simply passing another and inconsistent vote on the same subject. This is not recommended. It can

---

§31 [1]Opinion of the Justices, 291 Mass. 578, 197 N.E. 95 (1935).
For an early example of reconsideration, see Boston Town Records, May 25, 1778.

lead to confusion.[2]

§32. Who May Move Reconsideration

Some manuals[1] and by-laws[2] provide that reconsideration may be moved only by one who voted on the side that prevailed on the first vote. This rule is difficult to apply in a meeting where votes are taken by voice, by show of hand or by standing, or by secret ballot.[3] A few lionhearted moderators may look the mover in the eye, inquire how the person voted, and compel a truthful answer. This is a courageous course to take, but it involves some risk that the mover will stare right back and brazenly and untruthfully assert that he or she voted on the prevailing side previously. If the mover gets away with it, it is unfair to the honest voters. If other people on the floor know, or think they know, that the individual voted on the losing side, there will be an outcry, and the moderator will be right in the middle of it. Moderators can pass the buck to the floor by asking for a vote on whether X shall be permitted to move for reconsideration, but if X has the votes for reconsideration, he or she probably has the votes for the permission to make the motion for reconsideration; therefore, passing the buck to the floor is going to appear to X's opponents as a surrender to X. The safer, if less heroic, course is not to try to apply the rule at all, except after roll calls.

On roll-call votes, or in towns with lionhearted moderators, astute voters who sense that they are in a minority, and hope that it is only temporary, may vote contrary to their convictions on the first vote to preserve their right to move for reconsideration at a more favorable time. They may

---

[2] Attorney General v. Dole, 168 Mass. 562, 47 N.E. 436 (1897); Bullard v. Allen, 124 Me. 251, 127 Atl. 722 (1925).

§32 [1]Demeter 138; Robert 156. Contra: Cushing 208-209; Manual for the Massachusetts General Court, Note to Senate Rule 53.
[2] Amherst, Billerica, Brookline, Lenox, and Reading, for example.
[3] Bolton 40; Seavey, Massachusetts Town Officers 136 (1893); Deschler 417.

be wasting their vote, however. If the town has a by-law that forbids two motions to reconsider, they may be mousetrapped by an immediate motion to reconsider made by another voter on the prevailing side who really hopes that reconsideration will be defeated.

§33. Limits to Reconsideration

If the losers as well as the winners may move for reconsideration, there must be some limits on the right to move for reconsideration, in order to protect the meeting from frivolous, dilatory or hopeless last-ditch tactics by the minority, and many towns establish such limits by by-law. In the absence of a by-law, the courts are apt to forbid, for the democratic deliberations of a town meeting, some of the limitations that are permissible in other kinds of assemblies. For example, some authorities hold that if a vote must be adopted by more than a majority, the same fraction will be required to vote reconsideration.[1] At least one Massachusetts moderator and one New Hampshire judge have applied this rule and learned to their sorrow, on appeal, that in a town meeting, absent a by-law, a majority will suffice to vote reconsideration.[2] Many towns, however, have by-laws requiring a two-thirds vote for reconsideration of any motion.[3]

Again, the manuals say that if a motion to reconsider is defeated, it may not be made again.[4] In many towns a by-law

---

§33 [1] See an Opinion of the Attorney General of Massachusetts, 6 Ops. Mass. Atty. Gen. 515 (1922). Contra: Cushing 205-209; Demeter 138; Deschler 419; Robert 158.
[2] Adams v. Townsend Schoolhouse Committee, 245 Mass. 543, 139 N.E. 803 (1923); Frost v. Hoar, 85 N.H. 442, 160 Atl. 51 (1932). See also Opinion of the Justices, 291 Mass. 578, 197 N.E. 95 (1935). Athol has a by-law which requires more votes for reconsideration than were cast for the vote to be reconsidered.
[3] Arlington, Blackstone, Hamilton, Manchester, Northborough, Reading, West Bridgewater, Westminster, Weston, and Wrentham, for examples.
[4] Bolton 41; Demeter 143; Robert 158. The fact that the question has been decided once in the affirmative and once in the negative makes no difference. Manual for the Massachusetts General Court, Note to Senate Rule 53, Note to House Rule 71.

so provides.⁵ This can lead to dandy games. Where this is the rule, a member of the prevailing side, to foreclose reconsideration later when that side may no longer be in the majority, may move for reconsideration immediately following the initial vote, while its troops are still on (or in) hand, and vote it down. This slams the door on reconsideration later, and the mousetrap on that astute voter described above, who voted contrary to his or her convictions. Barring a by-law that establishes the rule of the manuals, however, this tactic will not work in town meetings. There a vote not to reconsider will not bind the town and bar it from reconsideration at a later time.⁶ In any event, there is considerable risk that the troops will become confused.

The question naturally occurs to everyone: What should the moderator do if one unsuccessful motion for reconsideration is immediately followed by another? Common sense would indicate that the second motion could be nothing but a desperate dilatory maneuver, and that the moderator would be justified in ruling it out of order until circumstances had changed or enough time had elapsed to make it reasonable to suppose that the town might have changed its collective mind.⁷

Some towns, which by by-law or tradition bar a second reconsideration, have been known to entertain a blanket motion at the end of the first session to reconsider all the articles acted on that evening, to prevent by a negative vote their being reconsidered at a later session. This practice

---

⁵ Amherst, Arlington, Hull, Manchester, Reading, Westborough, and Wrentham, for example.

⁶ Neil v. Ward, 103 Vt. 117, 153 Atl. 219 (1930); Denicore v. City of Burlington, 116 Vt. 138, 70 A.2d 582 (1950). See also Hunneman v. Grafton, 10 Met. 454 (Mass. 1845). The Denicore case was followed by a 1951 amendment to the Vermont statutes which inserted a requirement that petitions for special meetings to reconsider action of earlier meetings be filed within 30 days, and not more than once.

⁷ Some towns forbid reconsideration unless it is moved, or notice of it is given, within a certain time after the vote. Examples include Falmouth and Lexington (30 minutes); Billerica, Templeton, and Westminster (1 hour); and Stow (2 hours).

should not be permitted.[8] In the first place, it is presumably not legally effective, in view of the fact that a vote not to reconsider A, B and C is not equivalent to a vote not to reconsider A alone. In the second place, assuming it could be effective as intended, it would enable two people, the mover and the seconder, to put the whole meeting in the ridiculous position of having to vote for reconsideration of the whole evening's work in order to save its right to reconsider any part of it.

A motion to rescind is like a motion to reconsider. Accordingly, if a by-law or tradition forbids reconsideration twice, it forbids a motion to reconsider after a motion to rescind, or vice versa.

§34. Exceptions to the Power to Reconsider

Six exceptions to the general power of a town to reconsider or rescind are:

1. When the vote constitutes an acceptance of an offer and thus the creation of a binding contract.[1] Where the contract is not specifically enforceable, i.e., where the rights of the other party to it can be fully and adequately compensated for by monetary damages, it will not preclude reconsideration.[2] The voters may prefer buying off the other party to continuing the project.

2. When action has been taken that cannot be undone without affecting the rights of third parties, as, for example,

---

[8] Demeter (p. 140) says that reconsideration of more than one question (mass reconsideration) is prohibited, except by unanimous consent. A single objection, therefore, could defeat this maneuver.

§34 [1] Nelson v. Milford, 7 Pick. 18 (Mass. 1828); Hall v. Holden, 116 Mass. 172 (1874); Braintree Water Supply Co. v. Braintree, 146 Mass. 482, 16 N.E. 420 (1888); Cohasset Water Co. v. Cohasset, 321 Mass. 137, 72 N.E.2d 3 (1947); Marden v. Champlin, 17 R.I. 423, 22 Atl. 938 (1891). These and the cases in the following footnotes are mostly cases in which reconsideration was attempted at later meetings, but, in view of the strong language in Hunneman v. Grafton, 10 Met. 454 (Mass. 1845), it seems that the same result would have been reached had reconsideration been attempted at the same meeting.

[2] Garrett v. Fisher, 116 Vt. 323, 75 A.2d 674 (1950).

the execution of deeds or specifically enforceable contracts authorized by the vote.[3] The fact that rights have vested does not preclude reconsideration if the new action does not impair such rights. For example, if the town votes to elect three selectmen, and does, it may reconsider, at the same meeting, and elect two more to make it five. It may not subsequently reduce the number of selectmen.[4]

3. Where the vote constitutes a ratification of prior action by a town official or board.[5]

4. Where the vote constitutes an acceptance of an act of the legislature.[6]

5. Where statutes provide that an unfavorable vote precludes a second attempt for a specified period of time.[7]

6. Where the vote is self-executing, such as a vote to abolish a school district.[8]

These exceptions do not apply in a representative town meeting if, as is sometimes the case under the statute establishing the meeting, the vote does not take effect until after the meeting has dissolved.[9] If the vote has not taken effect, there is no substantive rule of law to prevent its reconsideration. Whether the vote is final or not can be a nice question.[10]

---

[3] Allen v. Taunton, 19 Pick. 485 (Mass. 1837); Hunneman v. Grafton, *supra*.

[4] Attorney General v. Dole, 168 Mass. 562, 47 N.E. 436 (1897).

[5] Brown v. Inhabitants of Winterport, 79 Me. 305, 9 Atl. 844 (1887); Arlington v. Peirce, 122 Mass. 270 (1877).

[6] Brucato v. Lawrence, 338 Mass. 612, 156 N.E.2d 676 (1959).

[7] For example, the purchase of a power plant, White Mountain Power Co. v. Bartlett and North Conway Lighting Precinct, 92 N.H. 210, 29 A.2d 468 (1942), or the amendment of a zoning by-law, Mass. Gen. Laws, c. 40A, §8. Fish v. Canton, 322 Mass. 219, 77 N.E.2d 231 (1948), describes a meeting at which a negative vote on a zoning amendment was reconsidered, without comment by the court, but the town clerk has stated that Canton did not accept §8 until the following year. See Kitty v. Springfield, 1961 Mass. Adv. Sh. 1409, 178 N.E.2d 580.

[8] Parker v. Titcomb, 82 Me. 180, 19 Atl. 162 (1889).

[9] See, for example, Mass. Gen. Laws, c. 43A, §10.

[10] Compare Sampson v. Treasurer and Receiver General, 282 Mass. 119, 184 N.E. 465 (1933), with Robinson v. Selectmen of Watertown, 336 Mass. 537, 146 N.E.2d 900 (1957).

§35. Rank and Application to Certain Motions

As we have already pointed out, main motions are not the only motions that may be reconsidered. Subsidiary motions to postpone indefinitely, to amend, to commit or refer, to postpone to a time certain, and to limit debate, and the privileged motion to fix the time to which to adjourn, may also be reconsidered. A motion to reconsider will have the rank of the motion to be reconsidered.[1] To the extent that these motions are debatable, a motion to reconsider one of them is also debatable.[2]

An amendment cannot be reconsidered after the main motion has been passed, without reconsidering the main motion. One motion to reconsider both will do.[3] By the same token, an amendment to an amendment cannot be reconsidered after the primary amendment has been adopted without reconsidering the primary amendment. If, after some action on an article, the subject has been referred to a committee, the action cannot be reconsidered until the subject has been retrieved from the committee by a vote to rescind the reference; but the motion to rescind the reference may be combined with the motion to reconsider the action taken, and with the motion for the desired action. This triple play should not be attempted if there is risk of confusing the meeting.[4]

A vote to lay on the table may be reconsidered,[5] since reconsideration is equivalent to a motion to take from the table. However, a motion to take from the table cannot be reconsidered. If a motion to take from the table is successful, another motion to lay on the table may be made after a proper interval, unless prevented by a by-law or tradition against repeated reconsideration. None of these motions, if adopted, may be followed immediately by its opposite, because it is not debatable and there can be no reasonable expectation that the

---

§35 [1] Demeter 140; Robert 157.
[2] Demeter 140; Deschler 420; Robert 157. Contra: Hackett 229.
[3] Robert 161.
[4] For example of a badly bungled attempt at such a triple play, see Blankinship v. Hadley, 11 Gray 431 (Mass. 1858).
[5] Deschler 420. Contra: Demeter 95, 228; Robert 107, 158.

meeting will change its mind immediately.

A motion to recess, adjourn or dissolve the meeting cannot be reconsidered. It would be grossly unfair to those who, following such a motion, had left the hall. After recess or adjournment, the meeting cannot act at all until it reconvenes in accordance with the terms of the vote to recess or adjourn. Dissolution is irretrievable.

Motions to divide the question and for the previous question cannot be reconsidered.

The only privileged motions that may be reconsidered are the motion to fix the time to which to adjourn and the motion to fix the time at which to adjourn.[6]

A motion to reconsider may not be amended, referred to a committee or postponed indefinitely,[7] and may not itself be reconsidered.[8] In a town meeting it is a waste of time to try to postpone it indefinitely. A simple "No" on the motion to reconsider will kill it for the moment, and as is shown above, even a vote never to reconsider is ineffective to kill reconsideration indefinitely.[9]

A motion to reconsider may be laid on the table or postponed to a time certain.[10]

The right to reconsider or rescind expires with the final dissolution of the meeting, and a later meeting cannot reconsider the action of an earlier meeting except pursuant to an article for that purpose in the warrant for the later meeting.[11]

Validation of a vote by the legislature does not prevent the town from reconsidering it;[12] nor does confirmation[13] or rescission[14] by the voters on a referendum prevent

---

[6] Demeter 98, 228.
[7] Id. at 140; Robert 157.
[8] Demeter 138; Manual for the Massachusetts General Court, Senate Rule 53, House Rule 71.
[9] See §33 *supra*, note 6.
[10] Demeter 140; Robert 157.
[11] Woodward v. Reynolds, 58 Conn. 486, 19 Atl. 511 (1890); Johnson v. Miller, 13 Conn. Supp. 116 (1944).
[12] Terrett v. Sharon, 34 Conn. 105 (1867).
[13] Denicore v. City of Burlington, 116 Vt. 138, 70 A.2d 582 (1950).
[14] Town of Trumbull v. Ehrsam, 148 Conn. 47, 166 A.2d 844 (1961).

reconsideration by town meeting members at a later meeting (pursuant to a proper article).

§36. Reconsideration by Ruse and by Thin Slices

Care should be taken by the moderator not to permit any properly applicable limits on reconsideration to be circumvented by the use of motions flying a different flag but amounting to reconsideration in substance. For an easy example: If a motion to dismiss is defeated, a motion for indefinite postponement should not be permitted except within the rules permitting reconsideration. If an affirmative motion is lost, a slightly rephrased motion is still a motion for reconsideration unless the question it presents is materially different.

What is material? The thin slice can raise a difficult question of judgment. If a motion to appropriate $5,000 is lost, a motion to appropriate $4,998 is probably not in order, but a motion to appropriate $4,500, or $5,500, might be. The problem really involves difficult questions of judgment for two people: the mover and the moderator. The mover has to estimate how much money the meeting might vote for. If the estimate is low and the motion carries, the mover may be stuck with less than could have been gotten. If the estimate is high and that motion loses, the mover may lose the more modest amount that might have been obtained had he or she aimed lower, and get nothing. In either case, whether that voter will have a chance to try again, to edge closer, will depend on whether the moderator thinks there is a dollar amount, not yet voted on, which the meeting would really prefer to any theretofore mentioned.

Obviously the moderator cannot permit a series of motions altering the amount by a dollar at a time like a penny-ante poker game, or oscillating over and under like an inept artillery battery. However, in Lamb v. Danville School Board, 102 N.H. 569, 162 A.2d 614 (1960), the Court sustained a vote to appropriate $95,000 after motions to appropriate $60,000 and $98,000 had been defeated, and Kenison, C.J., said:

"Mr. Justice Holmes' reminder 'that the machinery of

government would not work if it were not allowed a little play in its joints' (Bain Peanut Co. of Texas v. Pinson, 282 U.S. 499, 501, 51 S. Ct. 228, 229, 75 L. Ed. 482), has had particular application in this jurisdiction to town and school meetings." In each situation the moderator must decide whether the difference is material or penny ante.[1]

§37. The Tradition Against Reconsideration

Practice as to reconsideration is by no means uniform. Often it is governed by a by-law, as indicated above, and such by-laws, of course, differ greatly. In many communities a tradition or practice has grown up through the years[1] of shunning reconsideration, and in such communities the moderator will refuse to recognize a motion for reconsideration in the absence of some compelling circumstances that seem to justify a departure from the accepted practice. In such towns it is considered that motions for reconsideration substantially extend and prolong town meetings, and apparently their experience has indicated that no injustice has resulted from the practice of denying it.

In many towns where reconsideration is permitted, it is surrounded with restrictions protecting the prevailing side from what is there considered to be an unfair flank attack. Such restrictions prohibit reconsideration at late hours when the prevailing partisans are absent from the meeting or present in substantially fewer numbers. In a representative town meeting, the prevailing partisans include not merely the prevailing town meeting members but also the registered voters who are not town meeting members, since they are also entitled to participate in the debate and influence the discussion and the voting.

In any case, comparative attendance alone is not conclusive. The giving of advance notice that reconsideration is to be moved, the importance of the article, the quantity and

---

§36 [1]Aside from technical rules as to reconsideration, the moderator may always reject a motion which in his or her judgment is frivolous.

§37 [1]See §3 *supra*, note 5.

quality of the debate, the margin of the earlier vote, whether reconsideration is moved during the same session (and how soon after the action on the original motion) or a subsequent session, are all factors for the moderator to consider when tradition allows discretion to decide whether he or she will entertain a motion for reconsideration.

Moderators should always bear in mind that if they exercise discretion in this connection, they must (1) be consistent, and (2) make sure that the meeting understands their reasons for allowing reconsideration here and denying it there; otherwise their reputation for impartiality will suffer. Since one's reasons will rarely seem convincing to those whom one rules against, the average moderator will find it wiser not to be too sophisticated in such distinctions, but to refuse reconsideration — or allow it — in all cases but those that cry aloud for an exception.

It is a safe bet that in the long run the town will prefer to have the moderator err on the side of refusing reconsideration and get the voters home early, rather than err on the side of permitting the meeting to be protracted by repetition. Furthermore, although we have collected some instances where the moderator's judgment in this problem has been questioned in judicial proceedings, they are all cases in which he or she permitted reconsideration and the proceedings were brought to nullify the final vote. There are no reported cases, and probably no unreported cases, either, in which the moderator's refusal to permit reconsideration has been questioned, and there probably never will be. The reason is that the most the court could do would be to order the town to hold another meeting to reconsider the matter; it could not tell the town how to vote on reconsideration. And the proponents of reconsideration can usually obtain another town meeting to reconsider the matter by collecting signatures on a petition, which is much quicker, cheaper and surer than litigation.

Chapter 6

Subsidiary Motions

§38. In General

There are seven[1] subsidiary motions, ranking among themselves, from the highest to the lowest, in the following order:
- To lay on the table
- The previous question (i.e., to stop all debate and vote forthwith)
- To limit or extend the limits of debate
- To postpone to a time certain
- To commit (or refer)
- To amend (or substitute)
- To postpone indefinitely[2]

Subsidiary motions ordinarily apply to main motions only, but on occasion they may be made while other subsidiary motions are pending. Sometimes the second subsidiary motion is intended to apply to the main motion in competition with the first subsidiary motion, sometimes to apply to the first subsidiary motion, and sometimes to apply to both the main motion and the first subsidiary motion together. On other occasions there may be several subsidiary motions intended to apply, in competition with each other, to the first subsidiary motion.[3]

1. *Subsidiary Motions Competing with Each Other.* When subsidiary motions compete with each other for application to another motion (whether a main motion or another subsidiary motion), their "rank" determines the order in which they will be considered. The higher-ranking motion will be voted on before the lower. In fact, a lower-ranking motion may not even be entertained while a competing motion

---

§38 [1]Bolton, Cushing, Hackett and Jefferson do not consider "to limit debate" a subsidiary motion.

[2] We have already described this as a main motion, but it may be a subsidiary motion, too. See §30 *supra*.

[3] In some towns the moderator imposes a limit of two subsidiary motions at one time, of whatever kind. See A Handbook for Town Meetings 9 (League of Women Voters of Wayland, Mass.; undated).

of higher rank is pending. For example: (1) If a main motion is followed by a motion to commit, which is then followed by a motion to amend the main motion, the motion to amend may not be entertained; and (2) if a main motion is followed by a motion to amend, which is then followed by a motion to commit, action on the motion to amend is deferred until after action on the motion to commit. If the motion to commit is adopted, that disposes of the entire pending package. If the motion to commit is defeated, the motion to amend may then be acted upon.

2. *A Subsidiary Motion as Applied to Another Subsidiary Motion.* The order of rank given above will apply to several subsidiary motions made in competition with each other. It may be stated as a desirable general rule[4] that no subsidiary motion may be applied to another subsidiary motion of higher rank, with one exception: a motion to amend.[5] It may be applied to a motion to commit or to postpone to a time certain, but not to a motion for the previous question or to lay on the table, both of which are unamendable. Conversely, any subsidiary motion may apply to a subsidiary motion of lower rank, subject to what is discussed below, except that a subsidiary motion to postpone indefinitely may not be amended.

It follows that (1) in no case may a low-ranking subsidiary motion be entertained while a higher-ranking subsidiary motion is pending, whether the lower is intended to compete with or to apply to the higher (with the one exception described above respecting a motion to amend); and (2) a higher-ranking subsidiary motion may always be entertained and disposed of, notwithstanding the pendency of a motion of lower rank (with the exception described above: that a motion to postpone indefinitely may not be amended).

Inspection of the list printed at the beginning of this chapter will indicate that some of these subsidiary motions (to

---

[4] Cushing (p. 141) and Hackett (p. 88) make the general statement that subsidiary motions may not be applied one to another, but this statement is subject to so many exceptions as to be only half true, and not very useful.

[5] To illustrate: A motion to commit may not be applied to a pending motion to postpone to a time certain, but a motion to amend may be so applied.

postpone indefinitely, to commit, to postpone to a time certain and to lay on the table)[6] purport to defer action; two (to limit debate and the previous question) accelerate action; and one (to amend) neither defers nor accelerates. The subsidiary motions that defer action (to postpone indefinitely, to commit, to postpone to a time certain and to lay on the table) have obviously got to be applied, if at all, to the whole bundle of motions that may be pending. For example, if the bundle consists of a main motion and a motion to amend it, the motion to amend may not be committed or referred, laid on the table or postponed, without the main motion. The main motion may not be left in the air and it may not be acted on, because if it were, it would not be on hand to be amended when the motion to amend came back from committee, or from the table, or from postponement. Conversely the main motion may not be referred to a committee without the motion to amend.

On the other hand, the subsidiary motions that accelerate action (to limit debate and the previous question) do not need to apply to the entire bundle, as in the case of subsidiary motions that defer action. They may be applied to the immediately pending motion, or to a consecutive series of pending motions including the entire bundle, if desired, but beginning with the immediately pending motion. They need not be applied to a higher-ranking motion, since the higher-ranking motions are not debatable anyway. Thus, for example, a motion for the previous question need not be applied to a motion to lay on the table, since the latter is not debatable in any event.

The motion which neither defers nor accelerates (to amend) may be applied, regardless of rank, to all debatable motions except to postpone indefinitely (i.e., to amend, to commit or to postpone to a time certain), but may not be applied to the nondebatable motions (to limit or extend the limits of debate, the previous question, and to lay on the table). Generally speaking, any motion that may be debated

---

[6] The motion to lay on the table is usually used not to defer but to kill immediately. Even then, it is subject to the limitation described in the text.

may be amended,[7] and vice versa.

In 1789, the House of Representatives in Washington adopted a rule (Rule XVI, cl. 4) which, through imitation, has had influence far beyond the nation's capital. "When a question is under debate, no motion shall be received but to adjourn, to lay on the table, for the previous question (which motions shall be decided without debate), to postpone to a day certain, to refer, or to amend, or postpone indefinitely; which several motions shall have precedence in the foregoing order . . ."[8]

This enumeration includes six of the subsidiary motions listed above (excluding "to limit debate") plus one privileged motion, to adjourn. The General Court of Massachusetts has substantially similar rules,[9] and many towns have copied the national House[10] exactly in this respect. Others follow generally, but with additions, omissions and rearrangements.[11]

§39. To Postpone Indefinitely (as a Subsidiary Motion)

Basic Points: *A motion to postpone indefinitely requires a second and a majority vote; may be debated and reconsidered, but not amended; and may not interrupt the speaker.*

Form of Motion: *"I move that this matter be postponed indefinitely."*

The manuals say that this is the lowest-ranking subsidiary

---

[7] A motion to postpone indefinitely is an exception.
[8] House Document No. 459, 86th Cong., 2d Sess. 397 (1960).
[9] Massachusetts Senate Rule 46 (without the previous question); Massachusetts House Rule 80 (without "to postpone indefinitely"). Both houses add "to limit debate."
[10] Blackstone, Shirley, and Weston, for example.
[11] For example, Arlington omits "to postpone indefinitely," but Sudbury moves it up to a rank just below the previous question, and Westminster puts it between "to postpone to a time certain" and "to amend." Lexington and Westborough follow the Massachusetts Senate and House in introducing "to limit debate" just before "to postpone to a day certain." In Manchester "to postpone to a day certain" ranks below everything. Lincoln follows the national House, except that it specifies a two-thirds vote for the previous question.

motion[1] and that it can be made only while a main motion, and no other, is pending,[2] and many town by-laws follow House Rule XVI, 4, in assigning to this motion the lowest rank.[3]

"Should a member desire to consign a measure to the region of indefinite postponement, his way of going about to make the proper motion is simplicity itself. He has only to rise in his place, and when recognized by the speaker, to address the chair as respectfully as he knows how, saying 'Mr. Speaker, I move that the bill be indefinitely postponed.' If his motion be put to a vote and carried, the bill is indefinitely postponed, and the assembly, as it were, gambols into pastures new. If not - he subsides."[4]

A motion to postpone indefinitely (as a subsidiary motion) cannot be amended.[5] It may be postponed to a time certain or laid on the table.[6] The motion is subject to debate,[7] and, since the meeting may weary of it, it makes sense to say that the motion to limit (or extend) debate or the previous question may be applied to it.[8] It requires a majority vote.[9]

---

§39 [1] Bolton 39; Cushing 84; Deschler 400; Robert 152. This seems to be an example of a rule that is more arbitrary than logical. The effect of it is to deprive the motion of any usefulness. If the motion can only be applied to main motions, it can only serve, if it carries, to do what a negative vote on the main motion would do; or, if it fails, to cause two votes in a row on the same question and give the garrulous ones two opportunities to talk.

On the other hand, there would seem to be a useful function for the motion at other stages of the proceedings. Sometimes a minority of the meeting gets itself all wound up in motions to amend a proposition that the majority will not vote for in any condition, and the whole hopeless proposition could be cleared from the decks in one sweep by a motion for indefinite postponement, if it had a higher rank.

[2] Demeter (p. 64) assumes it can be made, but not voted on, while another subsidiary motion is pending.

[3] See §38 *supra*, notes 10 and 11.

[4] Hackett 100.

[5] Bolton 39; Cushing 85 (but see Cushing 142); Demeter 62; Robert 152. See §30 *supra*, note 3.

[6] Robert indicates (p. 152) that a motion to postpone indefinitely may not be committed, postponed or laid on the table, but gives no reason for this statement.

[7] Hacket 97.

[8] Robert 152.

[9] Demeter 62.

§40. To Amend (or Substitute)

Basic Points: *A motion to amend or substitute requires a second and a majority vote; may be debated, amended and reconsidered; but may not interrupt the speaker.*

Form of Motion: *"I move that the pending motion be amended by adding the following words: ...."*

As we have already pointed out, the article in the warrant and the main motion may propose amending an existing by-law.[1] Such a motion is a main motion and subject to the rules that apply to main motions. It is not to be confused with the subsidiary motion to amend another motion, which is the subject of this portion of the discussion. Usually the subsidiary motion to amend is applied to a main motion, but it may also be applied to a motion to amend[2] (within the limits to be described), or to motions to commit,[3] to postpone to a time certain[4] or to limit debate.[5] Those who confuse articles with main motions will sometimes try to "amend the article,"[6] but this is one thing that may not be done to an article. It may not be amended.

The amendment may consist of adding, deleting or substituting words in the motion to be amended. It may take the form of a motion to substitute a different motion, but a motion to substitute is still merely a motion to amend and is to be dealt with as such.

A motion to amend requires only a majority vote, even though the motion to be amended may require two-thirds or more.[7] It must be remembered that the main motion must always be acted upon after action on a motion to amend. It is especially easy to forget this when the amendment is highly controversial and the main motion is taken for granted. After all, some people may have voted for the amendment as the

---

§40 [1] See §23 *supra*.
[2] Bolton 37; Cushing 149; Robert 134; House Rule XIX.
[3] Bolton 36; Cushing 148; Deschler 401; Robert 125.
[4] Cushing 146; Demeter 85; Robert 121.
[5] Demeter 88; Robert 119.
[6] Fish v. Canton, 322 Mass. 219, 77 N.E.2d 231 (1948).
[7] Bolton 37; Robert 134.

lesser of two evils and would vote against the main motion in any form,[8] or the main motion may require a higher quantum of vote.

As with main motions, the principal problem facing the mover and the moderator, in motions to amend, is the problem of staying within the four corners of the article.[9]

The motion to amend may always be debated. Theoretically debate should be limited to the merits of the amendment. However, it is not always easy or desirable to impose a strict limit, and moderators may, if they desire, permit debate on the merits of the main motion as well.

The first amendment to a motion is called the primary amendment, or amendment in the first degree. It may itself be amended. An amendment to the primary amendment is called the secondary amendment, or amendment in the second degree. A secondary amendment may not itself be amended.[10] This is an arbitrary limit, designed to keep matters from getting too complicated. If any voter feels that with one more change the main motion could be made perfect, the moderator should advise that person to wait until the secondary amendment has been acted on, and to offer his or her amendment as a new secondary amendment. It is permissible for the voter to describe, during the debate on the first secondary amendment, the amendment he would really like to make, but the moderator must be sure that the meeting understands that it is not voting on it yet. Not more than one primary and one secondary amendment may be pending at one time. Subject to the foregoing there is no limit to the number of motions to amend (or substitute) which may be made.

A secondary amendment is voted upon before the primary amendment, and, of course, the primary amendment is voted

---

[8] However, a failure to put the main motion to a vote is not fatal if the action on the amendment leaves "no doubt that the sense of the meeting on the subject was really ascertained and declared." Leonard v. School District of Cornish, 98 N.H. 296, 99 A.2d 415 (1953). It is always desirable to avoid any question by putting the main motion to a vote.

[9] See §28 *supra*.

[10] Bolton 37; Demeter 66; Hackett 113-114; Jefferson 214; Robert 134; Massachusetts House Rule 89.

upon before the main motion,[11] except as indicated below with respect to figures.

It frequently happens that an amendment represents a retreat from an extreme position offered by the main motion or, vice versa, an advance from a cautious main motion, and an amendment to the amendment may represent a still bolder advance. In such cases, those who favor the proposition and would like to see it adopted at its boldest may be in something of a quandary. By reaching too far, they may prejudice their cause. Consequently, they may vote for a middle course out of tactical caution. There is nothing that the moderator can or should do to help them out of this quandary, with one exception. When the main motion and the several proposed amendments differ only in figures, three figures could be present on the stage at one time, with a fourth or fifth, or more, announced to be waiting in the wings. To vote on them in accordance with the rule stated above might mean quite a random sequence of high and low figures, and utter confusion for the voters and the moderator. The first figure to receive a majority might not be the figure the meeting really wanted most. By arranging the figures in their numerical order and starting at what seems to be the least popular end, the first figure to receive a majority will probably be the nearest to the figure the meeting wants.[12] For example, if it is a question of an appropriation, the least popular end of the series would probably be the high end, so the vote would be put first on the highest figure, then on the next highest and so forth until a figure is reached which obtains a majority. Conversely, if it is a question of selling town property and fixing the upset price, normally the low end of the scale would be the unpopular end, so the first vote would be taken on the lowest figure. Many towns relieve the moderator of the burden of determining which is the unpopular end of the scale by a by-law which, ignoring the foregoing analysis, provides that the largest sum

---

[11] See §23 *supra*.
[12] Jefferson 215.

shall be put first.[13]

As in the case of reconsideration by thin slices,[14] the moderator must always use some judgment as to whether there is enough difference between one figure and the next to justify taking the time of the meeting to vote on the second.[15]

"The moderator must maintain a careful record of the motions that are pending and put them to a vote in the proper order. Action must be taken on every motion. A common fault is the failure to put a main motion to a vote after action on a hotly-debated motion to amend when it is clear that the only real question is whether the meeting desires the original or the amended form. The main motion, however, must be put to a vote whether or not amended."[16]

If an amendment is an obvious improvement, is accepted by the maker of the main motion and is incorporated into the question finally put, it may be found to have been adopted by general consent, even though never formally voted on,[17] but this should be explicit and not left for inference. Otherwise some voters may not know just what they are voting on.

§41. To Commit (or Refer)[1]

Basic Points: *A motion to commit or refer requires a second and a majority vote; may be debated, amended and reconsidered, but may not interrupt the speaker.*

---

[13] Amherst, Blackstone, Lexington, Lincoln, Manchester, Shirley, and Westborough, for examples. So also does the Massachusetts Legislature: Manual for the General Court, Senate Pule 51 and House Rule 92.

[14] See §36 *supra*.

[15] Lamb v. Danville School Board, 102 N.H. 569, 162 A.2d 614 (1960).

[16] Bolton 15. See also Cushing 99-100; Robert 101.

[17] Sears v. Fuller, 137 Mass. 326 (1884).

§41 [1] "Commit" and "refer" are now synonymous, but in the seventeenth and eighteenth centuries it was a common practice to "refer" a matter "to the next meeting" or "to the May meeting." Boston Town Records, March 10, 1778, for example. In this sense "refer" means "postpone," and some traces of this usage may still be found. See Article 2, §4, of the Dartmouth by-laws, for example, in which "refer" appears to mean "postpone." We shall use it as equivalent to "commit."

Form of Motion: *"I move that the matter be referred to a committee to be appointed by the moderator, to study and report to the next (annual) meeting."*

"If the proposition will want more amendment and digestion than the formalities of the House will conveniently admit, they refer it to a committee."[2] The committee's functions may be to investigate and report, or it may be charged with carrying out substantive action on which the meeting has already made up its mind. A motion to commit should specify the committee, which may be one of the town's permanent boards or committees or may be a special committee to be appointed for the purpose.[3] If the latter, the motion must specify by whom it is to be appointed or elected. The motion may, but need not, contain specifications as to the personnel of the committee, such as "one member from each precinct" or "one member of the finance committee, one member of the planning board," etc.[4] For more on these matters, see Chapter 2, §12.

If and to the extent that the article permits it, but not otherwise, the motion may also contain an appropriation for the committee's expenses: for travel and the services of experts, etc.[5]

It is common and desirable to instruct the committee to report to the next special or annual town meeting.[6] When the next meeting arrives, it will naturally report if it is ready to do so and there is an article under which it may, but if it is not ready, or there is no such article, there will be no report, regardless of the instructions of the previous meeting. Some towns find it useful to require the committee to report to the moderator, or to some other specified town official, by a fixed date, to enable the report to be circulated and considered

---

[2] Jefferson 208. For an early example, see Boston's vote to appoint a committee "to treat with all the neighboring Townes concerning a convenient way of Fortifying at Castle Island." Boston Town Records, Nov. 11, 1643.
[3] Adams v. Plunkett, 274 Mass. 453, 175 N.E. 60 (1931).
[4] Brown v. Melrose, 155 Mass. 587, 30 N.E. 587 (1892).
[5] Ibid. "To see if the town will take any action . . ." will suffice even though money is not mentioned. Dunn v. Framingham, 132 Mass. 436 (1882).
[6] Boston Town Records, Jan. 9, 1657.

before the next meeting.

An unqualified vote to refer a matter to the selectmen has been held to confer authority not merely to determine what should be done but also to do it.[7] The vote should be clear on this point, as ambiguity will lead to litigation.

Occasionally the committee will be instructed to report to an adjourned session of the same meeting. In such a case, the moderator should see to it that any motion to adjourn is consistent with the committee's instructions.

The motion to commit may be made only when a main motion, one or more subsidiary motions of lower rank (to postpone indefinitely, and to amend), or incidental motions arising out of any of these, are pending,[8] and it must apply to all of them, including the main motion.[9] It may not be made when any other motion is pending, since all others are higher in rank. It is amendable[10] (with respect to the size, appointing authority, composition or instructions of the committee)[11] and debatable (but, theoretically, only with respect to these questions and the propriety of the committal).[12]

It may, together with all other pending motions, be laid on the table or postponed to a time certain,[13] and the previous question may be applied.[14] It may not be postponed indefinitely.[15]

It requires a majority vote.[16] It may be reconsidered or rescinded by a majority vote[17] unless the committee has taken

---

[7] Willard v. Newburyport, 12 Pick. 227 (Mass. 1831). See Littlefield v. Boston & Albany R.R., 146 Mass. 268, 15 N.E. 648 (1888).

[8] Cushing 148, 150; Robert 125.

[9] Bolton 36; Robert 126.

[10] Demeter 79; Robert 125.

[11] Cushing 148. As stated *supra* §38, this is an exception to the general rule that lower-ranking subsidiary motions may not be applied to higher-ranking motions.

[12] Bolton 36; Robert 125. Actually it is not always easy or desirable to impose a strict limit on the debate.

[13] Robert 125.

[14] Deschler 413; Robert 125.

[15] Deschler 400; Robert 125. But *see* §39 *supra*, note 1.

[16] Demeter 79.

[17] Adams v. Townsend Schoolhouse Committee, 245 Mass. 543, 139 N.E. 803 (1923). The statements of Demeter (p. 80) and Robert (p. 133) that a two-thirds vote is required do not apply to town meetings.

action which cannot be undone.[18] The committee is not obliged to wait until the meeting has dissolved before proceeding to act.[19]

§42. To Postpone to a Time Certain

Basic Points: *A motion to postpone to a time certain requires a second and a majority vote; may be debated, amended and reconsidered; but may not interrupt the speaker.*

Form of Motion: *"I move that consideration of this matter be postponed until after Article ___ has been disposed of."*

This may take the form of a motion to postpone one article until after some other article has been acted upon, and as such is a useful way of rearranging the order of the articles.[1] It may also take the form of a motion to postpone to a specified time of the clock, regardless of the state of the warrant. In the latter form, this is an awkward motion to handle in a town meeting, which may finish its business at any moment and adjourn without day or dissolve, and thus cease to exist. The motion should not be permitted in this form if the time stated is so far in the future that it is doubtful whether the meeting will have other business to occupy it until that time, making allowance for normal adjournments. The subject may be postponed to an adjourned session of the same meeting, but it may not be postponed to a different meeting.[2] If the current meeting dissolves without acting on the article, the article is dead, and a later meeting may not act on the subject without a new article in its warrant.[3]

---

[18] Hunneman v. Grafton, 10 Met. 454 (Mass. 1845).
[19] Ibid.

§42. [1] See §19 *supra*.
[2] Bolton 24.
[3] Reed v. Acton, 117 Mass. 384 (1875), cited by Bolton as a seeming exception, is the last expression of an earlier tradition when town meetings were held at least as often as monthly, it was every qualified voter's duty to attend, the warrant was not as important as it is now (see §1 *supra*) and the distinction between a new meeting and an adjourned session of an old meeting was not carefully observed.

A by-law fixing the order in which the articles may be considered may limit the use of this motion, but one town[4] evidently considers it quite consistent to have such a by-law, along with another that recognizes the motion to postpone to a time certain. In towns that use a lottery system for determining the order in which the articles are taken up (see §18), a motion to postpone action on a given article to a time certain should be ruled out of order, since the effect of the motion would be to defeat the lottery system.

Whenever the time stated is a later date, so that the meeting will have to adjourn at least once to be in session on that date, the motion to postpone should be preceded by a motion to fix the time to which to adjourn,[5] so that the meeting will not inadvertently adjourn to a later time.

Even though the meeting should run clear out of business before reaching the time to which something has been postponed, a motion to adjourn without day or to dissolve is out of order until the time has been reached. This is why the motion to postpone to a time certain should be handled with care. It may be reconsidered.[6] Bolton suggests[7] that reconsideration should be refused if it appears that it is sought to take advantage of interested persons who are absent, in reliance on the postponement, but he does not explain how the moderator is to divine this.

The motion may be applied directly to the article, and it may be made when any motions of lower rank are pending,[8] in which case it must apply to all of them.[9] It may not be made when a motion of higher rank (to limit or extend debate, the previous question, or to lay on the table) is pending.

The motion may be debated, and amended as to the time fixed, but the merits of the question to be postponed may be

---

In Rhode Island a matter may be postponed to, and acted upon at, an annual meeting, which is not limited by the warrant, except for disposing of land or making a tax. See §4 *supra*, note 4.

[4] Swampscott.
[5] Robert 121.
[6] Demeter 85.
[7] Bolton 35.
[8] Robert 121.
[9] Deschler 400.

debated only insofar as they affect the question of postponement.[10] It requires a majority vote.[11]

§43. To Limit or Extend the Limits of Debate

Basic Points: *A motion to limit or extend the limits of debate requires a second and a two-thirds vote; it may be reconsidered, but not amended or debated, and may not interrupt the speaker.*

Form of Motion: *"I move that debate on the pending motion (article) be limited to ___ minutes for each speaker."*

This motion may be made with respect to any debatable motion or series of debatable motions.[1] If not specified to the contrary, it applies only to the immediately pending question.[2] It is undebatable itself, and may not be amended, requires a two-thirds vote and may be reconsidered even though it has been applied to some speakers.[3]

The limit may be particular, as: ten minutes for each speaker; or general, as: one hour for the entire debate.

In view of the moderator's power to regulate the proceedings, it seems clear that he or she has the power to impose limits on debate of his or her own accord, without waiting for a motion.[4] Moderators may do this at the start of the debate or later, but if one allows some people to speak at

---

[10] Bolton 35. "A motion to postpone to a day certain can of course be debated, but upon such a topic there is really not much to be said. The question is simply whether to take this day or that, for the consideration of the bill. True, there are gentlemen gifted by nature who are able to offer a full line of remarks upon a theme even so contracted as this. They can take up a pocket calendar and ventilate their opinions at much length as to the superiority of one particular date over another; but it must be confessed that on these occasions the scope of genuine eloquence is limited." Hackett 97.

[11] Demeter 85.

§43 [1] Robert 118.
[2] Ibid.
[3] Id. at 119; Demeter 88-90. They are contra as to amendment.
[4] Me. Rev. Stat., c. 90A, §34 III; Mass. Gen. Laws, c. 39, §§15, 17; N.H. Rev. Stat. Ann., c. 40, §§4, 7; R.I. Gen. Laws, tit. 45, c. 3, §17; Vt. Stat. Ann., tit. 24, c. 31, §724.

length, one should be careful not to appear to discriminate against others. If the subject seems to have been pretty well explored, however, the meeting may welcome such a limit.

§44. The Previous Question

Basic Points: *The previous question requires a second and a two-thirds vote; may not be debated, amended or reconsidered; and may not interrupt the speaker.*

Form of Motion: *"I move the previous question."*

The phrase "I move the previous question" probably does more than any other to create the impression that a meeting is run by an inner circle of initiates who speak a secret language. There is no reason why anyone should be excluded from the secret. It does not mean that the mover wants to reconsider the question that has just been decided; it means that the person has heard all the talk he or she wants to hear on the pending question and desires to vote on it immediately.[1]

Some towns[2] do not permit debate to be cut off in this fashion. Other towns expressly recognize it in their by-laws.[3] It would seem to be out of order in Rhode Island, where the statute provides that the moderator shall "after having heard all the electors entitled to vote thereon who shall be desirous of being heard, cause the votes of the electors to be taken..."[4]

An argument could also be made against the use of the previous question in Massachusetts, where the constitutional authority for representative town meetings provides that the

---

§44 [1] For the history of the motion, see Cushing 80-84; Deschler 411-415; Hackett 90-92; Jefferson 218-221; and Robert 117. If the motion carries, the debate ends. "Those glowing sentences, that fervent appeal, that more than sublime climax, will all stand adjourned. No other course is open but to change a few sentences and work off the MS. at a future session in some other debate." Hackett 92-93.

[2] Wellesley, for example.

[3] Bedford, Lincoln, Manchester, and Westborough, for examples.

[4] R.I. Gen. Laws, tit. 45, c. 3, §20. The Massachusetts Senate does not recognize the previous question (Rule 46 bars all but seven enumerated motions, which do not include the previous question), but the House of Representatives does, allowing, however, not over ten minutes altogether or three to a member for debate, limited to reasons why the main question should not be put. Rules 79, 80, 81 and 82.

members are elected to "meet, *deliberate,* act and vote."[5] But this argument is opposed by what is probably the preponderance of the practice.

Where the motion is permitted, it may be applied to all of the motions then pending, or to any consecutive series of pending motions, provided that the series includes the motion immediately pending. Unless otherwise specified, it applies only to the motion immediately pending. It cannot be debated, and cannot be amended, committed or postponed.[6] It may be laid on the table.[7] It requires a two-thirds vote for passage,[8] and it cannot be reconsidered if adopted,[9] because it is undebatable and executed immediately, and there is no reason to suppose the meeting would change its mind without debate.[10]

If the motion for the previous question should fail, it may be renewed after a sufficient interval of debate to warrant the supposition that the meeting may have finally had enough.[11]

The moderator should never ask for the motion, nor accept a cry of "question" from someone who has not been properly recognized. There may be times, however, when the moderator might point out that the discussion is becoming repetitious and that further discussion would appear to be pointless. Also, if several consecutive speakers have spoken in favor of a motion, the moderator might shorten the discussion by pointing out that fact and asking if anyone

---

[5] Const., Art. LXX. The language of the Constitution is taken from Shaw, C.J., in Warren v. Mayor and Aldermen of Charleston, 2 Gray 84, 101 (Mass. 1854).

[6] The manuals say it may not be amended, and we are not disposed to attempt to change the rule. However, as an original question it may be wondered why a motion for the previous question which is expressly stated to apply to all the pending motions, including the main motion, should not be amendable to restrict its application (for example, to permit debate on the main motion).

[7] Robert 105, 112. Contra: Deschler 415.

[8] Bolton 34; Demeter 90; Robert 112.

[9] Massachusetts House Rule 71.

[10] Demeter (p. 93) and Robert (p. 112) say that it may be reconsidered before it has been executed (by voting on the motion to which the previous question is applied), and Deschler (p. 418) says it may be reconsidered once, but they do not give any reason for allowing this, and common sense indicates that an immediate motion for reconsideration can only be a move of desperation.

[11] Manual for the Massachusetts General Court, Note to House Rule 80.

wishes to speak in opposition.

In some towns where the moderator traditionally limits debate, under statutory powers, he or she may, in the exercise of a sound discretion, discourage the use of the previous question in favor of a short continuation of debate, or conversely terminate debate on his or her own initiative when it appears that the subject has been exhausted. Moderators should remember, however, that Mr. Doggett lost his temper and had to be evicted, in a famous stormy scene, as a result of being prevented on three different occasions from completing his remarks by the previous question.[12]

Finally, a person wishing to end debate should simply say, when recognized, "I call the question", and should not address the merits of the pending motion. The effect of a contrary rule would be to permit a speaker to state an opinion while attempting to prevent others from stating theirs.

§45. To Lay on the Table

Basic Points: *A motion to lay on the table requires a second and a two-thirds vote; may not be debated or amended or interrupt the speaker, but may be reconsidered.*

Form of Motion: "*I move that this be laid on the table.*"

"When the House has something else which claims its present attention, but would be willing to reserve in their power to take up a proposition whenever it shall suit them, they order it to lie on their table. It may then be called for at any time."[1]

The purpose of this motion in legislative assemblies was to enable the meeting to take up some more urgent business, meanwhile keeping the interrupted business close at hand ("on the table") so that it could be easily resumed when the more urgent business had been disposed of. For this reason the motion was given the highest rank, applying to or superseding every other subsidiary motion, was undebatable and required

---

[12] Doggett v. Hooper, 306 Mass. 129, 27 N.E 2d 737 (1940).

§45 [1]Jefferson 207.

only a majority vote.[2] If a town allows this motion for its original purpose to delay debate, it is important for the moderator to realize that a motion to adjourn is not in order until the motion that had been laid on the table is removed from the table and acted upon.[3]

Through the years the motion to lay on the table has lost its original purpose of temporarily deferring a debate and has come to be used as a motion to kill without further debate. Accordingly, moderators should treat the motion as one both to suppress debate and to dispose of the question.[4]

It is fundamental in parliamentary law that a two-thirds vote is necessary for a motion which eliminates debate, and therefore a two-thirds vote should be required by the moderator on a motion to lay on the table,[5] notwithstanding statements to the contrary in the manuals.[6]

To summarize, the motion has the highest rank of the subsidiary motions, is undebatable and requires a two-thirds vote.

If the motion carries, all pending motions go to the table with it.[7]

After an appropriate interval of debate, the motion to table, if lost, may be renewed;[8] or, if the motion was adopted, the subject may be taken from the table. To take from the table is the substantial equivalent of reconsideration, and accordingly it is not necessary to move to reconsider.[9] The

---

[2] Robert 107-108.
[3] Since this requirement is often neglected, it is suggested that the motion when used in the sense of delaying debate be treated as a motion to postpone to a time certain. See Bolton 32. The mover should be required to specify the time.
[4] Some towns (Amherst, for example) refuse to permit the motion, thus heeding Robert's comment: "This complete revolution in the use of the motion to lay on the table renders all the practice of Congress in regard to this motion useless for any ordinary deliberative assembly. It is the extreme of a 'gag law,' and is only justifiable in an assembly where it is impossible to attend to one-tenth of the bills and resolutions introduced." P. 108.
[5] See discussion in Bolton 33; Robert 109.
[6] Demeter 95; Robert 108.
[7] Cushing 144; Demeter 95; Robert 105.
[8] Manual for the Massachusetts General Court, Note to House Rule 77.
[9] See Robert 107.

manuals say that a motion to reconsider is out of order,[10] but the distinction is purely verbal, and the moderator may properly treat a motion to reconsider as a motion to take from the table.

Since a motion to take from the table is equivalent to reconsideration, any limits on reconsideration that prevail in the town (such as requirements of notice or a two-thirds vote) should apply, although the manuals do not so state.

A motion to take from the table may not be debated, amended or reconsidered and, as in the case of reconsideration, requires only a majority vote.[11] It is undesirable to entertain a motion to take from the table at any time except when no other business is pending. It should, therefore, rank as a main motion. It yields to incidental and privileged motions and to all the subsidiary ones, except that it cannot be amended and that, since it is not debatable, moving the previous question and moving to limit debate are unnecessary. It is hard to conceive of such a refinement as referring this motion to a committee. It is theoretically possible, but the committee would also, theoretically, be restricted to considering the advisability of taking from the table and not the merits of the matter to be taken.[12] The motion to take from the table is not in order unless some business has been transacted since the original motion to table was adopted.[13]

---

[10] Demeter 95; Robert 107.
[11] Bolton 34; Demeter 148; Robert 154.
[12] Contra: Robert 154. See Demeter's Table.
[13] Bolton 34; Demeter 149; Robert 154.

Chapter 7

Incidental Motions

§46. In General

Incidental motions relate to the conduct of the meeting with respect to the pending business. They are considered and disposed of before the motion out of which they arise,[1] because otherwise they would become moot. With respect to all other motions, they take the rank of the motion out of which they arise.[2] Incidental motions that compete for application to the same motion have no rank among themselves, but are decided as they arise.

For example, suppose a main motion, two incidental motions and then a subsidiary motion, made in this order and all applying to the main motion and pending at once. The subsidiary motion is acted upon first, since it outranks the main motion and therefore the incidental motions. If action on the subsidiary motion does not dispose of the matter, the incidental motions are acted upon in the order in which they were made, and finally the main motion is disposed of.

Incidental motions appropriate for town meetings are:
- Point of order
- Appeal
- Division of a question
- Separate consideration
- To fix the method of voting
- Nominations to committees
- Motions for leave to withdraw or modify a motion
- Suspension of the rules

Towns that have copied House Rule XVI, 4[3] into their by-laws would appear to have restricted the use of several

---

§46. [1] Jefferson 216.
[2] Bolton 28. Bolton's later statement (p. 29) to the effect that a motion to divide the question takes precedence over a motion to amend or postpone indefinitely is supported by Robert (p. 89), but seems inconsistent with his general statement on page 28. The general statement seems to be the better rule.
[3] "When a question is under debate, no motion shall be received but to adjourn, to lay on the table, for the previous question, . . to postpone to a day certain, to refer, or to amend, or postpone indefinitely; . . ."

incidental motions which are not necessary in Congress but are at least convenient in town meetings. One wonders if this was intentional. In Congress the division of a question is not made on a motion, but on the demand of one member,[4] and so is not barred by Rule XVI, 4; the method of voting is fixed by Rule 1, 5, and by the Constitution itself,[5] and withdrawal of a motion, where permitted at all, is a matter of right.[6]

Some towns follow through their adoption of Rule XVI, 4, with another by-law providing for the division of a question on the demand of one or more voters,[7] but many more do not. New England statutes generally allow a town considerable leeway in the method of voting,[8] and many towns have by-laws covering the subject to some extent,[9] but few of them cover it completely, so that there is a substantial area in which a meeting might find a motion to fix the method of voting useful.

If the meeting wishes to do any of these things that a by-law bars "when a question is under debate," when can it do them? To fix the method of voting might well be moved before the main motion is made, but to divide the question cannot be moved until there is a motion, or else there is no way of knowing whether it is divisible, and after the motion is made there is very little time, if any, before it is "under debate." Yet it is preferable to divide the question when it is first introduced,[10] and this is the only time to move for separate consideration.

There is not apt to be much time after the debate, either, in which to move to divide the question or to fix the method of voting, and yet these motions obviously have got to be made before the vote on the question, if at all. The sensible thing, therefore, for a voter in one of these towns who wishes

---

[4] Rule XVI, 6.
[5] Art. 1, §5.
[6] Rule XVI, 2.
[7] Lexington, Manchester, Shirley, and Westborough, for example.
[8] R.I. Gen. Laws, tit. 45, c. 3, §20, prescribes a method in certain areas.
[9] Fairfield, Conn., and Bedford, Blackstone, Lexington, Manchester, Milton, Reading, Shirley, Shrewsbury, Westborough, and Weston, Mass., for example.
[10] Robert 90.

to fix a method of voting or to divide the question, and who failed to make the motion before the debate, is to make his or her wishes known during the discussion and ask to be recognized by the moderator for this purpose at the close of debate.

§47. Point of Order

Basic Points: *A point of order does not require a second or a vote and may not be debated, amended or reconsidered, but may interrupt the speaker.*

Form of Motion: *"I rise to a point of order."*

The first thing to be said is that a point of order is not really a motion at all, but a question. (The question is often put in the form of an assertion.) This being the case, it escapes the interdiction of a by-law based on House Rule XVI, 4.[1] What sets it and the question of personal privilege (see §57) apart from any other questions which may be introduced into the debate is that they raise a question so important as to justify the interruption of a speaker. For this reason, it needs to be carefully defined, since some have the erroneous impression that it is merely a label which, by being prefixed to whatever the interrupter has to say, gives uninhibited license to break in and seize the floor. On a point of order, a voter may raise one or more of the following questions and no others:

1. Is the speaker entitled to the floor (for example, is the person a nonvoter, or a voter who has overstayed the time allotted by by-law)?

2. Is what the speaker is saying or proposing indecorous, frivolous, irrelevant, illegal or contrary to proper procedure?

3. Is any pending action frivolous, irrelevant, illegal or contrary to proper procedure?

A point of order may be a tactful hint from one who can see a point the moderator has missed, or it may be a bona fide inquiry.

---

§47 [1]See §38 *supra*.

Any attempt to use it as a device to usurp the floor should be dealt with firmly.

The proper way to raise a point of order is to rise and address the chair as follows: "Mr. Moderator, I rise to a point of order." It is imperative then to remain silent until the moderator says, "Please state your point of order."

A point of order resembles other motions in that it states a question, but, not being a motion, it need not be seconded; and whereas other questions are put to the meeting by the moderator, a point of order is decided by the moderator alone, without debate. There is no reason for the moderator to be rushed into a hasty decision. It is fine to be able to give the impression of having all the nice points of procedure at one's fingertips, but the effect is ruined if the quick answer is erroneous, and the meeting will usually follow more willingly the moderator who takes time to be right, rather than the hasty and erratic one. Furthermore, there are instances of august presiding officers who take time to look up the precedents.[2] The point should be decided, however, before proceeding further.

If the moderator needs factual information to decide a point of order (for example, if the point is whether or not a proposed bond issue is within the town's debt limit), he or she should inquire of the appropriate officials, or of others. If the information is not available, the moderator should recess the meeting or ask that the matter be postponed until the information can be obtained.

If the point raised is that the speaker is indulging in personalities, it may also be a question of privilege (see §57 *infra),* but there is no need to be overly particular about the label.

§48. Appeal

Basic Points: *An appeal requires a second and a majority vote, and may be debated (with exceptions) and*

---

[2] Deschler 306; Jefferson 172; Manual for the Massachusetts General Court, Note to House Rule 73.

§48 7: INCIDENTAL MOTIONS 111

reconsidered, but may not interrupt the speaker.
Form of Motion: *"I appeal from the ruling of the chair."*
In many assemblies, including town meetings in New Hampshire,[1] and probably in Connecticut and Rhode Island,[2] an appeal will lie to the floor from the ruling of the chair on a point of order.[3] Where the statutes provide that the moderator shall decide all questions of order and say nothing about an appeal,[4] there are two schools of thought as to appeals. One school holds that the meeting is supreme and the moderator merely its servant.[5] The better rule in Massachusetts is that the statute puts the burden on the moderator and it can not be avoided by letting the meeting decide.[6]

Adherents of the second school, however, may well consider it proper to take the advice of the floor on questions involving a mixture of law and fact where the facts may involve questions of judgment. Moderators who belong to the first school should never permit an appeal from a ruling based on a pure question of law when the result of reversing the ruling may be the taking of illegal action by the town. The meeting may be supreme, but it is bound by law, including substantive by-laws, which cannot be amended except

---

§48 [1] Hill v. Goodwin, 56 N.H. 441 (1876); Leonard v. School District of Cornish, 98 N.H. 296, 99 A.2d 415 (1953).
[2] Conn. Gen. Stat., tit. 7, c. 90, §7-7; R.I. Gen. Laws, tit. 45, c. 3, §21.
[3] Cushing 135; Demeter 116; Deschler 305; Jefferson 172; Robert 21.
[4] Mass. Gen. Laws, c. 39, §15; Vt. Stat. Ann., tit. 24, c. 31, §724. Maine has recently amended its statute. It formerly provided that the moderator "shall regulate the business of the meeting." Me. Rev. Stat., c. 91, §44. It now provides merely that the moderator shall "preside at the meeting." Me. Rev. Stat., c. 90-A, §34 III.
[5] Seavey, Massachusetts Town Officers 133 (1893).
[6] DeWolf, The Town Meeting 23 (1890). This school is aided in this construction by the circumstances that Rule 1, 4, of the federal House, Rule 2 of the Massachusetts Senate and Rule 2 of the Massachusetts House all provide that the presiding officer shall "decide all questions of order, subject to an appeal . . ." As a matter of statutory interpretation, the omission from the statute on town meetings of words deemed appropriate by the lawmakers in the rules that govern their own meetings is significant. Legislators are never supposed to use superfluous words, so if they thought it desirable to say "subject to appeal" in their own rules, the implication is that where they omit those words there is no appeal.

pursuant to an article.[7]

Where an appeal is allowed, it must be preceded by a point of order as a foundation for the appeal.[8] The moderator is entitled to have his or her attention directed to the question and make an express ruling on it before an appeal is taken. The appeal must be seconded[9] and must be taken at the time the decision is made.[10] If the appeal is allowed, the moderator puts the question: "Shall the decision of the moderator be reversed?"[11] An appeal is debatable except when it relates simply to indecorum, or transgression of the rules of speaking, or to the priority of business, or if made during a vote, or while the immediately pending question is undebatable.[12] When it is debatable, the moderator may speak on the question, without leaving the chair.[13] The appeal may not be amended.[14] It requires a majority in the affirmative to reverse the moderator's ruling,[15] and a tie vote sustains the moderator.[16] If the moderator is a member of the assembly in his or her own right, he or she may vote to make the tie.[17]

An appeal yields to privileged motions,[18] the previous question applies,[19] and an appeal may be laid on the table.[20] If it is laid on the table, the moderator's ruling is sustained.[21] The vote on an appeal may be reconsidered.[22]

---

[7] See §54 *infra*.
[8] Demeter 119.
[9] Id. at 120; Massachusetts House Rule 94; Robert 82 *(semble)*. Contra: Bolton 29.
[10] Bolton 29; Demeter 121; Robert 81; Manual for the Massachusetts General Court, Note to House Rule 94.
[11] But see Bolton 29; Demeter 120; Hackett 157-158; Robert 82-83.
[12] Robert 82.
[13] Demeter 121; Robert 82. They say that the chair may speak only twice, and others only once, but in town meetings the moderator's discretion is not so restricted.
[14] Bolton 29; Demeter 120; Robert 81.
[15] Demeter 120.
[16] Bolton 29; Demeter 121; Robert 83.
[17] Robert 83.
[18] Id. at 81.
[19] Demeter 121.
[20] Hackett 159; Robert 81; Manual for the Massachusetts General Court, Notes to Senate Rule 41. Contra: Note to House Rule 94.
[21] Hackett 159.
[22] Robert 82.

§49. Division of a Question

Basic Points: *A motion for the division of a question requires a second and a majority vote; may be debated and amended, but not reconsidered, and may not interrupt the speaker.*

Form of Motion: *"I move that the question be divided as follows:_____."*

When, and only when, a question is susceptible of division, a motion to divide it and vote on the parts separately is in order.[1] Each part must make sense (grammatically and otherwise) by itself,[2] but some leeway may be allowed to make purely grammatical adjustments. "The result will be the same as if motions to amend by striking out the several parts had been made and put to the question."[3]

The motion to divide a question may be applied only to main motions, amendments[4] and instructions to a committee,[5] because other motions are not susceptible of division. Preferably it should be debatable[6] and amendable[7] but it may not be reconsidered.[8]

Although Jefferson[9] and Cushing[10] suggest that division of the question can only be done by a vote of the meeting, Bolton suggests[11] that the moderator should divide the question, without waiting for a motion, if division will serve some constructive or valuable purpose. This is the better rule.

Some towns provide, by by-laws, for a division on the

---

§49 [1] See Perkins v. Crocker, 109 Mass. 128 (1872); Corey v. Wrentham, 164 Mass. 18, 41 N.E. 101 (1895).

[2] House Rule XVI, 6, puts it thus: if it include propositions so distinct in substance that one being taken away a substantive proposition shall remain. Compare Hackett 121.

[3] Cushing 93.
[4] Robert 89.
[5] Bolton 29; Robert 89.
[6] Contra: Bolton 29; Demeter 127.
[7] Bolton 29; Demeter 127.
[8] Bolton 29.
[9] Pp. 229-230
[10] Pp. 93-94.
[11] P. 29.

request of a stated number of voters.[12]

It is preferable to divide the question when it is first introduced[13] for the sake of orderly debate on each part separately, or, failing that, at the close of debate on the whole question, to avoid interruption of the argument. The debate may develop reasons, however, for dividing the question in the middle of the discussion.

The foregoing paragraphs contemplate final action on each part of the question. When all the parts have been acted upon, no further vote on the whole is necessary. However, notwithstanding this, any rules against reconsideration of final action should not be applied too strictly in this situation, as a subsequent amendment to a later part may require going back and making a corresponding amendment to a part already adopted.

§50. Separate Consideration

Basic Points: *A motion for separate consideration requires a second and a majority vote; may be debated and amended, but not reconsidered; and may not interrupt the speaker.*

Form of Motion: *"I move that we consider this paragraph by paragraph."*

A motion for separate consideration closely resembles a motion to divide the question, but differs in two respects: (1) it may be applied to a proposition, such as a building code, which falls naturally into parts but which is so interrelated that the parts will not stand alone (as is required for division); and (2) the action, if any, taken on each part is not final until the action on the whole proposition at the end. Thus an earlier section may be adjusted to fit a change in a later, without even

---

[12] Lexington (25) and Shirley (5). House Rule XVI, 6, Massachusetts Senate Rule 45 and Massachusetts House Rule 91 all provide for division on demand by one member.
[13] Robert 89-90.

going through the motions of reconsideration.[1] The moderator could submit the entire proposal for consideration, but if there are amendments to be made, they might be made at random. Separate consideration has the advantage of promoting orderliness. The lack of finality makes it safer for the moderator to take this step of his or her own accord, without appearing partial, though moderators should avoid a course that appears to invite amendments at one time and to discourage them at another. After separate consideration of all the sections, the moderator states that the entire proposition is open to amendment, and whole paragraphs may be added at the end and further amended. Eventually, a final vote is taken on the whole.[2]

If the moderator should offer the entire proposition as a package, a motion for separate consideration is in order from the floor. If a voter should offer a motion to divide the question, when it would be more appropriate to move for separate consideration because the parts will not stand alone, the moderator should explain the difference and require that a motion for separate consideration be substituted.

The motion for separate consideration should be debatable and amendable, but it may not be reconsidered.

§51. To Fix the Method of Voting

Basic Points: *A motion to fix the method of voting requires a second and a majority vote; may be debated, amended and reconsidered; but may not interrupt the speaker.*

---

§50 [1]See Boston Town Records, May 3, 4, 8, 9, 10 and 12, 1780, at which the proposed Constitution or "Frame of Government" was considered paragraph by paragraph. "The natural order in considering and amending any paper is, to begin at the beginning, and proceed through it by paragraphs; and this order is so strictly adhered to in Parliament, that when a latter part has been amended, you can not recur back and make any alteration in a former part . . . in numerous assemblies this restraint is doubtless important. But in the Senate of the United States, though in the main we consider and amend the paragraphs in their natural order, yet recurrences are indulged; and they seem, on the whole, in that small body, to produce advantages overweighing their inconveniences." Jefferson 188-189.

[2] Bolton 30; Demeter 131; Robert 92-94.

Form of Motion: *"I move that we vote on the pending motion by standing vote."*

Cushing and Robert do not recognize a motion to fix the method of voting prior to the vote, but Massachusetts does.[1] Mass. Gen. Laws, c. 39, §15, provides that if a vote declared by the moderator is immediately questioned by seven or more voters he shall verify it by polling the voters or by dividing the meeting, unless the town has "by a previous order or by by-law" provided another method. A number of towns which deal with the matter by by-law provide that the meeting may decide to vote by ballot.[2] Vermont provides for polling or dividing "unless the town has provided some other procedure in such cases."[3] This could refer to a by-law or to a specific vote, or, as is spelled out in Massachusetts, to both. Maine is similar.[4]

There seems to be no reason why the motion to fix the method of voting should not be debatable[5] or amendable.[6]

See Chapter 11 for a discussion of methods of voting.

§52. Nominations to Committees

Basic Points: *A nomination to a committee does not require a second, requires a plurality, and may not be debated, amended or reconsidered.*
Form of Motion: *"I nominate _____."*

The usual vote to refer a matter to a committee specifies that the committee shall be appointed by someone—the moderator, for example—but a vote to refer a matter to a committee to be elected by the meeting would not be out of

---

§51 [1] See Perkins v. Crocker, 109 Mass. 128 (1872). So does Demeter (p. 123). See §67 infra.

[2] Lexington and Shrewsbury, for examples. Some towns provide that a certain number of voters, or a percentage of those voting, may call for and get a ballot vote: Hanover (50), Hull (15), Middleton (5), North Andover (25%), Templeton (7), and West Bridgewater (8), for examples.

[3] Vt. Stat. Ann., tit. 24, c. 39, §724.

[4] Me. Rev. Stat., c. 90-A, §34 111, C.

[5] Contra: Demeter 123.

[6] Demeter 123.

order. Any voter may nominate, and no second is required.[1]

A motion to close nominations is a familiar bit of forensic display, but it is not in order until a reasonable time has elapsed,[2] and when a reasonable time has elapsed the moderator has the power to declare the nominations closed without a vote.[3] The motion is undebatable, may have no subsidiary motion applied to it, requires a two-thirds vote[4] and yields to privileged motions.[5]

If there are only as many nominees as places, they may be elected by a voice vote. This may seem unnecessary, but it should be done.

If there are two or more nominees for one place, a hand vote or a standing vote will do; the moderator should first make it clear that each voter should vote for only one candidate, and then call for "those in favor of A" and then "those in favor of B," and so forth. A plurality of those voting will elect, even though it may be less than a majority of those present, or indeed even of those voting.[6] If there are more than two places and more nominees than places, a ballot vote is recommended. On each ballot voters should write the name or names of their choices to the number of the vacancies, or "bullet the ballot" if they wish.[7]

---

§52 [1] Bolton 31. Demeter (p. 82) and Robert (p. 96) suggest other methods than nomination from the floor, such as nominations by the chair and nominations by a committee, but Bolton says that these are not appropriate to town meetings, and we concur.

[2] Robert 97.
[3] Bolton 31.
[4] Ibid.; Robert 96-97.
[5] Robert 97.
[6] Bolton 32. Demeter (p. 188) and Robert (p. 191) indicate that a mere plurality is insufficient in the absence of a by-law; that a majority of the votes cast is required. However, such a requirement involves run-off elections, and this is unnecessarily cumbersome for the election of a committee by a town meeting. See §6 *supra* (election of the moderator), and Chapter 11 (voting generally).
[7] To "bullet the ballot" is to refrain from exercising all the votes to which one is entitled, for the purpose of concentrating on one favorite candidate. For example, suppose there are five candidates for three places and voters wish particularly to see A elected. If they cast all the votes they are entitled to cast, their votes for B and C may be the votes that enable B and C to nose out A. In such a case they vote only for A and waste their other two votes. This would not be permitted where proportional

§53. Motions for Leave to Withdraw or Modify a Motion

Basic Points: *A motion for leave to withdraw or modify a motion does not require a second; requires a majority vote; may not be debated, amended or reconsidered; and may not interrupt the speaker.*

Form of Motion: *"I move for leave to withdraw (or modify) my motion."*

From time to time, one who has made the motion will wish to withdraw it. That voter may wish to save the meeting's time or avoid his or her own embarrassment, or may have a tactical reason, such as preserving a chance to make the motion again at a time more propitious for passage.

According to the manuals, it makes a difference whether the moderator has stated the motion to the meeting. Before that, the mover has a right to withdraw the motion, even though it has been seconded.[1] After that, leave to withdraw must be requested. This may be granted by general consent,[2] but a single objection will make it necessary to treat the request as a motion.[3] (The mover may move for leave; someone else may move to grant leave; or the moderator may choose to treat it as a motion.) It requires no second,[4] may be made while incidental and subsidiary motions are pending (and carries these with it), yields to privileged motions, cannot be amended or have any other subsidiary motion applied to it, is undebatable[5] and requires only a majority vote.[6]

It has been suggested that the moderator may use some judgment and spare the meeting the restatement of a motion that has just been stated by the mover. In such a case, the commencement of debate would serve to terminate the

---

representation is the governing principle. There voters would mark their first, second and third choices. Proportional representation may be a good thing in its place, but it is too complicated for the election of a committee by a town meeting.

§53 [1] Demeter 130; Robert 100-101.

[2] See Boston Town Records, March 14, 1780: "a debate arising on the motion, the question was withdrawn."

[3] Cushing 138; Demeter 130; Hackett 163; Robert 101.

[4] Robert 100. Contra: Demeter 130.

[5] Demeter 130; Robert 100.

[6] Demeter 130.

mover's absolute right to withdraw. In any event, the moderator should not be slow to discern general consent to withdrawal if it is clear that the reason for withdrawal is to save time or embarrassment. Moderators can be a little slower to discover such consent if the motion has been well debated and there is reason to believe that withdrawal is purely tactical.

After voting on a motion has commenced, it cannot be withdrawn except by unanimous consent.[7]

The fact that motions may be withdrawn illustrates another difference between motions and articles. The latter cannot be withdrawn, even by the sponsors. This is not an academic question, either. In a town that has accepted Section 8 of the Massachusetts Zoning Enabling Act,[8] no proposal to amend the zoning by-law which has been unfavorably acted upon by the town meeting may be considered again for two years unless recommended by the planning board.[9] Sometimes the sponsors would like to withdraw the article after they have felt the temper of the meeting, but they may not.[10]

The same rules that apply to withdrawal also apply to modification by the mover, except that the seconder has the right to withdraw that second. Sometimes a modification is suggested by someone other than the mover. Strictly speaking, this requires a formal motion to amend, duly seconded and voted on. However, if the mover accepts the suggestion, even after some discussion, and no one else objects, the modification may be treated as adopted by general consent.[11] This practice is so common that it sometimes gives rise to the

---

[7] Ibid.; Robert 100.
[8] Mass. Gen. Laws, c. 40A.
[9] See §34 *supra*, note 7.
[10] What may they do to keep their hopes alive for another meeting within two years? They may ask for postponement, but postponement beyond the life of the present meeting is the same as indefinite postponement and therefore unfavorable. A vote that the meeting "take no action" might be considered equally unfavorable, and a vote to lay it on the table certainly is. The safest thing they may do would seem to be to move to refer it to the planning board (or some other committee) for further study.
[11] Sears v. Fuller, 137 Mass. 326 (1884).

notion that the maker of the original motion, appearing to have the power to accept amendments, must also have the power to decline them. This is of course not the case. If a proponent declines to accept a proposed amendment, and someone wishes to press the point, then the formal process of amendment is followed.

§54. Suspension of the Rules

Basic Points: *A motion for suspension of the rules requires a second and a two-thirds or a unanimous vote, according to circumstances; may not be debated, amended or reconsidered; and may not interrupt the speaker.*

Form of Motion: *"I move that we suspend the rules, to permit _____."*

Rules relating only to the conduct of the meeting, such as the order of business, may be suspended,[1] but it requires a two-thirds vote unless there is unanimous consent.[2] Rules protecting absentees may not be suspended at all, and rules protecting minorities may be suspended only by unanimous consent.[3]

"By-laws which are merely directory may also be suspended,"[4] but "by-laws which are more than mere rules of parliamentary procedure cannot be."[5]

A rule requiring that notice be given of intention to move for reconsideration is an example of a rule protecting absentees; a rule providing for a ballot vote in certain circumstances, on the call of a specified number of voters, is an example of a rule protecting minorities. A by-law that requires the finance committee to make recommendations on

---

§54. [1] Bennett v. New Bedford, 110 Mass. 433 (1872). See DeWolf, The Town Meeting 27 (1890).

[2] Demeter 122-123; Hackett 164-166; Robert 83-87; House Rule XXVII; Massachusetts Senate Rule 63; Massachusetts House Rule 103. Cushing says that in the absence of a by-law providing for suspension of the rules, it may only be done by unanimous consent. P. 140.

[3] Robert 85.

[4] Young v. Westport, 302 Mass. 597, 20 N.E.2d 404 (1939).

[5] Loring v. Westwood, 238 Mass. 9, 130 N.E. 85 (1921). See Walsworth v. Casassa, 219 Mass. 200, 106 N.E. 847 (1914).

money articles is directory, but a by-law that provides that no appropriation may be made or by-law adopted unless the finance committee has made a recommendation is more than a mere rule of procedure. So, also, a by-law that prohibits a change in a personnel plan without a recommendation of the personnel board is more than merely procedural.

The motion may be made at any time when no question is pending, or while a question is pending, provided it is for a purpose connected with that question.[6] It requires a second.[7] It yields to all the privileged motions and to incidental motions arising out of itself, is undebatable and unamendable and may not have any other subsidiary motion applied to it, nor can it be reconsidered.[8]

§55. Inappropriate or Unnecessary Incidental Motions

Some of the manuals list a number of incidental motions not mentioned above, such as "Call for the Orders of the Day," "Objection to the Consideration of a Question," "Parliamentary Inquiry," "Request for Information," "To Reconsider and Have Entered on the Minutes" and "To Expunge."[1] They are not appropriate to town meetings. A town meeting has no "orders of the day," unless the warrant, plus a by-law requiring that the articles be considered in order, can be so construed, and, if so, a simple point of order will suffice to call attention to any departure. "Objection to the consideration of a question" serves no useful purpose that cannot be accomplished by a point of order (if the objection is that the main motion is illegal or irrelevant) or by moving the previous question (if debate is undesirable). "Parliamentary inquiry" and "request for information" are only fancy words for simple questions (for information as to

---

[6] Robert 84.
[7] Demeter 122. House Rule XXVII, 2, requires a second by a majority, by tellers if demanded.
[8] Demeter 122; Robert 84.

§55 [1] Cushing 152, 156, 158, 159; Demeter 99, 117, 118, 128, 142, 147; Robert 68, 87, 98, 99, 50, 165, 170.

procedure in one case and for any other kind of information in the other), and voters are more apt to ask the question if that is all they have to do than if they think the have to make a "parliamentary inquiry" or a "request for information." A vote "To reconsider and have entered on the minutes" serves, in continuing assemblies, to prevent hasty action. It compels the matter to be reconsidered on some other day.[2] It is out of order in a town meeting, which may dissolve before another day rolls around. A motion "To expunge" is out of order because the meeting has no control over the record. The town clerk has the exclusive power to make and to amend the record.[3] Perhaps the meeting may reconsider,[4] but that is all.

Congress has several interesting devices that are not appropriate to town meetings. One is the motion "To strike out the enacting clause," which, if carried, is equivalent to rejection.[5] Town votes do not contain enacting clauses. It should be apparent from §30 *supra* that there is no lack of other means of rejecting a main motion or an article. Another device, to move reconsideration and at the same time to move that reconsideration be laid on the table, is designed to lock the door.[6] Unless there is a special rule allowing it, the two motions could not be made at the same time in an ordinary society.[7] A third device is the motion "To strike out the last word." This is not meant seriously; it is intended to lengthen the time for debate.[8] A moderator may deal with this as a frivolous motion. The Massachusetts legislature kills bills politely by referring them "to the next annual session." This may not be translated into "the next annual meeting."[9] The proper motion is "To postpone indefinitely" or "To dismiss."

---

[2] Demeter 142; Robert 165.
[3] See §§7 and 17 *supra*.
[4] See §31 *supra*.
[5] House Rule XXIII, cl. 7; Hackett 112-113.
[6] Hackett 103.
[7] Robert 157.
[8] Deschler 454.
[9] See §42 *supra*.

Chapter 8

Privileged Motions

§56. In General

Privileged motions relate to the conduct of the meeting, regardless of whatever particular question, if any, may be pending, and so have priority over all other motions. There are only five privileged motions which are appropriate to town meetings, and they rank among themselves, from highest to lowest, in the following order:
- To dissolve or "to adjourn sine die"
- To adjourn to a fixed time, or to recess
- A point of no quorum
- To fix the time to (or at) which to adjourn
- A question of privilege

§57. A Question of Privilege

Basic Points: *A question of privilege does not require a second or a vote and may not be debated, amended[1] or reconsidered, but may interrupt the speaker.*
Form of Motion: *"I rise to a question of privilege."*

Questions of privilege relate first to the rights and privileges of the meeting collectively, its safety, dignity and the integrity of its proceedings; and second to the rights, reputation and conduct of the voters or town meeting members individually, in their capacity as voters or members.[2]

By the manuals, a question of privilege is the lowest ranking of the privileged motions,[3] but in Congress, and therefore presumably in those towns which follow House Rule XVI, 4,[4] a question of privilege is not a motion but a question (like a point of order)[5] and so escapes the bar of that rule. In Congress it takes precedence of all other questions except

---

§57 [1] Cushing 128; Demeter 101. Robert 67 contra.
[2] See House Rule IX.
[3] Bolton 25-28; Cushing 128; Demeter 101; Robert 66.
[4] See §38 *supra*.
[5] See §47 *supra*.

motions to adjourn.[6]

In Congress, questions of privilege range from matters of high constitutional prerogative, such as immunity from arrest and freedom of debate,[7] to the comfort and convenience of the members.[8] In town meetings, questions of privilege are usually limited to the latter.[9] If it is a mere matter of the temperature or ventilation of the room, a voter should refrain, within reason, from raising the question in the middle of debate,[10] but if it is a matter of noise, which prevents the speaker from being heard, the voter should speak up. A discreet call of "Louder, please" will usually suffice if the speaker's voice is too low, but if the problem is one of conversation or other disturbance nearby, the voter should rise, even interrupting the speaker if necessary,[11] say, "Mr. Moderator, I rise to a question of privilege," wait until the moderator directs him or her to state it, and then do so. Since it is not a motion, it need not be seconded.

In most cases, no vote is necessary. The matter can be dealt with by a simple request from the chair. To vote on whether or not to open or close a window does not greatly enhance the dignity of the meeting, but if necessary it is better than a squabble over it.

If a speaker indulges in personalities, the person attacked or any other person may rise to a question of personal privilege. The moderator should make it unnecessary by promptly calling the speaker to order. Occasionally the person raising the question of personalities may characterize the objection as a point of order. Strictly speaking, it is a question of privilege, and the moderator should simply treat it as such.

More serious questions of privilege are fortunately rare. In case of threats or attempted bribes, the meeting can do no

---

[6] House Rule IX.
[7] Art. 1, §6.
[8] Deschler 321.
[9] Proposals to blow up the assembly, whether real, as in Parliament on the first Guy Fawkes's Day, or feigned, as in Lynnfield town meeting on November 20, 1961, raise fundamental questions of privilege.
[10] Bolton 28.
[11] Robert 66.

more than express its opinion, so other proceedings are required to produce concrete results, but an expression of opinion by the meeting is not insignificant. A voter or member should always have the right to bring such matters to the attention of the town.

§58. To Fix the Time to (or at) Which to Adjourn

Bask Points: *A motion to fix the time to (or at) which to adjourn requires a second and a majority vote; may be debated, amended and reconsidered; but may not interrupt the speaker.*

Form of Motion: *"I move that when we adjourn we adjourn to . . .*

"I move that when the meeting concludes the business which is pending at eleven o'clock, we adjourn to . . "

Some of the manuals say that this motion is privileged only if made when some other question is pending; that if no other question is pending it ranks only as a main motion.[1] They do not say why we should be put to the trouble of remembering this, and in fact it makes very little difference. As a main motion it may be postponed to a time certain, or laid on the table; as a privileged motion it may not. Even considering it as ranking as a main motion, it is absurd to suggest postponing it indefinitely, referring it to a committee, moving the previous question, dividing it, or voting by ballot or roll call on it. On the other hand, even if it is privileged it is amendable.[2] There is not room for much debate on this motion, but what there is (Will the hall be available? Will there be a conflict with some important event?) is just as important whether the motion is privileged or not. A point of order is unlikely to arise, but it is hard to see why it would have to be dealt with in one case and not in the other.

The usefulness of a distinction is not readily apparent, and it is suggested, therefore, that for the sake of simplicity this motion should be treated as a privileged motion, whether

---

§58. [1]Bolton 26; Demeter 112; Robert 59.
[2] Robert 59.

other business is pending when it is made or not. However, in towns that follow House Rule XVI, 4, this motion is not in order while a question is under debate. The only utility of the motion to fix the time to which to adjourn is to forestall inadvertent dissolution. If the meeting has voted to consider a matter at a later date, the moderator would be well advised to suggest:

"Will someone move that when we adjourn we adjourn (stand adjourned) to (the date and place previously fixed)."

A motion then in the form "I so move" is sufficient.[3] Then, when the meeting votes to adjourn, it will be to the date and place fixed, and not result in a dissolution.

The motion to fix the time to which to adjourn is the only privileged motion that may be reconsidered. It requires a second,[4] is debatable[5] and amendable[6] as to dates and places, and requires only a majority vote.[7]

A motion that is not uncommon in town meetings, but which is not mentioned in any manual, is the motion to fix the time *at* which to adjourn, such as "I move that when the meeting concludes the business which may be pending at eleven o'clock, we stand adjourned until tomorrow night at 7:45 p.m." This motion, if carried, is self-executing, and at the time specified the moderator should declare the meeting adjourned, in accordance with the vote, without an additional motion.

In substance, this is a motion to fix the date to which to adjourn, combined with a motion to adjourn effective at the later hour specified. It cannot have the rank of the motion to adjourn because a point of no quorum necessarily outranks it. Accordingly it should be given the rank and all the other attributes of the motion to fix the time *to* which to adjourn.

---

[3] Bolton 26-27. See Boston Town Records, May 4, 1780: "Moved and Voted, that when this meeting is adjourned it shall be to Monday Morning 9 o'clock."
[4] Cushing 157; Demeter I 11.
[5] Bolton 26. Contra: a: Demeter I 11; Robert (table).
[6] Bolton 26; Demeter I 12; Robert 59.
[7] Demeter I 12.

§59. A Point of No Quorum

Basic Points: *A point of no quorum does not require a second or a vote; may not be debated, amended or reconsidered; and may not interrupt the speaker.*

Form of Motion: *"I rise to a point of no quorum."*

Bolton[1] is the only manual that classifies this as a privileged question,[2] but it seems clear that he is right. Since the meeting cannot take any action in the absence of a quorum except to adjourn to another time,[3] to take a recess[4] (which is the same thing)[5] or (in the discretion of the moderator when not prevented by a by-law) to dissolve,[6] the point of no quorum must necessarily supersede all motions other than these three.

If the immediately pending business is a motion to adjourn to another time, or to recess, an informal suggestion of no quorum may stimulate measures to obtain a quorum upon reconvening.[7] If the pending business is a motion to dissolve, a point of no quorum is superfluous and therefore out of order. A speaker may not be interrupted by a point of no quorum.[8]

Since a point of no quorum is not a motion but a question, it requires no second and escapes the bar of Rule XVI, 4. It is not debatable; no other motion may be applied to it.[9]

Although the earlier editions advised otherwise, the better view is that a point of no quorum is prospective only; that is,

---

§59 [1] Bolton 28.
[2] Demeter includes it among the incidental motions (p. 134), and Cushing and Robert simply do not classify it.
[3] Mass. Gen. Laws, c. 39, §13.
[4] Bolton 7; Cushing 32; Demeter 134-135; Robert 258-259.
[5] See §60 infra.
[6] See §61 infra. Many towns have by-laws that exclude a motion to dissolve until every article in the warrant has been acted upon. This applies when there is a quorum and a fortiori when there is not. Mass. Gen. Laws, c. 39, §13, and c. 43A, §5, are less than clear in this respect. They provide that less than a quorum may "adjourn from time to time." It could be argued that this implies no power to dissolve, but we see no reason of policy requiring this implication.
[7] Such as bell ringing, Boston Town Records, Sept. 29, 1778, or the services of "The Town Cryer." Id., June 29, 1780.
[8] Cushing 34; Robert 260. Contra: Deschler 21.
[9] Demeter 134.

the ascertainment of the absence of a quorum prevents the meeting from taking up any new business and from completing any unfinished business, but it does not affect any business completed before the point of no quorum is raised, no matter how short a time has intervened.[10]

After a count has established a quorum, the moderator need not entertain another point of no quorum after too short an interval unless there is reasonable ground for believing that there is a lack of a quorum.

§60. To Adjourn to a Fixed Time or to Recess

Basic Points: *A motion to adjourn to a fixed time or to recess requires a second and a majority vote; may be debated and amended, but not reconsidered; and may not interrupt the speaker.*

Form of Motion: *"I move that we adjourn to _____."*

The word "adjourn" has been used indiscriminately to describe any action from a short recess to complete dissolution. We recommend that a distinction be made between "adjourn" and "dissolve"; that "adjourn" be confined to a temporary suspension of the meeting, and that "dissolve" be used to refer to the final termination of the meeting, instead of "adjourn without day" or "adjourn sine die." There are two reasons for making this distinction. One is etymological: The word "adjourn" derives from the Latin word "adiurnare" which means "to fix a day," [1] and "to adjourn without day" is therefore a contradiction in terms.[2] The other reason is that it avoids confusion.

On the other hand, the terms "adjourn" (as defined above) and "recess" can be used interchangeably. They both connote temporary suspension.[3] We tend to use the word "adjourn" if

---

[10] Deschler 21; see also DelPrete v. Board of Selectmen of Rockland, 351 Mass. 344, 220 N.E. 2d 912 (1966).

§60 [1] Century Dictionary.
[2] Cushing 127 (1925 ed.).
[3] People v. Martin, 5 N.Y. 22, 26 (1851); Robert 64-65.

we expect to sleep before we reconvene[4] and to use "recess" if we expect to reconvene before we sleep, but nothing in law or the dictionary requires this distinction to be made. Accordingly, a motion to adjourn to a fixed time is identical with a motion to recess to a fixed time.

Such a motion, however worded, should have the highest rank of all motions except a motion to dissolve.

The manuals at this point make refinements the logic of which, if any, is mysterious. The first refinement they make is purely verbal: they distinguish between adjournment to a fixed time and a recess, and arbitrarily treat the former as a low-ranking main motion[5] and the latter as a highly privileged motion. Another peculiar refinement is that if the motion for a recess happens to be made when no question is pending, it is a mere main motion.

To treat the motion to adjourn to a fixed time as a low-ranking main motion is highly unsatisfactory as a practical matter. If it is a main motion, it follows that it cannot be made when any other question is pending. [6] This can be awkward. Eleven p.m. can arrive in the middle of a difficult question. It is unfair to the voters to keep them struggling with it until midnight or later, and unfair to the question to rush through a hasty decision on it.

Furthermore, a sophisticated parliamentarian can easily maneuver around the technical rule which assigns low rank to this motion in either of two ways: First the motion can be divided into two parts: (1) "to fix the time to which to adjourn at next Tuesday night at 7:45 in this hall," and (2) "To adjourn." Each of these motions has a high priority if any priority is needed.[7] No manual explains why it treats the whole motion as amounting to so much less than the sum of

---

[4] But see Blankinship v. Hadley, 11 Gray 431 (Mass. 1858), in which the meeting "adjourned" from morning to afternoon; and School District in Stoughton v. Atherton, 12 Met. 105 (Mass. 1846), in which the entire meeting "adjourned" for ten minutes to view the proposed new school site.

[5] Bolton 27; Demeter 109; Hackett 131; Robert 60; Manual of the Massachusetts General Court, Note to House Rule 79.

[6] Robert 51.

[7] Bolton 26-27; Demeter 97-114; Robert 59-60.

its parts. Second, the motion can be restated: "To recess to next Tuesday night at 7:45 in this hall."

It seems clear, accordingly, that no useful purpose is served by assigning this motion a low rank, and by assigning it a high rank we enable any voter, and not necessarily a sophisticated parliamentarian, to make the proper motion to get us home at a reasonable hour.[8]

The second refinement imposed by the manuals, i.e., that a motion to recess has no rank if made when no other business is pending, is the same refinement that they apply to the motion to fix the time to which to adjourn, which is discussed *supra* §58. For the reasons there given, this distinction should be ignored, and the motion to take a recess should at all times have its proper high rank.

If the vote is "To adjourn to Wednesday evening at 8 o'clock," it means the next Wednesday,[9] and custom can supply the place, if the vote omits that too.[10] Needless to say this brevity is not recommended. The motion should state fully and clearly the time and place.

Upon reconvening, the business that was pending at the time of adjournment or recess will come automatically before the meeting, subsidiary and incidental motions and all, just as if there had been no adjournment or recess.[11]

The motion to adjourn to a fixed time or to recess requires a second,[12] is debatable[13] and amendable[14] as to dates and places, and requires only a majority vote.[15] Of course it may not be reconsidered, if carried,[16] but the moderator's declaration of the vote to adjourn may be doubted, if without

---

[8] In towns with by-laws based on House Rule XVI, 4 ("when a question is under debate, no motion shall be received but to adjourn . . ."), there is no problem, because obviously the adjournment contemplated by the by-law is to a fixed time, and the by-law gives it the highest rank of all.

[9] First School District v. Ufford, 52 Conn. 44 (1884).

[10] Portland Water Co. v. Portland, 97 Conn. 628, 118 Atl. 84 (1922).

[11] Demeter 110; Robert 63. Contra: Cushing 127; Hackett 135.

[12] Demeter 107.

[13] Bolton 27; Cushing 125. Contra: Demeter 107; Robert 65.

[14] Bolton 27; Demeter 107.

[15] Demeter 107.

[16] Bolton 27; Demeter 107.

delay.[17] If lost, it may not be repeated until a reasonable amount of debate or business has intervened.[18]

The moderator always has the power to declare a short recess without a motion, under the power to regulate the proceedings, if, for example, the meeting appears to be growing restless, or if the moderator or the town counsel wants time to look up a precedent or whip a motion into proper legal form.

If an unqualified motion to adjourn is made before the business of the meeting is completed, the moderator need not rule it out of order, but may inquire, "To what time and place?" If several voices reply with several different times, the moderator may put the question first on whichever one he or she prefers.[19]

§61. To Dissolve or Adjourn Sine Die

Basic Points: *A motion to dissolve or adjourn sine die requires a second and a majority vote; may not be debated, amended or reconsidered, and may not interrupt the speaker.*

Form of Motion: *"I move that the meeting be dissolved."*

Dissolution ends the meeting altogether. The town cannot be brought together again except pursuant to a new warrant. Whatever may have been the rules respecting reconsideration of action taken or not taken, once the meeting has dissolved the action taken by it may not be reconsidered, except pursuant to an article for the purpose in the warrant for a future meeting.

In representative town meetings, the difference between adjournment and dissolution is even more significant. Much, if not all, of the important action voted will not take effect until a certain number of days after the meeting dissolves.

In open meetings, the distinction is less important, but the final motion properly should be "to dissolve."

A motion to dissolve the meeting (or to "adjourn without day," which has the same effect) is not in order as long as any

---

[17] Kaeble v. Mayor of Chicopee, 311 Mass. 260, 41 N.E.2d 49 (1942).
[18] Demeter 110; Robert 63. Contra: Cushing 127; Hackett 135.
[19] Hill v. Goodwin, 56 N.H. 441 (1876).

article in the warrant remains undisposed of.[1]

If there is no hope of ever attaining a quorum, the moderator might as well recognize the fact and accept a motion to dissolve, even if some business remains to be done.

When the motion to dissolve is in order, however, it has the highest rank of all. It is true that there is not much left for it to outrank, since the warrant has been disposed of. However, it is conceivable that after the last article has been acted upon, someone might move to reconsider some earlier action, or seek the floor on some question of privilege. Whatever might arise at this time, it will be superseded by a motion to dissolve.

Some manuals say that a motion to dissolve yields to a motion to fix the time to which to adjourn.[2] This is true when there is business yet to complete. The motion to dissolve is then out of order. When the motion to dissolve is in order, there is no need for a motion to fix a time to reconvene, and the motion to dissolve need not yield to a motion to fix, if one is made.

The motion to dissolve requires a second, is not debatable or amendable, requires a majority vote and may not be reconsidered.[3] It may be withdrawn.

Where a statute or a by-law forbids dissolution by less than a quorum, either expressly or by a strict construction of the authority to "adjourn from time to time," or where a majority of a quorum wishes to dissolve but is prevented from so doing by unfinished business and a determined minority, a vote to "adjourn to the night of the next annual town meeting" has often been used to achieve substantially the same result. (Although the business of the adjourned meeting stays alive, to be disposed of when the annual meeting rolls around, it is suspended in the meantime, and it cannot be deferred beyond the annual meeting, because the proponents may compel its insertion in the warrant for the annual meeting.)

If the business of the meeting is something which the town is required to transact, such as the election of officers

---

§61. [1] Jenney v. Alden, 79 Vt. 156, 64 Atl. 609 (1906); Bolton 27.
[2] Demeter 110; Robert 60. *Contra:* Cushing 157.
[3] Demeter 108; Robert 60.

and the appropriation of funds for the ensuing year, a motion to adjourn "to the night of the next annual town meeting" is as much out of order as a motion to dissolve.

The statutes establishing a number of representative town meetings provide that less than a quorum shall not adjourn a meeting over the date of an election of town meeting members.[4] This would rule out the "next annual meeting" device wherever the election precedes the meeting.

---

[4] Fairfield, Conn., and Reading, Mass., for example.

Chapter 9

Debate

§62. Decorum in Debate

And even as they did not like to retain God in their knowledge, God gave them over to a reprobate mind, to do those things which are not convenient; . . . full of envy, murder, debate, deceit, malignity, whisperers.
- Romans 1:29

We manage things better now. In King James's day debate may have been properly classified in the same category with murder, but murder is now virtually nonexistent in town meetings, and other forms of violence are rare.[1] We may not have stamped out envy, deceit and malignity, but at least they find expression, as a rule, in a civilized way. We will probably never succeed in extirpating whispering.

To avoid the temptation to violence or tumult, we have rules.

When the meeting has been called to order, every voter should find a seat and take it, as quietly as possible.

When people wish to speak they should rise in place and address themselves, not to the meeting or to any particular member, but to the moderator, who will call them by name if he or she knows it, or ask their names if he or she does not. It is a good rule to require everyone rising, no matter how well known, to state his or her name and precinct, or the street he or she lives on. Some of the voters present may be recent arrivals. It is helpful for them to be told the names of the veterans, and it also makes it easier for them to rise and identify themselves.

"Sometimes such is the mysterious nature of the workings of the human mind, there are more men in their seats who want to talk than there are of those who are anxious to listen.

---

§62 [1] But see 12 American Heritage 42 (Dec. 1960), for a literary account of a real donnybrook which reached the Supreme Judicial Court in Moloney v. Selectmen of Milford, 253 Mass. 400, 149 N.E. 317 (1925).

When an array of gentlemen rise at the same moment, and vociferate in concert, it becomes the instant duty of the presiding officer to quell the gale. He will see to it that all sit down again. His efforts to this end will consist largely of vigorous rappings, done with a hammer furnished for the purpose at the public expense. As soon as the chair becomes master of the situation, he will decide who shall have the floor."[2] If the moderator can determine who was first up, that person is usually entitled to the floor, unless he or she has already spoken on the subject or unless, by custom, the moderator first recognizes the sponsor of the article or a town official.[3]

No person should be permitted to speak at length unless a motion is pending. No one is to speak impertinently or beside the question, superfluously or tediously. No person is to use indecent language against the proceedings of the meeting, and no vote already passed is to be reflected on by anyone except on a motion to reconsider or rescind it. No one is to disturb another during a speech except for a point of order or question of privilege.[4] No one is to stand up to interrupt the speaker, or pass between the speaker and the moderator. The consequences of a measure may be reprobated in strong terms; but to arraign the motives of its advocates is against order, even though no names are mentioned.[5]

"My right honorable friend should not develop more indignation than he can contain."[6]

No person, in speaking, is to indulge in personalities. To make sure of this, the moderator is entitled to forbid any speaker to mention any person present by name, or to address anyone in the second person.[7] It is good practice, accordingly, to use such simple and easily recognizable expressions as "the previous speaker" whenever conveniently possible. This rule

---

[2] Hackett 43; Manual for the Massachusetts General Court, Note to Senate Rule 39.
[3] See §23 *supra*.
[4] See §47 *supra*.
[5] Jefferson 161-164.
[6] Taylor, Winston Churchill 219 (1952).
[7] Demeter 39-40; Hackett 62; Jefferson and Deschler 162; Robert 180; Manual for the Massachusetts General Court, Note to House Rule 73.

can be more rigorously enforced in assemblies like the House of Commons or the Congress where the members are expected to acquire a faculty for inventing and understanding the elaborate circumlocutions that the rule sometimes requires. In town meetings, however, the circumlocution is apt to leave a good portion of the meeting wondering whom in the world the speaker is talking about. The moderator may exercise a sound discretion, therefore, in the application of the rule. So long as the discussion is calm, courteous and dignified, it may be easier to follow if speakers are permitted to identify the remarks they intend to corroborate, explain or even to contradict as "Mr. Smith's remarks," rather than "The remarks of the next preceding speaker but one" or "The remarks of the person halfway down on the right-hand side." However, if the temperature of the debate begins to rise, the moderator has the right to use the rule as a pacifier.

There is never any occasion for one speaker to address another in the second person, and this should not be permitted.

Anyone who wishes to question another should address all questions to the chair. Subject to the foregoing considerations, the voter may indicate the individual whose answer is desired. Cross-examination is out of order.

"Where a member is charged with committing a breach of decorum, his attention is invited to the subject by the presiding officer in a few well chosen remarks, after which the offender is permitted an opportunity to offer an explanation, should he happen to have one on hand."[8]

Carlyle notwithstanding ("The substitution of tobacco smoke for parliamentary eloquence is by some held to be a great improvement"),[9] it is improper[10] and, in Massachusetts, illegal to smoke — or carry intoxicating liquor — in a town meeting.[11]

Enforcement of Order. In the beginning, the meeting itself

---

[8] Hackett 63.
[9] 2 History of Frederick the Great 74.
[10] House Rule XIV, 7; Hackett 172-173.
[11] Mass. Gen. Laws, c. 54, §73. Note that this empowers the moderator to cause the offender to be removed, but not confined. Compare c. 39, §17.

maintained its own order. "If any man shall behave himself offensively at any Towne meeting, the rest of the freemen then present, shall have power to sentence for his offence. So be it the mulct or penaltie exceede not twentie shilings."[12]

This gives rise to interesting speculation as to what happened when approximately half the meeting thought the other half was misbehaving. Eventually it was decided to vest this power in the moderator,[13] and there the power resides to this day. "No person is to speak without leave of the moderator. If a person, after warning from the moderator, persists in disorderly behavior the moderator may order him to withdraw from the meeting, and, if he does not withdraw, may order a constable or any other person to remove him and confine him in some convenient place until the meeting is adjourned."[14] This means what it says.[15] To minimize the possibility of successful lawsuits, the moderator should carefully follow the steps set out in the statute before ordering that someone be removed and confined.

If a by-law limits the number of times, or the length of time, one person may speak, another person cannot transfer his or her rights to the person whose time has run out.[16]

§63. Slander

A member of Congress is protected by the Constitution[1] from suit for slander for utterances "in any Speech or Debate in either House." Voters and town meeting members do not

---

[12] The Body of Liberties, c. 56 (1641).
[13] Massachusetts Province Laws, c. CXVII (1715).
[14] Conn. Gen. Stat., tit. 7, c. 90, §§7-8; Me. Rev. Stat., c. 90A, §34 IIIA; Mass. Gen. Laws, c. 39, §17; N.H. Rev. Stat. Ann., c. 40, §§7, 8, 9; R.I. Gen. Laws, tit. 45, c. 3, §19; Vt. Stat. Ann., tit. 24, c. 31, §725. See also Conn. Gen. Stat., tit. 53, c. 943, §53-172.
[15] Doggett v. Hooper, 306 Mass. 129, 27 N.E.2d 737 (1940). See Boston Town Records, Jan. 23, 1635: ". . . whosoever at any publique meeting shall fall into pryvate conference, to the hindering of the publique businesses, shall forfeit for every such offense 12d."
[16] Manual for the Massachusetts General Court, Note to House Rule 73.

§63 [1] Art. 1, §6.

have the same sweeping exemption. However, there is a limited privilege in town meeting. A statement otherwise defamatory is not actionable if it is made in good faith, without malice, in the reasonable belief that it is true, and is material and pertinent to a matter legitimately before the meeting for action.[2]

---

[2] Bradford v. Clark, 90 Me. 298, 38 Atl. 229 (1897); Bradley v. Heath, 12 Pick. 163 (Mass. 1831); Smith v. Higgins, 16 Gray 251 (Mass. 1860). See Shattuck v. Allen, 4 Gray 540 (Mass. 1855); Howland v. Flood, 160 Mass. 509, 36 N.E. 482 (1894); Retailers Commercial Agency, Inc., petitioner, 1961 Mass. Adv. Sh. 755, 174 N.E.2d 376.

Chapter 10

Conflict of Interest

§64. In General

"Where the private interests of a Member are concerned in a bill or question he is to withdraw. And where such an interest has appeared, his voice has been disallowed, even after a division. In a case so contrary, not only to the laws of decency, but to the fundamental principles of the social compact, which denies to any man to be a judge in his own cause, it is for the honor of the House that this rule of immemorial observance should be strictly adhered to."[1]

How does this apply in a town meeting?

The enormous practical difficulties of enforcing a rule against interested voting in a town meeting hardly need to be stated. Mr. Jefferson did not explain how he proposed to enforce his rule in the Senate, where instances of interest would be relatively rare. In a town meeting, the questions that would not involve one or more voters directly would be the rare ones.

In an open town meeting, where every voter may attend, an interested vote is considered to be no threat to the integrity of the meeting. It acts in a legislative, not a judicial capacity, and individuals have a right to vote for their own interests.[1a] Their neighbors might even think them not quite bright if they did not. A group of personally interested voters might have a more decisive influence on the outcome of a question, but even here, there has probably always been a feeling that these things balance out in the long run. To some people, the term "pressure group" is a term of opprobrium, but as the Rockefeller Panel Report on "American Democracy: The Power of the Democratic Idea" (1960) has pointed out, the politics of democracy is the politics of pressure groups.

Logrolling and interested voting are accepted in an open meeting. The only limits placed on these activities are limits imposed by a respect for the opinions of one's neighbors as to

---

§64 [1] Jefferson 171.
[1a] Town of New London v. Davis, 73 N.H. 72, 59 Atl. 369 (1904).

what is fair and decent, and not limits imposed by parliamentary rules. For example, the local merchant who votes against enlarging a commercial zoning district for fear of competition is not likely to fool the neighbors as to his or her motives. Such persons will carry much less weight in town than those at the opposite extreme who, with all their children grown and moved away, lead the fight for a new school.

In a representative town meeting, however, the situation is different. It may be taken for granted that town employees will go to an open town meeting and vote on their own salaries, but if they become town meeting members in a representative meeting and vote on their own salaries, they provoke serious consideration of the conflict-of-interest question.[2] In a small town with a large representative meeting, where the town meeting member represents comparatively few voters, the analogy to the open town meeting may be strong. This does not explain away the conflict, but perhaps explains the acceptance of the conflict.

In 1961, Massachusetts adopted a Code of Ethics that prohibited an officer or employee of an agency from having any interest which conflicted with the proper discharge of his or her duties in the public interest.[3] This was replaced on May 1, 1963, by a "Conflict of Interest Law"[4] that purports to govern the conduct of "municipal employees," a term that is defined, in the act, broadly enough to include even the moderator, but which expressly excludes elected members of a town meeting. Does this give elected members a free hand? No other terms are defined in any relationship to a town meeting.

---

[2] Lincoln, Some Notes on Representative Town Meetings, 33 Mass. L.Q. 31 (1948); Tilden, Separation of Powers and the Representative Town Meeting, 42 id. 24 (1957). In several Connecticut towns a town employee is expressly disqualified, by the act creating the representative meeting, from serving as a member; Hamden, Trumbull, Wallingford, Darien, Westport and West Haven are examples. For a discussion of "office" and conflict of interest see Reilly v. Ozzard, 33 N.J. 529, 166 A.2d 360 (1960).

[3] See Mass. Gen. Laws, c. 268A, inserted by Acts of 1961, c. 610. "A continuing problem of a free government is the maintenance among its public servants of moral and ethical standards which are worthy and warrant the confidence of a free people."

[4] Mass. General Laws, c. 268A, inserted by Acts of 1962, c. 779.

Most of the discussion of the problem, formal and otherwise, revolves around town employees. Everyone can see them and can see the problem. In their case, at least, there is no hypocrisy. They never pretend that there is no conflict. The serious moral problem is raised by the town meeting member who conceals the fact that he or she has a substantial interest in the corporation that owns the land which is to be taken for a school or to be rezoned from residential to industrial use. This applies to open as well as to representative meetings.

What, if anything, should the moderator do about all this? It seems clear that it would be excessively quixotic to try to bar anyone from voting on account of interest. Further, a moderator who once began could never stop. If a town employee were barred from voting on his or her salary, all the persons interested in a zoning question would have to be barred from voting on that question, and the mere ascertainment of who was interested might be an intolerable burden. Finally, it may be none of the moderator's business. The town meeting members are the judges of the election and qualification of their members.[5] This may apply only to qualifications generally, and not to qualification for a particular vote, but it seems to indicate that, if anyone may judge in a particular instance, it is not the moderator.

If in any representative meeting each town meeting member represents a comparatively large number of voters, so that the analogy to an open meeting is weak, and the town wishes to regulate the conflict of interest problem, it should do so by a by-law and not expect the moderator to do it. The by-law should be carefully drawn so as to impose its sanctions, if any, outside of the meeting. It should not impede the conduct of the meeting by imposing voting qualifications (the least of which would take much time to check), and it particularly should not be so drawn as to allow any retroactive doubt to be cast on the validity of a vote once taken. The hardest part of such a by-law, and not the least important, would be to define a conflict of interest. Some towns have adopted a by-law that provides for disclosure by a speaker

---

[5] Mass. Gen. Laws, c. 43A, §5.

with a potential conflict.⁶ As suggested above, the definition of parties interested in zoning proposals would be very difficult.⁷

§65. For the Moderator

Should moderators ever hold other town offices? In some towns they do—for example, doubling as town counsel, but this can bring on its own set of problems. This is acceptable provided that the dual employment is not itself a violation.¹

The office of selectman or member of the planning board, and other such policy-making offices, however, seems less compatible. It is the function of such officers to furnish leadership to the town, particularly in controversial matters, and this leadership may be better evidenced in the sponsorship of articles and in debate upon the floor, not from the chair.

To be simultaneously moderator and town clerk seems to be both physically impracticable and contrary to the implication of the statute² which provides that the moderator shall swear the clerk and the clerk shall swear the moderator.

The ability to preside fairly and impartially over a town meeting is fundamental for the moderator. Building a reputation for impartial handling of matters can enhance one's ability to run an effective meeting. If any matter comes before the meeting in which the moderator is interested, or appears to be interested, he or she should step down from the platform

---

⁶ Belmont General By-laws, Article 2, §2-7-4. "A Town Meeting Member who speaks on any motion in which the speaker or his or her immediate family has a direct financial interest shall first disclose such interest to the meeting. The words 'direct financial interest' shall include, but not be limited to, employment as an attorney or consultant with respect to the matter."

⁷ See McNamara v. Borough of Saddle River, 60 N.J. Super. 367, 158 A.2d 722 (Law Div. 1960), *aff'd per curiam,* 64 N.J. Super. 426, 166 A.2d 391 (App. Div. 1960), in which a zoning ordinance was invalidated because a borough councilman owned property within two hundred feet of the property involved, even though, or perhaps because, he had been very active on the issue prior to his election. See also a criticism of this case in 75 Harv. L. R. 423 (1961).

§65 ¹ Mass. Gen. Laws, c. 268A, §20.
² Mass. Gen. Laws, c. 41, §107. §65.

and designate someone else to preside during the consideration of and voting on that article. In Massachusetts the conflict of interest statute[3] applies. Failure to understand its requirements can lead to civil and criminal penalties and to the invalidation of actions taken in violation of the statute.

The statute defines conflict in a number of ways. Foremost is when the moderator, a member of his or her immediate family, a partner, or a business in which the moderator serves as officer, director, trustee, partner or employee has a financial interest in a matter pending before the town meeting.

"Immediate family" is defined as the employee, his or her spouse, their parents, children, brothers and sisters.[4] Curiously, a spouse's brother is included; a brother's spouse is not. Examples of conflicts include presiding over a vote to set one's son's or daughter's salary if he or she works for the town, and presiding over a zoning article that will allow a real estate deal in which the presiding officer or a family member has an interest to close. It is a conflict to preside over an article that affects a matter in which the presiding officer is representing a client.[5] It is not a conflict to preside over an article where that officer's interests are the same as many other taxpayers', such as an appropriation that will affect the tax rate, or to preside over a budget article that includes among other line items the moderator's salary or that of a family member. (Note, however, that this refers to the vote on the budget as a whole. Debate, an amendment or a vote on the specific budget line item does present a conflict.[6]) This prohibition includes presiding over a vote on an appropriation that benefits an organization on which the moderator serves as a board member.[7]

Other conflicts include acceptance of gifts or

---

[3] Mass. Gen. Laws, c. 268A.
[4] Mass. Gen. Laws, c. 268A, §1 (e)
[5] Ibid., §17.
[6] *Graham vs. McGrail*, 370 Mass. 133, 345 N.E. 2d 888 (1976).
[7] Ibid., §19 (a).

compensation of substantial value[8] incompatible with one's responsibility as moderator[9], holding a second municipal contract[10], or any other action that creates the appearance of or potential for undue influence.[11]

When in doubt one may consult with town counsel, and obtain an opinion in writing. Although Section 22 of the statute provides that one is entitled to such an opinion, it does not seem to protect a moderator if he or she acts in reliance thereon. It is preferable to seek an opinion from the State Ethics Commission in accordance with Section 10. The Commission may currently be contacted at One Ashburton Place, Room 619, Boston, MA 02108, telephone (617) 727-0060.

A moderator should not preside over an article that presents a conflict. Disclosing the conflict to the meeting, coupled with a subsequent lack of objections, is not a remedy in the eyes of the law. The appropriate action is to step down, and allow the town's procedure for providing a substitute moderator to operate. There is no requirement that the nature of the conflict be disclosed. As noted in the first section of this chapter, voters attending a town meeting are exempt from provisions of the conflict-of-interest law. This means that a moderator who has stepped down as described here is not prevented from speaking as a voter or from voting on the matter. However, any form of coaching or guiding the substitute moderator should be strictly avoided.

Good moderators do not take any action that could create the appearance of a conflict. This is a nebulous standard, but common sense should provide a reliable guide. They do not take a public position on a controversial article unless they intend to step down. They do not speak from the podium on the merits of a motion. They do not preside over an article that they sponsored (even one relating to changes in town meeting procedure). Acts such as the foregoing, if taken in

---

[8] Substantial value is defined from time to time, and in Massachusetts currently (June 2001) it is defined as $50.00 or more.
[9] Ibid., § 23(b)(1) and (2).
[10] Ibid., § 20(a).
[11] Ibid., § 23(b)(3).

good faith, may be acceptable to many in the community, but can be difficult to defend if even a single complaint is lodged.

Whether the town has classified the office of moderator as that of a special municipal employee can be of significance. In many situations special municipal employees are subject to less restrictive conflict of interest rules. The classification is made by vote of the board of selectmen and is filed with the town clerk. It is the office of moderator that is classified, not a particular incumbent. To be eligible to be classified as a special municipal employee the moderator must be compensated for less than 800 hours per year or by the terms of the office be permitted to engage in private employment during normal working hours.[12]

§66. For Attorneys

As noted at the end of §64, some towns have by-laws requiring attorneys who have been retained to speak on a question to disclose the fact.[1] In an open meeting, this seems like no more than a counsel of common sense. Why should it not apply to anyone, a member of the bar or not, who undertakes to express, for personal gain, a viewpoint not his or her own?[2,3]

Apart from by-laws and customs, is there any law against employing a voter or town meeting member as a spokesman? The answer is clearly no, as far as voters are concerned. The doubt that existed as to town meeting members under the earlier Massachusetts statutes[4] seems to have been resolved in the negative by the repeal of those statutes and the express exclusion of elected town meeting members from the Conflict of Interest Law.[5]

---

[12] Ibid,, § l(n).

§66 [1] Framingham, Hardwick, Manchester, Shirley and Templeton, for example.

[2] Framingham's by-law requiring disclosure covers not just attorneys, but any professional retained to speak on an article.

[3] See Commonwealth v. Avery, 301 Mass. 605. 18 N.E.2d 353 (1938), in which a selectman, not, apparently, a member of the bar, behaved very badly.

[4] Mass. Gen. Laws, c. 268, §§7, 8, repealed in 1962.

[5] Mass. General Laws, c. 268A, inserted by Acts of 1962, c. 779.

Chapter 11

Voting

§67. In General

Votes may be taken by voice, by show of hands, by standing, by roll call or by balloting.

The expression "dividing the meeting," which appears in Mass. Gen. Laws, c. 39, §15, and Vt. Stat. Ann., tit. 24, c. 31 §724, derives from the practice in Parliament. There, the division is literal; one party leaves the chamber. In America, however, the practice is not followed to this extreme. Instead, first the "Yeas" rise in place, and then the "Nays." The division is figurative.[1]

Under most of the governing statutes[2] the moderator has the power to regulate the proceedings of town meetings and to decide all questions of order, and it would seem to follow that the moderator may initially determine the manner in which votes are to be taken. In Connecticut representative town meetings, by statute, any elector may request a roll call vote and, if the request is supported by enough of the members present and voting, the vote is taken by roll call.[3] In New Hampshire, at a special meeting, a vote to appropriate money or to reduce or rescind an appropriation must be by ballot.[4] In Rhode Island, whenever any question is pending, in any town meeting, that involves an expenditure of money, or the incurring of liability by the town, or the disposition of town property, the vote must be taken by ballot, if a ballot is called for and the call is seconded by at least one fifth of the electors present who are qualified to vote on the pending

---

§67 [1] Compare Jefferson 241-243 with Rule 1.5 of the House of Representatives.

[2] Mass. Gen. Laws, c. 39, §15; N.H. Rev. Stat. Ann., c. 40, §4; R.I. Gen. Laws, tit. 45, c. 3, §17; Vt. Stat. Ann., tit. 24, c. 31, §724. Me. Rev. Stat., c. 91, §44 ("Said moderator shall regulate the business of the meeting") was superseded in 1957 by c. 90-A, §34 IIIA ("As soon as he has been elected, the moderator shall preside at the meeting").

[3] For example, Conn. Sp. Act No. 27 of 1953, §11 (Trumbull, 20 percent of the members must support it); Conn. Sp. Act No. 60 of 1953, §5 (Hamden, 10 percent); Conn. Sp. Act No. 313 of 1953, §10 (New Canaan, 10 percent).

[4] N.H. Rev. Stat. Ann., c. 31, §5.

question.[5]

On routine matters, or where, from the manner of the debate or otherwise, it would appear that there is no substantial doubt as to the result, the vote will always be taken by voice vote or by informal show of hands.[6] In either case, the moderator will merely estimate the vote, and not attempt to count it. On a contested matter, a call for a voice vote will often be deemed an invitation to the voters (and in a representative meeting, to the gallery) to attempt to influence the ears of the moderator (and thus the declaration of the vote) by decibels rather than numbers of those entitled to vote. In such cases the moderator will avoid a good deal of grief by calling for a show of hands. To guard against the casting of votes by non-voters, many towns issue colored cards or slips of paper to voters as they check in, and the moderator asks for a display thereof when taking votes.

If a vote is immediately questioned by seven or more voters ("I doubt it," "I doubt the vote," "I question it," by seven voters rising in place is the method), the moderator must verify the vote "by polling the voters or by dividing the meeting unless the Town has, by a previous order or by by-law, provided another method" (Massachusetts); "by polling the voters or by a method directed by the legislative body" (Maine); "poll the voters or divide the meeting, unless the town has provided some other procedure in such cases" (Vermont); or "make the vote certain by a poll of the voters" (New Hampshire). Seven is the magic number. The differences seem to be that in New Hampshire a poll (roll call) is the only method of verification; in Maine the meeting may prescribe another method on the spur of the moment; but in Massachusetts and Vermont the moderator may choose a poll or a division unless the town has previously provided otherwise.

Moderators are under no obligation to declare a vote if they are in doubt. They may simply state that "the chair is in doubt," and order a division.

---

[5] R.I. Gen. Laws, tit. 45, c. 3, §20.
[6] For an early instance of a vote "by lifting up of hands," see Boston Town Records, Sept. 16, 1636.

Once the vote has been taken by polling or dividing, either on the moderator's own motion or after his or her declaration has been questioned, the counted vote, as declared by the moderator, may not be questioned.[7]

In the case of a voice vote or a vote by show of hands, the moderator will determine the vote. If the vote is taken in any other manner, the moderator should enlist the assistance of tellers, who in some towns are sworn by the moderator or by the town clerk to the proper performance of their duties.

If there is a standing vote, it would be helpful to divide the hall into appropriate sections and to appoint at least two tellers for each section, who will count each row together and agree on their count before they proceed to the next row. And if there is a public-address system, it will increase public confidence in the count if the tellers successively announce their counts into a microphone, rather than delivering the same to the moderator, so that the voters may hear the tallies at the same time the moderator does and may thus check the moderator's arithmetic.

The tellers should be reminded by the moderator to include their own votes in their tallies, since a teller is not disqualified from voting. However, it would seem to be good practice for tellers to refrain from debating. If a teller wishes to speak, the moderator should excuse him or her and appoint a substitute teller for the remainder of the meeting.

It would be wise to remind the tellers also to count the votes of those (such as the town clerk and members of the board of selectmen and finance committee) who may be eligible to vote but sit on the platform or at tables or other locations separate from the ordinary seating of voters. For a discussion of voting by the moderator, see §6 *supra*.

Normally, in the event of doubt, it should be possible to take an accurate vote—expeditiously and efficiently—by a standing vote, without resorting to a roll call or balloting. These take time and should be avoided so far as possible.

---

[7] DeWolf, The Town Meeting 23 (1890). This was the almost unanimous opinion of the Massachusetts Moderators' Association, expressed at an annual meeting duly called and warned, with a proper article covering the subject, on November 4, 1960. See Hill v. Goodwin, 56 N.H. 441 (1876).

§67 11: VOTING 149

Attainment of a majority means that there are more voters in favor than opposed. Thus a tie vote means that a majority has not been achieved, and the motion fails. Where a two-thirds vote is required, all that is necessary for passage is the attainment of at least two-thirds of those present and voting. Thus, if there are 150 present and voting,
- a count of 75 aye and 75 nay means that the motion fails on a majority vote,
- a count of 76 aye and 74 nay means that the motion has achieved a majority,
- a count of 100 aye and 50 nay meets the requirement for a two-thirds vote.

If the number voting is not divisible by 3, and the number of votes required to achieve a two-thirds vote is thus not a whole number, the required number is rounded up to the next largest whole number. Thus, if 100 are present, 67 votes are required to achieve a two-thirds vote.

Human nature being what it is, a number of voters may be influenced one way or the other by the choice of one of these methods: by the secrecy of the ballot or by the pitiless publicity of the roll call. Even if in fact no one's vote is so influenced, the losers will think so, and think they lost because of the method of voting selected. If the moderator selected it, they will suspect him or her of partiality. For this reason, the moderator should stick to standing votes unless a statute, a by-law, a vote of the meeting or a highly unusual situation requires a roll call or a ballot.

Considerable controversy has developed on the issue of secret ballots. May the town meeting vote for one or the moderator order one? Perhaps there is not much doubt that either may in open town meetings, but in the case of representative town meetings there is a substantial body of opinion that elected town meeting member should be required to vote publicly so that their constituents may know how they vote. This opinion holds to the belief that in representative town meetings secret ballots should be held to be against public policy.[8] There is a contrary view that town meeting members, like voters in open town meetings, should be permitted to vote in secret, particularly on issues affecting municipal employees, so that they may not be in a position to reward or punish members for their vote.

If the town is small and the meeting is large, the members do not feel like representatives to a legislature. They feel like ordinary voters who have been reduced somewhat in numbers, out of necessity, by a thinning process which does not change their status as ordinary voters any more than selection for jury duty does. No one suggests abolishing the tradition of secret jury votes. If the town is large and the meeting is small, the analogy to a legislature is felt more strongly. It is interesting to note that the Founding Fathers did not consider that a congressman's constituents had a right to have his vote recorded. They considered it to be his right, but only if he could get enough of his colleagues to agree,[9] except when overriding a veto.[10] The state constitutions of Connecticut, Maine and Rhode Island follow the same formula.[11] New Hampshire's provides for yeas and nays at the call of one member,[12] and Vermont at the call of five representatives or one senator.[13] Massachusetts requires yeas and nays only

---

[8] In 1960 the Massachusetts General Court required all votes at Stoughton town meeting to be by voice or standing vote. Mass. Acts of 1960, c. 394. Query: Does this prohibit a roll call? In 1961 the Massachusetts General Court passed an act prohibiting the secret ballot in all representative meetings unless two-thirds of the members present and voting thereon vote that a secret ballot be had, but the Governor vetoed it and the General Court sustained the veto. H. 2345, H. 2646 and H. 2790. In 1962, a similar bill failed to pass the Senate. H. 3367. In 1963, however, it passed both houses and the present Governor and is now law. Mass. Gen. Laws, c.39, §15, third paragraph. The prohibition applies to "voting in the exercise of the corporate powers of the town or on any motion."

[9] "The Yeas and Nays of the Members of either House on any question shall, at the Desire of one fifth of those Present, be entered on the journal." U.S. Constitution, Art. 1, §5.

[10] U.S. Constitution, Art. 1, §7.

[11] Conn. Const., Art. Third, §12, Art. Fourth, §14; Me. Const., Art. IV, §§2, 5; R.I. Const., Art. IV, §8.

[12] Pt. 2, Art. 24.

[13] C. 11, §9.

when a veto is being overridden.[14] Furthermore, the Twelfth Amendment to the Federal Constitution provides that the electoral college shall vote by ballot for president and vice-president, and if no person has a majority, the House of Representatives shall choose the president by ballot.

Bolton describes two methods of taking a ballot vote: "A common method is to have tellers distribute slips of paper and then collect them after the voters have written Aye (or Yes) or No on them. This method, however, is open to serious abuse, as it is impossible to keep a close enough check. A better method, if opportunity is afforded in advance, is to have a paper, perforated in the middle, on one half of which is printed Aye (or Yes) and on the other No. Tellers then direct the voters to a ballot box, row by row, keeping track of them to prevent repeating. The ballots are handed to the voters as they near the ballot box. Each voter tears the ballot in half at the perforation, deposits his vote in the ballot box, places the other half in some container, and returns to his seat. ... If more than one such vote is anticipated, different colors may be used, and a sufficient number of each color should be printed before the meeting." We concur in recommending the second method.

If a town employs the practice of issuing voter slips upon check-in, the process of taking a secret ballot is simplified. The voter slip becomes the ballot upon which "yes" or "no" is written. Since the voter was identified as such in order to receive it, no check-in is required at the ballot box. Upon casting the ballot, the checkers issue the voter a new slip of a different color, which becomes the voter credential for the balance of the meeting (or the next secret ballot!). If this system is used, the moderator should make clear that all voters must cast a ballot, and receive a new colored slip, in order to vote on other matters following the secret ballot. Those wishing to abstain simply cast a blank ballot.

If the system just described is not in use, then the checklist is used to prevent repeating. In a larger meeting, two checklists, one for names starting with letters A through L and

---

[14] Pt. 2, c. i, §I Art. 2.

one for M through Z, may expedite the vote. If the requirement of a ballot vote catches the town clerk unprepared with printed perforated paper, a perfectly satisfactory substitute, is to hand each voter a blank slip and a pencil as he or she approaches the ballot box. It takes very little longer to write "Yes" or "No" than to tear a slip in half. These suggestions are not designed to foreclose other systems, which may be better suited to the physical accommodations or the predilections of particular towns. The important considerations are two: that the vote be secret, and that everyone be able to see that no one has an opportunity to cheat. Of scarcely less importance is the recommendation that the procedure calling for a secret ballot be anchored in a by-law, or at the very least, in a well-known and consistently applied local practice. This is surely in the public interest, but it also protects the moderator from the appearance of arbitrariness or favoritism in calling for secret ballots.

There is not much room for variation in the manner of conducting a roll-call vote. Either the moderator calls the roll and the clerk notes the replies, or vice versa. It is a good idea to require each voter to rise in place and respond "Yes," "No" or "Present," so that everyone can see that no one is taking advantage of an absentee to vote twice. A handy way to keep a running tally is to note ayes on the left and nays on the right, and then to put a "1" to the left of the first person who votes "Yes," a "1" to the right of the first person to vote "No," a "2" to the left of the second person to vote "Yes," and so forth. Thus:

Yes		No
1	Little	
	Brown	1
2	Dakin	
3	Robertson	
	Johnson	2
4	Trustman	
	Wadsworth	3

At the end of the call, the moderator may read the totals of the yeas and nays without going back to count.

When by some special provision of statute (rather than by a rule of parliamentary law, such as in the case of a motion for the previous question or by the terms of a gift to the town)[15] a two-thirds, four-fifths or nine-tenths vote is required, a count must be taken and recorded, unless the vote is unanimous; or, if a two-thirds vote is required by statute, unless the town has provided, by by-law or by procedural vote adopted at a town meeting, that a count need not be taken.[16] The moderator's declaration that a motion was passed by a two-thirds vote should be recorded in the records of the meeting.

Two Massachusetts towns[17] adopted by-laws requiring that the meeting adjourn to a subsequent date to vote by secret ballot at the polls on any motion to authorize certain borrowing. The Secretary of State's Election Division has ruled that such an adjourned session must be considered an election requiring compliance with election laws for registration of voters and absentee ballots. Because town meeting votes must be taken at a town meeting and not an election, such a procedure must be authorized by special statute, if at all.

Votes may be dispensed with where it is apparent that there is unanimous consent. For example, if no one makes a motion under an article, the moderator may, after a decent interval, take this as a unanimous vote that no action be taken and go on to the next article. The better practice, as noted earlier in Chapter 5, § 30, is to avoid any ambiguity by voting on a motion to take no action. However, if a proposal is made which seems obviously desirable, the moderator may state that it will be adopted "unless there is objection," and the absence of an objection will demonstrate affirmative acquiescence.[18]

While the moderator's declaration of the quantum of the vote is binding, subject only to being doubted once in the case

---

[15] Nelson v. Georgetown, 190 Mass. 225, 76 N.E. 606 (1906).
[16] Mass. Gen. Laws, c. 39, §15.
[17] Hamilton and Manchester-by-the-Sea.
[18] The meeting may even decide, by a mass movement, without a vote, to move outdoors. Brown v. Inhabitants of Winterport, 79 Me. 305, 9 Atl. 844 (1887). This procedure is not recommended for general adoption, however. It could lead to a sadly split meeting.

of an estimated vote by voice or show of hands, his or her declaration of the effect of the vote is merely an expression of opinion.[19]

It is good practice, whenever the vote is in fact unanimous, to declare it as such and ask the town clerk to record it as such. If it later turns out that the moderator and the town counsel have overlooked a requirement for a two-thirds vote, the record of the declaration of unanimity will save the day.

No vote may be received after the moderator has declared the result.[20]

---

[19] Bedard v. Cunneen, 111 Conn. 338 (1930); Ogden v. Selectmen of Freetown, 258 Mass. 139, 154 N.E. 555 (1927).

[20] Manual for the Massachusetts General Court, Senate Rule 57.

Appendix

Quantum of Vote

As stated *supra* §27, the vote required to pass an affirmative main motion is a matter of substantive law, and is usually a majority. A by-law may not increase or decrease this, but the legislature, by general or special statutes, may impose different requirements. However, rules of procedure (standing, adopted by the meeting, or imposed by the moderator) may increase or decrease the vote required for procedural action, and in this connection a vote to reconsider is procedural.

We have made no attempt to list special statutes, and in Connecticut and Rhode Island there are no general statutes that alter the requirement of a majority vote in any case. In the other four states, the votes listed below will, as a matter of general law, require something in excess of a majority, and the record must show that the moderator declared an actual count, or declared the vote to be unanimous. In all but two of the following, the required vote is two thirds of those present and voting. As indicated below, unpaid bills in Massachusetts and gas and electric plants in Vermont require something different.

MAINE

To enact a zoning proposal that is disapproved by the Planning Board, two thirds. *Me. Rev. Stat., c. 90-A, §61-B4.*

MASSACHUSETTS

To abandon or discontinue a project for which a loan has been issued, if no liability has been incurred, two thirds. *Mass. Gen. Laws, c. 44, §20.*

To accept §12 of Chapter 40 (public baths or washhouses), two thirds. *Mass. Gen. Laws, c. 40, §12.*

To accept §85 of Chapter 32 (requiring the retirement of police officers and firefighters incapacitated in the line of duty), two thirds. *Mass. Gen. Laws, c. 32, §85.*

To accept §88 of Chapter 32 (authorizing pensions to widows, or children under 16, of persons killed aiding police officers or firefighters in their duties), two thirds. *Mass. Gen. Laws, c. 32, §88.*

To acquire or sell a town gas or electric plant, two thirds, by ballot using the voting list, at two successive meetings. *Mass. Gen.. Laws, c. 164, §§36 and 68.*

To adopt or change zoning by-laws, two thirds. *Mass. Gen. Laws, c. 40A, §5.*

To appropriate from the stabilization fund, two thirds. *Mass. Gen. Laws, c. 40, §5B.*

To grant or increase certain pensions or annuities, two thirds. *Mass. Gen. Laws, c. 32, §§95-97.*

To incur debt under a general or special act, unless otherwise provided therein, two thirds. *Mass. Gen. Laws, c. 44, §2.*

To incur debt under §7 of Chapter 44, two thirds. *Mass. Gen. Laws, c. 44, §7.*

To incur debt, other than temporary loans, under §8 of Chapter 44, two thirds. *Mass. Gen. Laws, c. 44, §8.*

To incur debt to satisfy a judgment against the collector of taxes or the treasurer, if the tax rate for the current year has been fixed, two thirds. *Mass. Gen. Laws, c. 41, §43A.*

To lay out a way not shown on a plan approved by the Planning Board (where the Subdivision Control Law is in effect), two thirds. *Mass. Gen. Laws, c. 41, §81Y.*

To pay unpaid bills of previous years which may be unenforceable because of the insufficiency of an appropriation, at the annual meeting, four fifths; at a special meeting, nine tenths. *Mass. Gen. Laws, c. 44, §64.*

To appropriate money for the purchase or taking of land or easements generally, two thirds. *Mass. Gen. Laws, c. 40, §14.*

To reconstruct, extend or enlarge a town gas or electric plant, two thirds. *Mass. Gen. Laws, c. 164, §41.*

To remove the art commissioners, two thirds. *Mass. Gen. Laws, c. 41, §83.*

To rescind a vote to use official ballots, two thirds. *Mass. Gen. Laws, c. 41, §6.*

To take or purchase land for a public domain, two thirds. *Mass. Gen. Laws, c. 45, §19.*

To accept §90A, §90C and §90D of Chapter 32, authorizing an increase in the pension of certain former municipal employees, two thirds. *Mass. Gen. Laws, c. 32, §90A, §90C, and §90D.*

To transfer municipal land (excluding land acquired for park purposes) to another board or to another municipal purpose, two thirds. *Mass. Gen. Laws, c. 40, §15A.*

To sell or abandon land or easements acquired other than by purchase, and held for a particular purpose (e.g. schools, playgrounds) in charge of a board or committee other than the selectmen, two thirds. *Mass. Gen. Laws, c. 40, §15.*

To establish per capita limits on yearly contributions to meet the costs and expenses of a regional planning district, two thirds. *Mass. Gen. Laws, c. 40B, §7.*

To establish an historic district, two thirds. *Mass Gen. Laws, c. 40C, §3.*

To make changes or additions to an official map prepared or

approved by a planning board and adopted by a town meeting, two thirds. *Mass. Gen. Laws, c. 41, §81F.*

To approve proposed amendments to a Town Charter, two thirds. *Mass. Gen. Laws, c. 43B, §10.*

To approve the acquisition of property within a town by a regional school district, if the regional district school committee has authorized the incurring of debt for the acquisition, two thirds. *Mass. Gen. Laws, c. 71, §16.*

To approve an economic development plan, two thirds. *Mass. Gen. Laws. c. 121 §6.*

NEW HAMPSHIRE

To acquire or establish a municipal utility plant, or to ratify a contract by the selectmen therefor (except that a contract for a water utility may be ratified by a majority), two thirds. *N.H. Rev. Stat. Ann., c. 38, §§5, 8 and 11.*

To alter town lines, two thirds. *N.H. Rev. Stat. Ann., c. 51, §9.*

To change the purpose of a capital reserve fund, two thirds. *N.H. Rev. Stat. Ann., c. 35, §16.*

To dissolve a village district, two thirds. *N.H. Rev. Stat. Ann., c. 52, §21.*

To issue bonds or notes, other than tax anticipation notes, two thirds, in general. *N.H. Rev. Stat. Ann., c. 33:8.*

VERMONT

To acquire, construct, ratify a contract for or abandon a municipal gas or electric plant, three fifths, by ballot, and not less than 30 percent of all the voters. *Vt. Stat. Ann., tit. 30, §§2904, 2908 and 2920.*

To authorize the selectmen to fix taxes for new industrial or commercial owners for 10 years, two thirds. *Vt. Stat. Ann., tit. 24, §2741.*

To issue bonds for improvements other than public schools, two thirds. *Vt. Stat. Ann., tit. 24, §1755.*

To issue "poor relief bonds," two thirds. *Vt. Stat. Ann., tit. 24, §1766.*

To take property of any religious, charitable or educational society, unless held by it for commercial purposes, without its consent, two thirds. *Vt. Stat. Ann., tit. 24, §2804.*

To validate a bond issue, two thirds. *Vt. Stat. Ann., tit. 24, §1756.*

It is apparent that the Massachusetts legislature has less confidence than any other in the good sense of its constituents, when they are assembled in town meeting.

Bolton, in his Appendix, notes that many of the foregoing votes can be taken only at an annual meeting. We have omitted this notation because (1) it is only one of many limits on the powers of towns; (2) there are many more votes that need only a majority which, in Massachusetts, may be adopted only at annual meetings, and (3) it is the town counsel's job to see that such matters are excluded from the warrant for a special meeting.

In New Hampshire, however, the difference between an annual and a special meeting not authorized by the Superior Court may introduce a different voting requirement. At a special meeting not authorized by the Superior Court, at least half of all the registered voters must vote, by ballot, on proposals to raise or appropriate money, to reduce or rescind an appropriation, to issue bonds or notes except tax anticipation notes, or to create a housing authority. N.H. Rev. Stat. Ann., c. 31, §5; c. 52, §4; c. 197, §3; c. 33, §8; c. 203, §4. A special meeting cannot be authorized to change the purpose of a capital reserve fund or to alter town lines. N.H. Rev. Stat. Ann., c. 35, §16; c. 51, §9.

ADDENDUM

THE TOWN MEETING

Its Development as a Form of Government

Joseph Harrington, Jr.
Moderator, Town of Wenham

The Town Meeting form of government, while extremely old, is not well known nor understood outside of rural and suburban New England. People, with the easy mobility of today, move into "town meeting country" from the big cities, or from outside New England, and find themselves at a loss to understand the local government in their new home towns. Furthermore, there is no readily available source to which they can turn to inform themselves. This chapter has been included in Town Meeting Time to supply at least a portion of the background information.

Our town meeting of today is the end product of a continuous evolution in local government which has been going on uninterruptedly for well over 1500 years, of which the last 1000 are reasonably well documented. To understand town meetings fully, we should review this evolution. We will find that the town meeting has been perfected by trial and error over the centuries to become a nearly perfect medium by which individuals may exercise effective control over their immediate environments.

The world of 400 AD could be divided into the Roman Empire — self defined as the civilized world — and the rest of the world, or the barbarians. Roman government followed the complex, codified Roman law; it was based on an aristocracy supported by slavery; it served a commercial world dominated by heavy concentrations of wealth; it was administered by a highly structured court bureaucracy, and enforced by the swords and the hobnailed boots of the Roman legions. For 500 years the Pax Romana lay upon the Mediterranean and the European world from Constantinople to London, and on the surrounding high seas.

But Roman law ran only as far as the lance tips of the

outermost Roman legions, roughly from the Black Sea along the Danube and the Rhine, past Vienna, Munich, Cologne, and Rotterdam, and in Britain as far north as Hadrian's Wall. North of that line on the continent lived people loosely described as the Germanic tribes, although they had no governmental unity. Their level of civilization was not far different from that of the Indian tribes of our western plains and deserts in the mid-19th century — the Navajos, Sioux, Apaches, and Blackfeet. They had no written law, because these people could neither read nor write. But they did observe a common legal system, based on tribal customs and precedents, and passed down from generation to generation in an oral tradition, parts of which we know as the sagas. All the experience and accumulated wisdom of the past was thus handed down from age to age.

It was a basic tenet of a tribesman that he and his opinions were as good as any man's, and he stood ready to prove it with war club and broad axe against anyone, anytime, anywhere. He was his own master, and as prickly an individualist as ever existed. Yet in those savage days no one could survive alone; the family or the clan had to have some unity to survive. So the tribesman compromised between absolute freedom and a modicum of security. He achieved this by what was apparently a spontaneously generated and universally accepted set of principles:

Every man had a right to be heard in council.

When all had been heard, they voted, and the majority ruled.

Every man was bound by the majority's decision.

The councils were held — not to make laws nor to interpret them — but to solve a problem of that day and hour, in the light of the immediate circumstances, but with the guidance of the ancient tribal customs and wisdom; and custom had a very strong voice.

Now why dwell at length on these few people so remote from us in time and space? Because they had two characteristics which, in spite of their small numbers have given them a major impact upon our lives and times. First was their basic governmental philosophy outlined above — a philosophy with such basic "rightness" that it still appeals to free men. Second was their proclivity for spreading their influence over the world, at which, on a per capita basis, they were the all time champions.

Let us now go back to April of the year 410. Rome was being pressed so hard by the Goths, Vandals and Huns that she withdrew the last legion from Britain, and the Roman fleet from the English Channel. The colony of Britain was rich, lush, effete, and defenceless; it lay like a ripe plum ready for the picking. The northern tribesmen climbed into their longboats, crossed the Channel, and descended upon it, raiding, looting, raping and burning with such vigor and thoroughness that the pages of British history are left nearly blank for four hundred years.

The Angles, the Jutes, and the Saxons, having destroyed Roman Britain, decided they liked what was left, the rich farmland. They moved in, seized farms, settled down, and made excellent farmers and colonists. As they had been at home, every man was a law unto himself. They banded together when necessary for their common defense. When they needed a leader, they elected their best man king. If he turned out to be a bad king, they disposed of him and elected another man king. When the king's mission was accomplished he reverted to private status. It never entered their minds for one moment that one man had a divine or inherited right to rule over others.

Over the next four hundred years, England emerged as an Anglo-Saxon agricultural community, partially Christianized and reasonably wealthy. Larger and larger areas were consolidated into kingdoms, a system of local government was evolved, and some off-island trading was instituted.

During this same four hundred years another group of northern tribesmen were making themselves felt. Winter nights in northern Europe were long and cold, well suited to eating, drinking, and the telling of sagas. But each spring there would come a day when the sun felt warm, the snow in the barnyard turned to slush, the ale had all been drunk, the last of the flour was weevily, and a warm wind blew up the fjord from the ocean. No Norseman could resist; he re-sharpened his sword, got out his helmet and shield, enlisted in a ship's company, and joyously set off on the ocean for a summer of raiding, looting, fighting, and high adventure. He went "a-viking," whence the name Vikings. He was quite impartial about whom he fought-other Norseman were as acceptable as the Roman fleet. For six centuries these Viking raids had harried the coasts of Europe from the eastern Baltic clear around to the very gates of Rome. At one time or another during this period the Vikings invaded Europe and laid siege to Paris; they invaded Spain and fought the Moors to a bloody standstill: they crossed Russia and whipped the Magyars to a frazzle, and then went on to lay siege to Constantinople; they occupied Corsica and half of northern Italy. Not for nothing did all of Christianity include in its daily litany of prayer the phrase "From the fury of the Norsemen, Good Lord, deliver us."

And they were sailors as well as fighters. They thought nothing of climbing into their open longboats and, without compass or chronometer, sailing off across the foggy North Atlantic. They successively discovered Iceland, Greenland, and Newfoundland. And everywhere they touched they left their imprint-blond haired, blue eyed descendants, and a love of freedom.

Anglo-Saxon England had defended itself against these Viking raids, but in 865 the Danes erupted, and in 35 terrible years conquered and settled the midlands of England. By the end of that century, in 896, the combined Danes and Saxons, now allied, struck the remaining Vikings such a blow that England enjoyed 170 years thereafter of peace. During that time the Angles, Saxons, Danes, together with the Welsh, Picts, and Scots (none of whom were distinguished for pacifism) gradually worked out the beginnings of a democratic, harmonius government and civilization. They did it the hard way, by trial and error, selecting and rejecting as time tested their experiments.

Under the leadership of Alfred the Great, Athelstane, and Edgar, peace was restored, the government was organized, and some laws were codified. England was divided into shires, headed by a shire reeve (or sheriff, as we pronounce it), the officer responsible to the Crown. Each shire was divided into smaller units called "hundreds" or "ridings," and these in turn into towns or boroughs or burgs. Each shire, hundred or town had its court, and at the top the King had his court called the Witan.

The town courts or manor courts attended to affairs of local administration, minor squabbles, self defense, and tax collection. Some land was organized into manors, under a squire or knight who was supported by his yeomen, and in return furnished them with armed protection. The yeoman or freeman owned his land. A village headman was chosen by the townsmen, or by the lord if the town was a manor town. All yeomen in a free town and all tenants on a manor were duty bound to attend the town or manor court. They were "suitors" to the court. On all matters brought before the court they heard the complaints and the testimony, and — well knowing the local circumstances — could make decisions on what was right. They were witnesses, jury, and judge all in one, presided over by the lord or the headman.

Graver matters were handled in the hundreds courts which met monthly, or in the shire courts which met twice a year. Theoretically all yeomen were suitors to these courts, and could vote on all matters. Actually it was difficult to get all men to the higher courts, and gradually it became accepted that only those directly involved in a cause attended. Local citizens who well understood the environment made up the court, and all joined to cast the deciding vote. Neither the lord, sheriff, nor the King had despotic power. The power of the manor court flowed from the participation of the village assembly — all those who owned land. Their rights to the soil and the enjoyment of its fruits (subject to the lord's dues) were protected and enforced by the courts, as were traditional customs of the society. Thus was the King's peace protected.

Meanwhile the Norsemen, finding England a hazardous target, turned their attention to the continent. They captured northwestern France and laid siege to Paris. They settled down here too, and quickly absorbed the best of French culture, together with some of the feudal system, without losing any of their vigor. The feudal system was a military hierarchy, a legacy from the old Roman social structure. It converted the French Normans into a formidable military power by combining feudal discipline with Norse enthusiasm for a good fight.

Once again, and for the last time, England was invaded, this time by the Normans under Duke William, in the year 1066. It took five bloody years to bring Anglo-Saxon-Danish England, plus Wales, Scotland and most of Ireland under Norman rule. William imposed the Roman-derived feudal system of land tenure on his unified domain. He had a following of vassals of many ranks — dukes, earls, and barons — whose armed knights supported his conquests. To reward them, each in his degree was given a piece of English land. In turn, William demanded a compact and efficient army. The Saxons and Danes, so closely geared to the land by their ancient customs and basic culture, lost all their rights and became virtually slaves attached to the land on which they dwelt.

The Norman barons were an unruly and quarrelsome lot, and William very shrewdly decided to preserve where possible the basic Saxon-Danish system of local government. He retained the yeoman militia system, and the obligation of attendance at town, hundreds, and shire courts. Thus he had a ready foil for the feudal system of his troublesome barons, a counter system applicable to the vast majority of the population and endowed with the great strength of ancient custom. While his feudal lords and their courts formed the aristocracy and the backbone of England's military strength, the shire knights and their untitled serfs formed the economic and agricultural backbone of the country. They were the elements of continuity by which the solid basis of government worked out so well by the Saxon kings, based on the old Norse principles, was perpetuated into Norman England. Thus Duke William sowed the seeds of the system of checks and balances which still serves us well. And for several hundred years the kings of England maintained themselves by that precarious balance of power.

There were times when the barons rode roughshod over a weak king, and plunged the country into a period of bleak repression of liberty. There were times when a powerful king dominated the barons and led the country into foreign wars, crusades and intrigues. But regardless of how the pendulum swung, there was always the solid foundation of the English yeoman and the country squire governing themselves as of old in their manor courts and village assemblies.

As the yeomen, squires, and shire knights became more self sufficient, the feudal aristocracy became more dependent on their goodwill as well as on their feudal dues. As a result they gained more and more rights to self government. And they were far from defenceless, as they had once been, against the armored knight on horseback. An English yeoman could, with his long bow, drive his clothyard arrow straight through an armored knight at a distance of 250 yards; and their marksmanship was excellent. For this and for other reasons, feudalism finally crumbled to dust. But the king was still the king, now standing at the top of a pyramid which had its base in the village assembly, where every man had his voice and his vote, and the majority still governed.

As time passed, the village assemblies focused their attentions on local matters — the election of their own officers, the raising of taxes, and the governance of their own municipality. Other matters were handled in the higher courts, and at the top of his structure was the King's court, the Parliament — literally, the talking place. Any citizen could take a complaint to the higher courts and be heard; he could even appeal to the King himself. This system of government was deeply imbedded in the habits and the thought processes of English people.

In the early 1600's, little bands of Englishmen came to settle on the American continent. Those who came to Massachusetts Bay came not for adventure, as in Virginia, nor for commercial reasons, but primarily to avoid persecution or domination by the government. But when they stepped ashore and their ship sailed away, they found themselves not only free of the persecution, but also of all the customary support of an established government. They had 3000 miles of cold gray Atlantic at their back, and what turned out to be 3000 miles of howling wilderness before them. The animals, and most of the Indian inhabitants of that wilderness, and the climate, were definitely unfriendly.

What could have been more natural to these Englishmen than to continue to order their affairs after the ancient traditions so deeply imbedded in their natures? Literally, they knew no other way, nor did it occur to them to invent one.

And like the Norsemen and Germanic tribes of 1200 years earlier, they had to cooperate in order to survive. The Pilgrims held a town meeting even before they had debarked from the Mayflower.

Town meetings were held in the new towns — Plymouth, Boston, Salem, and Gloucester whenever there was a question to be decided. Meetings were held at irregular intervals, but frequently — sometimes every Monday morning. Town officers were elected with titles and duties identical to those used in England — clerk, sheriff, bailiff, constable, hay warden, hog reeve, pound keeper, shepherd and cowkeeper, jurymen, surveyors of highways, and fence viewers.

The title Moderator was also an import from England. Since at least 1573 it had been the title used for the person who presided and preserved order at a town meeting. Apparently a moderator was elected by each meeting from those present, to preside for the duration of that meeting. By 1685 a moderator was elected at the annual town meeting for a year's term.* The term "select men" was however distinctly an American invention; for years it was written as two words. The administrative function delegated to the select men had apparently been fulfilled in England by other functionaries left behind when the move to America took place. The American innovation put these functions in the hands of elected citizens. By 1670 these selectmen were authorized to call town meetings.* It was the constable's duty to notify all freemen to attend each meeting. His authority to do so was called a warrant; in Connecticut it was (and still is) called a warning.

As in England, attendance at town meetings was obligatory for all freemen who owned land in the town. The Town of Wenham levied a fine of 2s-6d for absence from "our Generall Towne meeting on the first Mondays in January by nine of the clock," and a fine of 1s-6d for absence from other town meetings. The old Norsemen held their folkmoot out of doors, regardless of the weather; they seem to have been completely insensitive to physical discomfort. In New England there was no lack of other discomforts, so town

---

* This date refers to the records of Wenham, Massachusetts.

meetings were held indoors, in a town meeting house that served for religious services on Sundays as well as business meetings on other days. Holding both types of meetings in one building was calmly accepted, as the division of Church and State even in New England was by no means complete until 1833. Until 1694 no man could be a voter unless he was a land holder and a church member. The town called and paid the minister, and built the meeting house. The severely spartan church liturgy called for no pictures, statues, or symbols in the house of worship, so there was no conflict between the use of the room for secular as well as religious meetings. The moderator did not ascend the pulpit to preside, but instead stood on the deacon's seat, directly in front of the pulpit and facing the floor of the house. The clerk sat facing him on the front pew, which was normally reserved on Sunday for the old and deaf.

So we can see that our town meeting of today is a lineal descendant of the old Anglo-Saxon and Norse folkmoot. We still govern our towns by the ancient rule of the equal right to speak, with the majority's vote prevailing. We still elect our moderator from year to year to keep order in the meeting, and our selectmen to run the town's affairs between meetings. We conduct the meetings under a formalized protocol known as Parliamentary Law, derived from the usages of the highest English court, the Parliament. As Massachusetts towns we hold our charter from the highest court in Massachusetts, the Great and General Court of Common Pleas of the Commonwealth of Massachusetts, familiarly referred to as the Legislature. The town meeting's functions are threefold: to elect the officers of the town; to make and amend the local laws, or by-laws, governing the town; and to provide funds and direction to the town's officers for the conduct of the town's affairs.

Abraham Lincoln described American democracy as a .... "government of the people, by the people, and for the people". . . . And so it is. But in city, state, and the federal governments, the government is *by* elected representatives of the people. We elect our representatives on the belief that, when faced with a problem, they will vote in the majority of cases as we ourselves would vote. But in a New England town, the government is literally by the people governed, acting on each problem as they individually deem wise. No more perfect form of democracy exists.

Basic to the concept of the town meeting form of government is the presence of the eligible voters in one place at one time, so that they may hear the problems presented for solution, and the arguments for and against any proposed solution. They may ask questions, debate the issues, modify or amend the solution, and ultimately vote aye or nay. Such a forum is possible only when the town is small enough so that such a meeting is physically possible. When the community is larger than this size, then those who meet to debate must be the selected representatives of the townspeople. The town meeting form is not suitable for large cities, counties, and the nation, where our elected representatives act in other forms of government which still preserve the fundamentals of democracy.

The town meeting has of course changed with the passage of time; indeed, that is one of its strengths. It is even now in a state of evolution, which is to say that it may not yet be perfect, but it is perfectible. And yet it seems to be an unmatched medium by which individual people may exercise effective authority over those things that are within their immediate range of interest, competence, and concern.

We have come a long way from the rugged individual independence of the Anglo-Saxons and the Norsemen. There were times in the Middle Ages when the light of democracy flickered very low indeed. But it survived by reason of its initial vigor and its apparent fitness to the task of the government of free people. Folkmoot, manor courts and town meetings have been part of the life stream of freedom for 1500 years and more. Today democracy takes many forms, each probably well suited to its people and its locality. We in New England can be proud of our heritage, and proudly carry on its ancient and well tested form, which seems to suit us so well.

INDEX 171

[References are to pages]

Absentees
attendance once compulsory, 3
fines for, 3
number immaterial if quorum present, 20
rules protecting, 120-121
town meeting members, 8
Abstainers from voting counted toward quorum, 20
moderators who abstain, 25
Acceleration of action, 90
Acceptance
of act of the legislature, 82
of amendment, 96
of report, 38-39, 51-52
Accountant, town clerk certifies appropriations to, 28
Action
motions which defer and motions which accelerate, 90
"take any other," 67
Adjourn. *See also* Dissolution; Recess
exception to votes subject to referendum, 75
fixing time to or at which to, 125-126
sine die, 131
Adjournment
by less than a quorum, 20, 132-133
conformed to any instructions to a committee, 98
conformed to any postponement to a time certain, 99-100
for balloting by all voters, 153
in general, 128-133
no reconsideration of, 84, 128, 130
voluntary, 19
Administrative functions, 4
Advisory committee, 31-33. *See also* Finance committee
Affirmative main motions
brief, 61, 71-72
detailed, 61, 66-72
necessity for, 66-72

Alternative in an article
makes brief affirmative out of order, 72
makes referendum on negative vote useless, 75
Amendability
equated with debatability, 91
particular motions. *See* inside front cover and Basic Points heading section on that motion
Amendment
amendment of, 93-95
article, impossibility of amending, 65, 71, 93
form of motion, 93
in general, 61-63, 93-96
lay on the table, motion unamendable, 89
neither defers nor accelerates, 95
of brief affirmative main motion, 71-72
of budget recommendations, 54-57
of by-law, 93
of commitment, 63, 89, 93
of figures, 95
of indefinite postponement, 73-74, 89-91
of main motions, 66
of negative main motion, 72-74
of postponement to a time certain, 89
of record, 27, 121-122
previous question, motion unamendable, 89
primary, 94
rank of motion, 88-91
reconsideration of, 94
referendum on, impossible, 76
secondary, 94-95
Annual meetings
adjournment to, 132
anthem and prayer, 49, 57
articles petitioned for, 13
notice required, 3

172 INDEX

[References are to pages]

Annual meetings (*cont.*)
  requirement of, 3
  Rhode Island rule as to notice, 3-4, 12, 99-100
  time of year to be held, 15
Annual reports, 51
Anthem, 49
Appeal from chair's ruling, 110-112
Application of motions
  in general, 62-63, 66, 88-91, 107-109
  reconsideration, 83-85
Appointment of committees
  advisory, appropriation, budget, finance, or warrant committee, 31-34
  others, 35-39
Appropriation committee, 31-33. *See also* Finance committee
Appropriations
  budget items, 54-57
  certification to assessors by town clerk, 28
  for committees, 97
  limits
    by article, 68-70
    by recommendation of committee, 32-33, 34-35, 39
  no dissolution before necessary appropriations made, 132-133
  requested by school committee, 34-35
  when necessary but not called for by article, 67
Arrest and confinement, 24, 40, 137
Articles
  budget, 54-56
  custom of recognizing sponsor, 61
  editing, 13
  history of, 3
  illegal, 13, 30
  in general, 12-14
  interpreted in liberal manner, 67
  may not be withdrawn, 119
  may propose amending by-laws, 62, 93
  motion may differ, 66-71
  motion must stay within scope, 66-71, 94
  no amendment of, 66, 72, 93
  not self-starting, 61, 71
  order of, 52-54, 99
  rearranging the order of, 52-54, 99
  required for reconsideration of action at another meeting, 84, 131
  sponsors not bound by recommendation of finance committee, 72
  to hear reports, 35-39, 51-52
  town counsel's duties, 30-31
Assessors, town clerk certifies appropriations to, 28
Assistant moderator
  overflow meetings, 23-24, 47
  temporary substitute while moderator debates, 142-143
Attendance once compulsory, 3
  See also Absentees
Attorney General, 30
Attorneys
  conflict of interest, 145
  moderators who are not, 10

Balcony, 47
Ballot. *See also* Method of voting; Voting
  adjournment for balloting by all voters, 153
  bulleting, 117
  committee elections, 116-117
  contrast with roll call, 146
  election of temporary clerk, 48
  makes it difficult to apply rule that reconsideration must be moved by one on prevailing side, 78
  method of taking, 151-152

INDEX 173

[References are to pages]

motion to fix method of voting, 115-116
representative meetings, 149-150
Blanket motion to reconsider, 80-81
Board of education, 34-35
Board of finance, 31-34
  See also Finance committee
Bond counsel, 20, 28, 30
"Borrow," included in "raise," 67
Bribes, 124
Brief affirmative main motion, 71-72
Brief negative main motion, 72-77
Broadcasting, 58-60
Budget
  reading the article, 54-57
  school committee or board of education, 34-35
  sometimes prepared by selectmen, 29
Budget committee, 31-34.
  See also Finance committee
Bulleting the ballot," 117
By-laws
  amendment of, 62, 93, 111
  copied into record by town clerk, 28
  covering
    action on committee reports, 51-52
    adjournment, 130
    admission of nonvoters, 41-43
    alteration of finance committee's recommendations, 33, 120-121
    attorneys, 145
    ballot votes, 120, 149-152
    certain motions to be in writing, 61
    conflict of interest, 141-142, 145
    dissolution without finishing warrant, 19-20, 127, 132
    division of the question, 113-114
    election or appointment of finance committee, 32

    election of other committees, 117
    filling vacancies, 38
    hour for the meeting, 15-16
    incidental motions, 107-108
    indefinite postponement, 92
    largest sum first, 95
    limits on reconsideration, 78-81, 83, 86, 120
    method of voting, 108, 116, 147, 149
    motions permitted "when a question is under debate," 91, 108
    notice of the meeting, 14-15
    order of articles, 52-54, 100, 121
    point of no quorum, 127
    point of order, 109
    postponement to a time certain, 100
    previous question, 102-103
    quorum, 17-20
    secret ballots, 152
    equating "refer" with "post pone," 96
    following House Rule XV1, cl. 4, 91-92, 107-108, 123
    in general, iii-v, 11-12
    limiting debate, 109, 137
    made by the meeting, 4
    New Hampshire, not permitted to regulate proceedings in, 11
    suspension of, 120-121
    zoning, 67, 82, 119

Call for the orders of the day, 121
Chair. *See* Moderator
Chairmen of committees
  appointment of, 37-38
  custom of first recognizing, 61
  moderator confers with, 44
  of finance committee, 44, 61
  of other committees, 51
Charts, 34
Checkers, 40, 46

[References are to pages]

Clerk. *See* Town clerk
Close nominations, motion to, 117
Collector of taxes
  arrest by, 28
Commit. *See also* Select
  committees
  essential elements of motion, 35-36, 96-97
  form of motion, 97
  in general, 88-91, 96-99
  motion
    defers action, 90
    may be amended, 96
    rank of, 88-91, 96-99
  reconsideration of, 96-98
Committees. *See also* Finance
  committee; Select committees
  appointment of, 31, 35-39
  conflict of interest of, 37
  nomination, election of, 116-117
  of the whole, 39
  quorum, 38
  reports of, 38-39, 51-52, 97
  rules of, 38
Commons, House of
  cautious about strangers, 41-42
  circumlocutions to avoid
    second person, 135-136
  dividing the meeting, 146
  members expected to know
    detailed rules, 10
Competing motions, 88-91
Complimentary resolutions, 50
Conditions precedent, 45, 65
Confinement, 24, 137
Conflict of interest
  attorneys, 145
  committees, 37
  in general, 139-142
  log rolling, 139
  moderator, 142-145
Congress
  conflict of interest, 139
  members expected to know
    detailed rules, 10
  questions of privileges, 124
  recorded votes, 150
  right to have gallery cleared, 42
  Rules of the House as a source, v, 91
  slander in, 137
Consideration
  by paragraphs, 114-115
  objection to, 121
  of articles, 52-54
Constable
  makes return of warrant, 49
  may sometimes preside until
    moderator elected, 23
  removes disorderly persons at
    direction of moderator, 24, 40
  serves warrant, 40
Constitution
  of United States
    Congressional privilege, 123-124
    contains many parliamentary rules, v
    protects congressmen from slander suits, 137
    yeas and nays and ballots, 150
  of Connecticut
    yeas and nays in legislature, 150
  of Massachusetts
    amended to allow
      representative town meetings, 6
    imposes obligation to
      maintain public schools, 34
    initiated and ratified by town meetings, 4, 115
    precludes previous question, 102-103
    yeas and nays in legislature, 150
  of New Hampshire
    yeas and nays in legislature, 150
  of Rhode Island
    establishes the "financial town meeting," 1, 18
    yeas and nays in legislature,

INDEX

[References are to pages]

150
of Vermont
yeas and nays in legislature, 150
Contracts
implied authority, 71
ratification, 67-68, 74
rescission, 81
Council, in Rhode Island, 1
Counsel. *See* Attorneys; Bond counsel; Town counsel
Courts. *See also* judges
cannot compel reconsideration, 87
construing obscure votes, 71
hold legislature supreme, 5
now have judicial functions of town meetings, 4
town meetings once called, 20
Cross-examination never permitted, 136
Custom. *See also* Tradition
broadcasting and recording, 58
complimentary resolutions, 50
inviting guests, 50
opening meeting by anthem and prayer, 49-50
reading of articles, 54
recognizing sponsor of article, 61, 135
recognizing town official, 61, 135
seconding, 63-64

Debatability and amendability, 90-91
Debate. For debatability of particular motions, *see* inside front cover and Basic Points heading section on that motion
always sensible and practical, 2
by moderator, 25, 112, 142-143
by registered voters in representative town meetings, 43, 86
by strangers, 41-43
commencement of, limits withdrawal of motion, 65, 118-119
House Rule XVI, cl. 4, limits motions receivable during, 91
in general, 2, 25, 62, 134-138
limiting or extending the limits of, 43, 101-102, 102-104
main motions, 62
on amendments, 94
reconsideration and rescission, 83
restatement of motion during, 64
subsidiary motions, 90-91
the previous question, 102-104
Declaration of vote, 24, 147-148, 153-154
Decorum
in general, 134-137
point of order, 109-110
privilege, 123-125
Deferment of action, 91-92
Detailed affirmative main motions, 66-71
Details, article need not contain, 67, 71
Dismiss, 72-77, 122
Disorderly conduct, 24, 40, 42, 104, 123-125, 134-137
Dissolution. *See also* Adjourn; Recess
after postponement to a time certain, 99
by less than a quorum, 132-133
in general, 131-133
of a representative meeting and referendum, 8, 20
reconsideration of, impossible, 84, 131-132
Districts. *See also* School districts
basis for electing members of representative meetings, 7
compared with towns, 1
Division of the meeting, 24-26, 116, 146-148

176 INDEX

[References are to pages]

Division of the question
  budget recommendations, 55
  by moderator, 113
  in Congress, 108
  in general, 113-114
  in the face of by-law, 108-109
  no reconsideration, 84, 113
Dollars, essential detail in motion to appropriate, 70, 71, 75
Doubt, 24, 116, 130-131, 147, *See also* Voting.
Duties. *See also* Powers
  of checkers, 40
  of clerk
    ascertaining quorum, 19
    bringing gavel, ballots and ballot boxes, 46
    certifying appropriations, 28
    mailing copies of the warrant, 14
    presiding until moderator elected, 23, 29
    recording all votes, 26-27
    Rhode Island, issuing warrant in, 13, 29
    swearing moderator, 23, 49
  of constables presiding, 23
    removing disorderly persons, 24, 40
    return of warrant, 49
    serving warrant, 40
  of finance committee, 31-33. *See also* Finance committee
  of moderator
    appointing committees, 32, 36-38
    appointing finance committee, 32
    ascertaining quorum, 19
    avoiding conflicts of interest, 142-145
    checking quantum of vote required, 66
    in general, 20-26
    investigating conditions precedent, 44, 45, 65
    keeping record of motions, 26, 45, 96
    limiting debate, 102, 104, 134-136
    maintaining order, 20-21, 24, 40, 43, 124, 136-137
    preparing for meeting, 44-48
    quelling the gale, 135
    reading articles, 54
    reading return of warrant, 48-49
    receiving votes, 17-18, 48
    stating motions, 64
    swearing clerk, 26, 49
    verifying the vote, 115-116, 146-147
  of pages, 40, 47
  of school committees, 34-35
  of select committees, 35-39
  of selectmen
    counting ballots, 48
    designating place, providing space and equipment, 46
    issuing warrant, 12-13, 28-29, 44, 46, 52
    preparing for meeting, 28-29
    presiding, 23, 27
    submitting budget, 29, 32
  of tellers, 40, 148
  of town counsel
    checking the quantum of vote required, 66
    in general, 30-31

Editing articles, 13
Education, board of,
  in general, 34-35
  New Hampshire, represented on finance committee in, 31
Effective date of votes in representative meetings, 8, 20, 82
Election
  no dissolution before, if necessary, 133
  of advisory, appropriation, budget, finance or warrant committees, 31-32
  of other committees, 116-117
  of a temporary clerk, 48, 49

Index

[References are to pages]

of the moderator, 22-24
Elector, 18, 146. *See also* Voters
Employees of town, votes affecting, 140, 141, 150
Enacting clause, striking out, 122
Enforcement of order, 20, 24, 40, 43, 124, 137
Equipment for meeting, 46-47
Ethics, 139-145
Exceptions to the power to reconsider, 81-82
Expunge, motion to, 122
Extend limits of debate, 101-102

Figures, Amendments of, 95. *See also* Dollars
Filling blanks. *See* Figures
Finance committee
  by-laws on altering recommendation of, 120-121
  chairman sometimes moves the budget by brief reference to the report of, 55
  custom of first recognizing chairman of, 61
  in general, 31, 34
  moderator confers with chairman of, 44
  recommendations of, 32-33, 61, 72, 120-121
  what sponsors of article may do about negative recommendation of, 72-73
Financial town meeting in Rhode Island in general, 1, 18
Fines
  for absentees, 3
  for tardiness, 3
  for whispering, 137
Fix method of voting. *See also* Voting
  in Congress 108,
  in general, 115-116
  in the face of by-law, 108-109
Fix the time to or at which to adjourn
  in general, 125-126
  reconsideration of, 84, 125-126

Flag salute, 49
Floor
  advice of, 111
  appeal to, 110-112
  giving floor. *See* Recognition
  passing buck to, 78
  point of order not license for seizing, 109-110
  questions from, 24
Four corners of an article, 66-69
Frivolous motions
  questioned by point of order, 109-110
  too thin a slice, 85-86, 96
  to strike out last word, 122

Gallery
  and voice vote, 147
  for visitors, 47, 50
  right of a member to clear, 42
Gavel, 46, 135
General Court, rules of, v, 9, 91. *See also* Legislature
Graphs, 34

Hall
  availability and arrangement of, 46-47
  capacity outgrown, 5, 23
Hands, show of, 146-148, 154
History of town meetings, 1-5
House Rule XVI, cl 4, 91, 92, 108, 109, 123, 126, 127

Illegal
  action not permitted, even where appeal to floor is permitted, 111
  article, 12
  meeting, 12-16
  motion, 61-63
  proposal questioned by point of order, 109-110
Inappropriate motions, 121-122
Incidental motions
  appeal, 110-112
  division of question, 113-114

INDEX

[References are to pages]

Incidental motions (*cont.*)
  fixing method of voting, 115-116
  for leave to withdraw or modify a motion, 118-120
  in general, 62, 107-109
  nominations to committees, 116-117
  on reconvening, 130
  point of order, 109-110
  separate consideration, 114-115
  suspension of rules, 120-121
Indefinite postponement
  amendment of motion, 73, 89, 92
  as negative main motion, 72-77
  better than "to the next annual meeting," 122
Individuals, protection of by rules, 10, 120-121
Information, request for, 121
Injunction against illegal meeting, 13
Interest, conflict of
  attorneys, 145
  committees, 37
  in general, 139-142
  moderator, 142-145
Interruption, not permitted
  except for point of order or question of privilege, 109, 123,125
Invitees, 41-43, 47, 50, 52

Judges. See *also* Courts
  moderators distinguished, 21
  precedents established by, 10
  town meeting is judge of members' qualifications, 7, 141
Judicial functions, 4
Justice of the peace
  may call meeting on petition, 15
  may preside until moderator elected, 23
  may swear the clerk, 49

Land, Disposing of, Notice Required, 4

Lay on the table
  in general, 104-106
  may be reconsidered, 83
  no amendment of, 90-91, 104
  not debatable, 90-91
  to reconsider and, not in order, 122
Leave to withdraw or modify a motion, 107, 118-120
Legislative functions, 1, 4
Legislature
  blows hot and cold, 33
  held supreme, 5
  may authorize representative meetings, 5
  validation of town vote by does not bar reconsideration by the town, 84
Limit debate
  accelerates action, 90
  amendment of, 101
  in general, 101-102
  moderator may, 20, 24, 104, 135-137
Limited town meetings
  See Representative town meetings
Limits to reconsideration, 79-81
Liquor, 136
Log rolling, 139.
  See also Conflict of interest

Main motions
  amendment of by-laws as, 62, 93
  finance committee's recommendations as, 33
  in general, 66-87
  must be voted on after an amendment, 96
  rank of, 62-63, 66
  scope, 66-71, 94
Majority. See also Quantum of vote
  encroachment by, 9
  for amendment, 93
  for commitment, 96, 98
  for indefinite postponement, 92

INDEX 179

[References are to pages]

for postponement to a time certain, 101
for reconsideration, 79
for taking from the table, 106
is quorum of a committee 38,
not required for election to committees, 116-117
suffices for most votes, 66, 155
vote on figures, 95
Mandamus
  to compel meeting, 13
  to correct record, 51
Manuals
  not necessary to follow, 10, 64
  sometimes contrary to law, v
  sometimes disagree, 73, 78, 83, 103, 112, 117, 118, 123, 126, 127, 130-132
  sometimes inapplicable, 64, 78, 98, 112, 116-118
  sometimes inconsistent, 73, 92, 107
  sometimes not useful, 89
  sometimes wrong, 61, 79, 113
  used as sources, iv-v
Meeting within meeting, 57
Members of representative meetings
  as officers, 49, 140-142
  at large, 29
  election and qualification of judged by other members, 7, 141
  ex officio, 29
  quorum, 17
Method of voting. *See also* Ballot; Voting
  division of the meeting, 24, 115, 116
  hands, show of, 146-147, 153
  in general 146-154
  motion to fix, 108-109, 115-116
  roll call. *See Roll* call
  voice votes, 146, 152-154
Microphones, 41, 47, 64
Minority
  protection of, by rules, 9, 120

reconsideration moved by, 78-80
Moderator. *See also* Duties; Powers
  and town counsel
    moderator bound to follow advice of, when, 30
    moderator consults, 30, 44, 66, 71
    moderator may also be, 142
  appoints committees, 32, 35-38
  ascertains quorum, 19
  checks quantum of vote required, 66
  conflict of interest, 142-145
  Connecticut, issues warrant in, 13
  consults selectmen, 44
  custodian of tradition, 10
  declares quorum, 19, 48
  declares vote, 24, 116, 147-148
  division of the question, 113
  election of, 22-24
  enforcement of order
    a question of privilege, 123-125
    assisted by constable, 40
    control of gallery, 41-43
    history of the power, 20-21, 136-137
    no person to speak until recognized, 134-135
    present statutes, 24
    rule against using the second person or indulging in personalities, 135-136
  establishes precedents, 10
  indispensable, 17
  in general, 20-26
  investigates conditions precedent, 45
  limits debate, 101-102, 137
  lion-hearted applies rule that reconsideration must be moved by one on prevailing side, 78
  need not attempt to avoid nega-

[References are to pages]

Moderator (cont.)
tive main motions unless bound by statute, 76
nominations by, 116
notes, 26, 44-45
oath of office, 23
of representative meeting issues warrant in Connecticut, 13
presides, 24
opening the meeting, 48 et seq.
order of articles, 52-54
powers and duties, 24-26
preparation for meeting, 44-47
reading the articles, 54
receiving votes, 18
recess, 57, 128-131
rules out repeated unsuccessful motion for reconsideration, 80-81
states effect of defeating negative main motion, 73
states effect of silence, 74, 153,
states motions, 63-64
swears the clerk, 26, 48
verifies the vote, 115-116, 146-148
voting by, 25-26
Modification of a motion, 118-120
Monitors, 40
Motions. *See also* Affirmative main motions; Application of motions; Frivolous motions; Incidental motions; Main motions; Privileged motions; Rank of motions; Subsidiary motions
adjourn to a fixed time or recess without day, 128-131
amend or substitute, 93-96
appeal, 110-112
brief affirmative main motions, 66, 71-72
brief negative main motions, 72-77
commit, 96-99
competing, 88-91
consider by paragraphs, 114-115
detailed affirmative main motions, 66-71
dissolve, 131-133
divide the question, 113-114
extend limits of debate, 101-102
fix method of voting, 115-116
fix time to or at which to adjourn, 125-126
in general, 61-63
inappropriate motions, 121-122
indefinite postponement as main motion, 72-73
indefinite postponement as subsidiary motion, 91-92
lay on the table, 104-106
limit debate, 101-102
modification of, 118-120
negative main motions, 72-77
nominations, 116-117
no quorum, 127-128
point of order, 109-110
postpone to a time certain, 99-101
previous question, 102-104
qualified motion to adjourn, 128-131
question of privilege, 123-125
recess, 128-131
reconsider, 77-87
refer, 96-99
rescind, 77-87
scope, 66-71, 94
seconding, 63-64
separate consideration, 114-115
stating, 64, 118
substitute, 92-96
suspend the rules, 120-121
take from the table, 105-106
withdrawal, 65, 118-120
written, 61
Mousetraps, 78-80

Names, 134-136
Negative main motions, 72-77

INDEX 181

[References are to pages]

"Next annual meeting"
  adjourn to the night of, as equivalent to dissolve, 132-133
  postpone an article to, not in order, 73, 121-122
Nominations to committees, 116-117
No quorum, 19-20, 127-128, 132
Notes by moderator
  made prior to meeting for guidance, 44
  of motions and speakers during meeting, 26
Notice of a meeting
  in general, 12-16
  of committee meeting, 38
  once not needed, 3-4
Notice of reconsideration, 80, 86, 120

Oath of office
  by moderator, 23
  by tellers, 40
  by temporary town clerk, 48
  by town clerk, 26-27
  by town meeting members, 49
Objection to consideration of a question, 121
Officers
  swearing in of, 49
  town meeting members as, 49, 139-145
Officials' attendance at meeting, 46
Opening the meeting
  in general, 48-51
  two in one night, 57-58
Order
  of articles, 52-54, 100
  of voting on amendments, 94-96
  point of. *See* Point of order
Orders of the day, 121
"Other action in relation thereto," 68
Overflow, 23-24, 47

Pages, 40-41, 47
Parliament, *See* Commons, House of
Parliamentary inquiry, 121-122
"Pass" a word to be avoided
  ambiguous use by legislature, 74
  use "adopt" or "accept" (favorable) or "dismiss" (unfavorable) with respect to articles, 71, 74
  use "hold" instead, in budget procedure, 55
Personal privilege, 123-125
Personalities prohibited
  question of privilege, 123-124
  question raised by point of order, 109-110
  second person to be avoided, 135-136
Petitions
  for articles in the warrant, 13, 30
  for referendum, 8, 75-76
  for special town meeting, 15, 80, 87
Physical equipment, 46-47
Place of meeting
  stated in warrant, 12
  who fixes, 16, 47
Plurality for election
  of committees, 117
  of moderators, 23
Point of no quorum, 19-20, 127-128, 132
Point of order
  and question of privilege, 124
  foundation for appeal, 111-112
  in general, 109-110
  no interruption except for, 135
  rank of, 63, 109
  replaces "Call for Orders of the Day," 121-122
Police, 46
Political parties, affiliation of town meeting candidates, 7
Polling the meeting. *See Roll* call
Posting warrant, 14

182 INDEX

[References are to pages]

Postpone indefinitely
  as negative main motion, 72-74
    amendment of, 73
  as subsidiary motion, 88-92
    amendment of, 73-74, 89-90, 92
    defers action, 90
    reconsideration of, 83-84, 91
Postpone to a time certain
  amendment of, 89, 92, 93
  defers action, 90
  form of motion, 99
  in general, 99-101
  no commitment of, 90
  rank of motion, 88-91
  reconsideration of, 83-84
Postpone to next annual town meeting, 73, 122
Powers. *See also* Duties
  of clerk
    in general, 26-28
    in Rhode Island, to issue warrant, 13
    to correct the record, 27, 121-122
    to preside until moderator elected, 23, 29
    to swear moderator, 23, 49
  of finance committee, 31-34
  of moderator
    appointing assistant moderators, 23-24
    appointing committees, 32, 36, 38
    changing order of articles, 52-54
    closing nominations, 117
    compelling truthful answer, 78
    Connecticut, issuing warrant for representative town meeting in, 13, 28-29
    debating, 25, 142
    deciding questions of order, 24, 111-112
    declaring the vote, 20-21, 24, 116, 147-148
    denying reconsideration, 85-87
    discovering unanimous consent, 65, 119, 154
    dispensing with verbatim reading, 54
    dividing the question, 113-114
    enforcing order, 20-21, 24, 40, 43, 123-124, 134-137
    forbidding indulgence in personalities, 135-136
    in general, 24-26
    limiting debate, 101-104, 137
    recessing, 57-58, 128-131
    requiring motions to be in writing, 61
    speaking in debate, 25
    swearing the clerk, 26, 48-49
    taking up by paragraph, 114-115
    terminating debate, 102-104
    tyrannizing, iv
    voting, 25-26
  of select committees
    in general, 35-39
    to act, 97-98
    to report, 38-39, 51-52, 97-98
  of selectmen
    administrative functions, 4
    in general, 28-29
    to count ballots, 48
    to determine order of articles, 52-54
    to edit warrant, 13-14
    to issue warrant, 12-16, 28-29
    to preside, 23, 29
    to submit budget, 29
Prayer, 46, 49, 57
Precinct
  basis of electing members of representative meetings, 7
  speaker states name and precinct on being first recognized, 134
Preparation for meeting, 44-48

INDEX

[References are to pages]

Previous question
  accelerates action, 90
  in general, 102-104
  no amendment of, 90, 103
  no reconsideration of, 84
Primary amendment, 94
Privilege
  as defense against slander suit, 137
  question of, 110, 123-125
Privileged motions
  in general, 62, 123
  point of no quorum, 127-128, 132
  question of privilege, 110, 123-125
  rank, 123
  to adjourn to a fixed time, or to recess, 128-131
  to dissolve or adjourn sine die, 131-133
  to fix time to or at which to adjourn, 125-126
Procedure
  in general, 8-11
  of committees, 38
  questions as to, 24-25, 46, 122
Property qualifications in Connecticut, 18
Public address system, 46, 64
Purpose of warrant, 67

Qualifications
  of moderator, 21-22
  of town meeting members, 7, 141
  of voters, 18
Qualified motion to adjourn, 128-131
Quantum of vote. *See also* Majority. For quantum of vote on a procedural motion, *see* inside front cover and Basic Points heading section on that motion
  for reconsideration, 79
  main motion, 66, 73
  notes on, 44

sometimes higher for main motion than for amendment of it, 94
substantive motion, 155-159
to change order of articles, 53
to elect committee, 117
to override finance committee, 33
"Question!", 103
Question. *See also* Point of order; Previous Question; Request for information
  by voter before meeting, encouraged by moderator, 46
  from floor, 24-25, 103, 123-124, 136
  of privilege, 123-125
  of moderator's declaration of the vote, 24, 146
  parliamentary inquiry, 123-124
  point of order as, 109
Question of privilege, 123-125
Quorum
  abstainers counted toward, 19-20
  actions that may be taken in the absence of, 19-20, 127, 131, 132
  declaration of quorum on opening the meeting, 48
  effect of lack of quorum on previous business, 128
  in general, 17-20
  no quorum, 127-128
  of a committee, 38

"Raise" includes "borrow" 67
Rank of motions
  incidental motions, 62, 107-109
  indefinite postponement, according to the manuals, 91-92
  indefinite postponement, the better rule, 92 n.1
  in general, 62-63

[References are to pages]

main motions, 63, 66
Rank of motions (*cont.*)
   privileged motions, 123
   reconsideration, 77, 83
   subsidiary motions, 88-91
Ratification
   implied by acceptance of report, 38, 51-52
   no reconsideration of, 82
   under an article to authorize, 67
Reading the articles, 54
Receiving reports, 51-52
Recess. *See also* Adjourn; Dissolution
   effect on pending business, 130
   equivalent of "adjourn" to a fixed time, 128-129
   form of motion, 128
   may be voted by less than quorum, 19-20, 127, 132
   no reconsideration of, 84, 128, 130
   of one meeting to proceed with another on same night, 57, 58
   to avoid by-law which prevents strangers from speaking, 43
   to look up precedent, 110
Recognition
   assistant moderator may not grant without permission, 24
   customs as to, 61
   no one may speak without, 24
   previous request for, 109
Recommendations
   limits on alteration of, 32
   of advisory, appropriation, budget, finance, or warrant committee, 32, 39, 61
   of other committees, 38-39, 121
   of planning board, 44
   of school committee, 34-35
Reconsider
   and have entered on the minutes, 120-121
   and lay on the table, 121
Reconsideration.
   See also Rescission. For reconsiderability of particular motions, *see* inside front cover and Basic Points heading section on that motion
   blanket, 79-80
   debatability of, 83
   in general, 77-87
   limits on, 79-81
   not barred by validation or confirmation by legislature or voters at large, 84-85
   not implied in "the previous question," 102
   notice of, 80, 86-87, 120
   only occasion for commenting adversely on earlier vote, 135
   possibility of, as a reason for having two meetings at one time, 15
   rank of, 77, 83
   to permit higher ranking motion after matter disposed of by a lower ranking motion, 63
   tradition against, 86-87
Reconvening
   effect on pending business, 130
Record
   of action on reports, 51-52
   of election of clerk, 48
   of meeting
     collateral attack on not permitted, 27
     correction only by town clerk,
     not by meeting, 27, 122
     kept by town clerk, 27-28
Recording by tape or stenographer, 58-60
Refer. *See* Commit; Select committees
Referendum
   by voters at large on action by representative town meeting, 8, 75-77

INDEX

[References are to pages]

device to achieve the equivalent in open meeting, 153
does not prevent reconsideration by members at another meeting, 84-85
on negative vote, 75-76
on subsidiary motion, 76
only means of participation by all voters, 153
reconsideration notwithstanding, 84-85
Relevance, 66-72
Reports
in general, 51-52
of finance committee, 34, 54, 61
of other committees, 38-39, 52, 53, 96-99
Representative town meetings
attorneys attending, 145
cannot achieve participation by all voters except pursuant to referendum, 153
conflict of interest, 140-142, 145
deferment of effective time of vote may permit reconsideration, 82
election of moderator, 22-23
in general, 5-8
quorum must finish warrant and dissolve to give effect to any business, 20
referendum. *See* Referendum
required by constitution to *deliberate,* 102
right of registered voter to make or second a motion, 61
right of registered voter to speak, 43
secret ballots, 150
some may not adjourn over date of an election, 133
statute specifies quorum, 17
swearing new members, 49
voting by moderator, 25-26
Representatives. *See* Town meeting members
Request for information
before meeting, encouraged by moderator, 46
from the floor
always addressed to chair, 136
encouraged by moderator, 24-25
need not be formal, 121-122
Rescission. *See also* Reconsideration
exceptions to power of, 81-82
in general, 77-87
limits to, 79-81
of appropriation in New Hampshire, at special meeting,146
rank of motion, 77, 83-85
tradition against, 86-87
who may move, 78-79
Resolutions, complimentary, 50. *See also* Motions
Return of the warrant, 48-49
Roll call
after motion to fix method of voting, 115-116
as a limit on moderator's power, 24-25, 147
contrasted with secret ballot, 148-149
in general, 146-149
makes it possible to apply rule that reconsideration must be moved by one on prevailing side, 78-79
method of taking, 152
on moderator's own initiative, 147-148
Rules
necessity for, 8-12
of committees, 38
of decorum, 134-137
rank of motions set by, 62-63
suspension of, 120-121

School Committee
has one member on finance

[References are to pages]

Committee (*cont.*)
  School committee in New Hampshire, 37
  in general, 34-35
School districts
  in general, 1
  in New Hampshire, 34-35
Scope of articles, 66-71, 94
Secondary amendment, 94
Seconding. For the necessity of seconding a particular motion, see inside front cover and Basic Points heading section on that motion
  in general, 63-64
  withdrawal of, 118
Second person, use of, 135
Secret ballot
  by all voters, 153
  contrasted with roll call, 148
  election of a committee, 119
  election of moderator, 23
  election of temporary clerk, 48
  in general, 146-147
  in representative meetings, 149-150
  makes it difficult to apply limit on who may move reconsideration, 78
  method of taking, 151
  preparation for, 46, 151
  when required in Connecticut, New Hampshire and Rhode Island, 146-147
Select committees. *See also* Commit
  election of, 117
  in general, 35-39
  motion to refer to, 96-99
  reports of, 38-39, 51-52, 97
Selectmen. *See also* Duties; Powers
  as members at large, ex officio, in representative town meetings, 28-29
  as moderators, 142
  designate place, provide space and equipment, 46
  determine order of articles, 52-53
  have administrative functions formerly exercised by town meetings, 4
  in general, 28-29
  meeting may not instruct as to warrant, 73
  moderator confers with, 44, 46
  prepare warrant, 12-14, 28, 44, 73-74
  ratification of action of, 67, 74
  senior may preside until moderator elected, 23, 29
Separate consideration
  in general, 114-115
  in the face of by-law, 107-109
Show of hands, 146-147, 153-154
Silence, 74, 153-154
Sine die, 100, 131-133
Slander, 137-138
Smoking, 136
Special meetings
  anthem and prayer at, 49
  authorized, 3
  called by selectmen, 13, 15
  changing views on attendance and necessity of warrant articles, 3-4
  for reconsideration, 87
  illegal purpose, 13
  on petition, 13, 15
  quorum for, 17
  time and place, 16
  two in one night, 57-58
Sponsors of articles
  custom of recognizing, 62
  not bound by recommendation of finance committee, 72
Standing votes, 146-148
Stating the motion
  in general, 63
  withdrawal after, 118
Strangers
  accommodations for, 47
  attendance and speaking by, 41-43

INDEX

[References are to pages]

Striking out enacting clause or last word, 122
Subsidiary motions
  amend (or substitute), 93-96
  commit (or refer), 96-99
  in general, 62, 88-91
  lay on the table, 104-106
  limit or extend limits of debate, 101-102
  on reconvening, 130
  postpone indefinitely, 91-92
  rank of, 88-91
  referendum on, 75
  the previous question, 102-104
Substitute. *See* Amendment
Substitutes
  for moderator, 17
  for town clerk, 17
  for voters, none, 17
Swearing newly elected officers, 49-50

Table
  to lay on
    in general, 104-106
    purports to defer action, 90
    reconsideration of, 104-106
  to take from
    in general, 104-106
    reconsideration of, impossible, 83, 104-106
"Take any other action in relation thereto," 68
Take no action, 72-77
Tape Recording, 58
Tardiness, fine for, 3
Tax,
  imposed at "financial town meeting" in Rhode Island, 18
  liability for, as voting qualification in Connecticut and Rhode Island, 18
  notice required, Rhode Island rule, 4
  poll and old age assistance tax payment as voting qualification in Vermont, 18
  request for excuse from disqualifies from voting in New Hampshire, 18
Tellers
  appointment of, 40-41
  use of, 40-41, 148
  voting by, 148
Temporary
  moderator, 17, 23, 25
  town clerk, 17, 48
Term of office
  of moderator, 22-23
  of town meeting members, 7
Threats, 124-125
Tie, moderator voting to make or break, 25-26, 112
Time
  allowed for debate, 101-102
  certain, postponement to, 99-101
  fixed by law and by-law, 15-16
  of meeting stated in warrant, 12
  to or at which to adjourn, 125-126
Town clerk. *See also* Duties; Powers
  assists in determining quorum,19
  brings gavel, ballots and ballotboxes, 46-47
  certifies appropriations, 27
  election of temporary, 48
  helped by written motions, 61
  indispensable, 17
  in general, 26-28
  issues warrant in Rhode Island, 13,28
  mails copies of warrant, 14
  may amend record, 27, 121-122
  moderator confers with, 44
  oath of office, 26-27
  presides until moderator elected, 23,29
  records adjournment, 19
  records all votes, 26-27
  swears the moderator, 24, 49
Town council, in Rhode Island, 1
Town counsel

188 INDEX

[References are to pages]

Town counsel (*cont.*)
  assists in preparing warrant, 13-14, 30-31
  in general, 30-31
  moderator bound to follow advice of, when, 31
  moderator confers with, 30, 44, 66, 71
Town employees, 140-141, 150
Town meeting history, 1-5
Town meeting members
  absentees, 8
  as office holders, 49, 140
  at large, 8
  election of, 7-8
  ex officio, 8, 29
  meeting has authority to determine election and qualification of, 7, 141
  number of, 7-8
  political parties, 8
  quorum, 17
Town report. *See* Reports
Tradition. *See also* Custom
  against reconsideration, 80, 86-87
  legislative function retained by meeting, 4
  moderator as custodian of, 11
  of amending negative main motion, 73
  of electing moderator as first order of business, 22-23
  of inserting article for reports, 57
  of not more than two subsidiary motions at one time, 88
Treasurer
  moderator doubles as, 142
  town clerk certifies appropriations to, 28
Two meetings in one night, 57-58

Unanimous consent
  suspension of rules, 120
  to an amendment, 96
  to blanket reconsideration, 80
  to hearing stranger, 41-42
  to withdrawal of motion, 68, 119
Unanimous vote, good practice to declare, 154

Vacancy
  in office of moderator, 23
  in office of town meeting member, 8
Validation, of a vote does not bar reconsideration, 84-85
Vested rights, 81-82
Visitors
  accommodations for, 47
  attendance and speaking by, 41-43
Voice votes, 146-147, 152-154
Voters. *See also* Referendum
  admission to meeting, 40
  conflict of interest of, 134-142
  device to obtain participation by all, 153
  in general, 17-20
  purpose of warrant to warn of business to be acted upon, 67
  questions by, 24-25, 46
  right to attend and speak at representative town meetings, 8, 43, 86
Votes, quantum of. *See* Quantum of vote
Voting
  ballot, 146, 149-154,. *See also* Ballot
  division, 24-26, 115-116, 146
  in general, 146-154
  method of, 108-109, 115-116, 146-154
  moderator, 21, 25-26
  on figures, 95
  roll call or poll, 24-25, 78-79, 115-116, 146-148, 152
  show of hands, 146-148, 154
  tellers. 148
  voice, 146-147, 150-154
Voting lists, 18, 40

INDEX

[References are to pages]

Warning. *See* Warrant
Warrant
 clerk brings, 46
 constable posts, 40
 history of, 3-4
 in general, 12-16
 moderator, preparatory study by, 44-45
 order of articles, 52-54, 120-121
 purpose of, 67
 representative meetings, 8
 return of, 48-49
 selectmen prepare, 12-14, 28, 73-74
 sometimes called warning, 12
 two meetings in one night, 57-58
Warrant committee, 31-34. See also Finance committee
Withdrawal of motion
 in Congress, 107
 in general, 65, 118-120
Without day, 100, 131-133
Women
 as moderators, 22
Written motions, 45-46, 61, 63-64

 skipping metes and bounds in zoning articles, 54
 withdrawal of proposal, 119

Yeas and nays
 and abstainers counted toward quorum, 19
 methods of counting, 146-154
 roll call sometimes required in Connecticut, 146

Zoning
 conditions precedent, planning board recommendation as, 45
 conflict of interest on questions of, 139-142
 constitution of committee to consider, 37
 reconsideration of unfavorable vote on, 82, 119
 scope of articles concerning, 67-68